THE BATTLE OF
PRESTONPANS
1745

About the Author

Martin Margulies is a law professor emeritus at Quinnipiac University School of Law in Connecticut. He is the author of *The Early Life of Sean O'Casey*. He lives in Sandy Hook, Connecticut, but spends as much time as he can in his holiday home on the Hebridean island of South Uist.

THE BATTLE OF
PRESTONPANS
1745

MARTIN MARGULIES

TEMPUS

This book is dedicated to my parents, Max and Mae Margulies, who alas are not here to read it; to my wife and sons, Beth, Max and Adam Margulies, who suffered through its writing; and to my friends and neighbours on Scotland's Isle of South Uist, many of whom know more about its subject matter than I do, which is not surprising, since their ancestors were there.

First published 2007

Tempus Publishing Limited
The Mill, Brimscombe Port,
Stroud, Gloucestershire, GL5 2QG
www.tempus-publishing.com

British Library Cataloguing in Publication Data.
A catalogue record for this book is available from the British Library.

ISBN-10: 0 7524 4035 7

ISBN-13: 978 0 7524 4035 4

Typesetting and origination by Tempus Publishing Limited
Printed in Great Britain

CONTENTS

ACKNOWLEDGEMENTS

I gratefully acknowledge the invaluable assistance of the Rev. Tom Hogg, minister of Tranent kirk, who drove me around the Prestonpans battlefield, photocopied and gave me copies of archaic materials about the battle which I would never have found on my own, answered my questions, and taught me about collapsing bottle mines. I am also grateful to Sue Falconer, Senior Ranger of Pentland Hills Regional Park, and Bill Patterson of the Scottish Place-Name Society, both of whom helped me identify locales that were described by obsolete names in older sources; to Sue King of the National Police Library in Bramshill, England, for information about the genealogy of the Cope family; and to East Lothian Local History Officer Craig Statham, for attentions that went far beyond the call of duty. I cannot adequately express the extent of my debt to the Quinnipiac University law library staff, especially Tina DeLucia and Larry Raftery, who have assisted me over the years with this project and many others. I appreciate, too, the patience and guidance of my editors Jonathan Reeve and David Gruar and their colleague, Sophie Bradshaw. None of these kind and generous people is responsible for my errors.

I am indebted as well to Steve Lord, whose *Walking With Charlie* – see the Select Bibliography – provided me, literally, with a road map to the battlefield, and to the late John Prebble, historian and prose-poet, whose magnificent books awakened my interest in Scotland and its history.

PROLOGUE

They came bounding through the mist toward the cannon. Some of them wielded muskets, others brandished cruder devices that had long since vanished from conventional European warfare.

Lieutenant-Colonel Whitefoord and Master Gunner Griffith from Edinburgh Castle prepared to fire on them. There would be just a single round, because the crews had fled and carried off the powder flasks, leaving the two officers to work the pieces alone, with no means of re-loading. But that round would surely suffice, for Highlanders were proverbially afraid of cannon.

Running from one gun to the next, Whitefoord and Griffith managed to touch off the entire battery. The effect was not as anticipated: though the Highlanders wavered, they kept coming. And now it was the government troops who were afraid.

INTRODUCTION

The level, open field outside Prestonpans village, East Lothian, is tranquil today, as it has been throughout most of its history. But once, briefly, it was a battlefield, and no ordinary battlefield either: rather, a human slaughterhouse, a repository for severed limbs and spilled entrails, produced by weapons that no ordinary army would have employed.

The battle of Prestonpans was fought on 21 September 1745, some seven miles east of Edinburgh, between British government forces led by Lieutenant-General Sir John Cope and the rebel followers of Prince Charles Edward Stuart. It was not a major engagement by eighteenth-century standards. Though historians disagree about the precise numbers, it appears that scarcely above 4,500 men were involved – fewer than 2,500 in each army – and that no more than 350 were killed, mostly on the losing government side. In contrast, when French, British and allied troops clashed at Fontenoy during the War of the Austrian Succession (to which Prestonpans and its aftermath were sidebars) in May of the same year, 100,000 men took part and almost 15,000 perished.[1] Blenheim, at the beginning of the century, was bloodier still: of its more than 100,000 combatants – English, French, Dutch, Austrian and Bavarian, among others – approximately 20,000 were slain.[2] It was not, then, the scale of the slaughter that made Prestonpans so horrific; it was the nature of the wounds, and of the instruments that inflicted them.

Despite being small-scale in numbers and casualties, Prestonpans had important consequences. It was the first set-piece battle of the 1745 Jacobite Rebellion – popularly known as the '45 – and its unexpected outcome, a swift, humiliating rout of the government troops (the severed limbs and spilled entrails were theirs), shocked and demoralised the ruling Hanoverian regime and its supporters. On Charles Edward, it had the opposite effect: it gave him an inflated view of his soldiers' capabilities, which is scarcely surprising; raised, as he had been, in princely self-absorption, he was given to supposing that he could make things so by wishing them so. His propensity for wishful thinking was not irrelevant either to the decisions that he made subsequently or to the rebellion's ultimate failure.

That failure, however, was seven months away. In the battle's immediate aftermath, Scotland fell wholly under rebel control, except for Edinburgh and Stirling Castles, some fortresses and barracks, and scattered pockets in the north-east where tiny detached companies still roamed on recruitment missions, and England was opened to invasion, which followed in due course. The invasion may or may not have posed a threat to the British state – historians disagree about that too[3] – but at the very least it forced the regime to take the rebellion seriously and recall units home from the continent in order to confront it, further undermining Britain's already precarious position in the Austrian Succession war. Prestonpans also set in motion a chain of events that culminated in high drama – the drama of Charles's march on London and his unwilling about-face at Derby – and even enduring legend: the legends of Culloden Moor, and the Prince in the Heather, which have left their marks on Scottish literature and consciousness and which fuel the Scottish tourist industry to this day.

And, of course, Prestonpans produced a song. Of the song, more in a moment.

Just one year after the battle, the picture had changed dramatically. The rebellion had been crushed at Culloden, the Duke of Cumberland's redcoats were ruthlessly stamping out its embers, and Prince Charles was slipping from hiding place to hiding place in Scotland's western Highlands. In that anniversary month of September 1746 a military board met on five separate occasions in the Great Room of the Horse Guards in London under the presidency of Field Marshal George Wade, builder of the famous roads that had opened up the Highlands earlier in the century. The board's mandate, according to a warrant issued by King George II, was 'to examine into the Conduct, Behaviour, and Proceedings of Lieutenant-General Sir John Cope' and two of his subordinate officers, Colonel Peregrine Lascelles and Brigadier-General Thomas Fowke, and to render an 'Opinion [of] what is proper to be done thereupon'.[4] This was not a court martial in the formal sense – rather, the board was only charged with finding facts and making recommendations – but it is clear, from the warrant's ominous concluding phrase, that a court martial would have followed if the board had judged Cope harshly. Cope, anxious to clear his name, had invited the inquiry, and the King, who seems to have been well disposed to him, issued the warrant in part to satisfy him and in part to appease the public, which was not well disposed to him at all.[5]

Indeed, some members of the public had judged him harshly already. John Home, a fresh-minted Edinburgh University graduate who went on to become a noted historian and dramatist, described him as 'one of those ordinary men who are fitter for any thing than the chief command in war, especially when opposed, as he was, to a new and uncommon enemy'.[6] Home's friend and school fellow Alexander Carlyle, later a famous minister, questioned whether Cope 'had any will of his own'.[7] Both men were writing years after the event, but there is no reason to suppose that their sentiments were any different in the autumn of 1745. To Horace Walpole, author, diarist and failed politician, Cope was a pitiable soul 'who, with no shining abilities, and no experience, and no force, was sent to fight for a crown'.[8] Arguably, none of these gentlemen was positioned to make such assessments, for it was Walpole, not Cope, who lacked any military experience; as for Home and Carlyle, though they joined the College Company of the Edinburgh Volunteers – a band of enthusiasts who mobilised to protect the city against Charles and his marauders in the days just prior to the battle – those doughty warriors disbanded before it took place, and Carlyle himself, who lived nearby, slept through it at a neighbour's house. (Home, on the other hand, at least saw action subsequently, being taken prisoner at the Battle of Falkirk in January of the following year.) Their dearth of military credentials did not, however, inhibit them from being critical. Benjamin Robins, the brilliant military engineer and inventor who published the board's report anonymously, was at first equally scathing: in his preface to the report he acknowledged having imputed the Prestonpans debacle, and the misfortunes it wreaked upon the kingdom, 'entirely…to the Misconduct of Sir *John Cope*', and opined that his view represented the nation's.[9] Robins would shortly change his mind, but the others did not.

And then there was the song. It was written soon after the battle by Adam Skirving (1719–1803), a tenant farmer and sometime balladeer who lived and farmed not far from the battlefield, and its lyrics and jaunty tune, familiar to many who know nothing else of the affair, have fixed Cope's name in the annals of infamy. In particular, it perpetuates the legend that an over-confident Cope fled in unseemly haste after he was literally caught sleeping when the rebels attacked at dawn:

Cope sent a challenge from Dunbar,
Come fight me Charlie an' ye daur;
If it be not by the chance of war
I'll give you a merry morning.

CHORUS:
Hey Johnnie Cope are ye waukin' yet?
Or are ye sleeping I would wit?
O haste ye get up for the drums do beat,
O fye Cope rise in the morning.

When Charlie looked the letter upon
He drew his sword the scabbard from,
'So heaven restore to me my own,
I'll meet you, Cope, in the morning'.

Cope swore with many a bloody word
That he would fight them gun and sword;
But he fled from his nest like an ill fear'd bird
And Johnie he took wing in the morning.

Sir Johnie into Berwick rade
Just as the devil had been his guide;
Gien him the warld he would na stay'd
To foughten the boys in the morning.

Says the Berwickers unto Sir John,
O what's become of all your men?
In faith says he, I dinna ken,
I left them a' this morning.

Says Lord Mark Car ye are na blate;
To bring us the news o' your ain defeat:
I think you deserve the back o' the gate;
Get out o' my sight this morning.[10]

The views of Home, Carlyle, Walpole and Skirving are echoed by at least some modern historians. The *Dictionary of National Biography* characterises Cope's efforts as 'ludicrous'.[11] (Its recent successor, the *Oxford Dictionary of National Biography*, is kinder.)[12] Peter de Polnay, writing in the middle of the twentieth century, dismisses him as 'not much of an officer'.[13] Katherine Tomasson and Francis Buist, authors of *Battles of the '45*, chide him for exhibiting 'a distinctly casual attitude with regard to his artillery'.[14] In a 2004 study, Evelyn Lord decries his 'ineptitude'.[15] Rupert C. Jarvis, one of the more distinguished commentators on the military aspects of the '45, defends some of the decisions Cope made prior to the battle, but Prestonpans itself, he says, 'is another story'.[16]

The members of the military board, however, had access to more evidence than Skirving and his contemporaries, and perhaps even to more evidence than some of the moderns – de Polnay, for one – troubled to scrutinise. What is more, their military expertise was undeniable. Nor were they likely to gloss over Cope's shortcomings in deference to a brother officer: as Admiral Sir John Byng – shot on his own quarterdeck by order of a court-martial barely a decade afterward – would learn to his cost, mid-eighteenth-century British military tribunals could be unsparing even of the highest. The board, therefore, would not have been averse to using Cope the way Byng would be used: as a scapegoat to appease popular wrath. But the board did nothing of the sort; on the contrary, Cope and his two subordinates emerged from its investigation with honour.

The remainder of this book will be given over to examining whether Skirving or the board had the right of it. My qualifications to undertake this inquiry might be questioned, for I am not a professional historian, and I have had no more military experience than Walpole (and rather less than Home or even Dr Carlyle). But I am a law teacher by profession, and have been a litigator, and I know well, therefore, how one can prepare for confrontation meticulously, anticipate every foreseeable contingency, make all the right decisions – and then have one's plans collapse catastrophically in the face of the unexpected and unimaginable.

The dates of all events occurring in Great Britain are rendered in the Old Style, that is to say, eleven days behind the corresponding date of the Gregorian Calendar, which was in general use on the continent. Thus, 21 September, the day of the battle, would have been 2 October in continental parlance. It would be almost another decade before Protestant Britain would adopt this Popish innovation.

Characterising the antagonists is a trickier matter. The '45 is often envisioned as a conflict between England and Scotland, which it was not, and the rebel army is in consequence thought to have been a Scottish army, or more narrowly a Highland army, which it was not. As for the supposed England versus Scotland dichotomy, there were Scots aplenty among the government forces – for instance, the afore-mentioned detached companies – and there were even some English who chose to fight for the rebels, mostly in the ill-fated Manchester Regiment, although those who were captured probably regretted the choice, because their treatment was usually sanguinary and severe. There were also many other Englishmen, and Englishwomen too, who wished Charles Edward well or said they did, but who lacked the necessary zeal to risk their lives and estates in his cause. As for being a 'Highland' army, there is this much truth to the notion: at Prestonpans nearly all the rebels were indeed Highlanders, but thereafter their ranks were augmented by Lowlanders and by 'volunteers' from the French army – the latter mainly of Scots or Irish origin – to the point where Highlanders were in the minority. Even then, to be sure, the Highland troops occupied the front line in the two remaining major battles, Falkirk and Culloden, with the others playing supporting roles, and all of them except the French wore Highland dress of one sort or another. But to call this a 'Highland' army is to ignore its national, and even international, character.

Accordingly, I shall refer to Charles Edward's forces as rebels, as I have done hitherto, or as Jacobites, which they were called because they gave their allegiance to the descendants of the deposed King James (in Latin, *Jacobus*) II of England and VII of Scotland: specifically, to James's son James Francis Stuart, whom they regarded as their rightful king, and grandson Charles Edward Stuart, whom they regarded as the heir apparent. Their opponents I shall describe as the government army, or as Hanoverians, based on their allegiance to the ruling House of Hanover, which had displaced the Stuart line – in the Jacobite view, illegitimately, since the Jacobites gave their allegiance to the descendants of the deposed King James.

I shall not refer to Charles Edward Stuart by his best-known nick-name, Bonnie Prince Charlie, except by way of irony. 'Bonnie' he was not. Alcoholic, narcissistic, paranoid and a spouse and partner abuser, he was a pleasant enough fellow when he got what he wanted, but so are most people. The true test of character is how one behaves in adversity, and by this measure he fails miserably. And yet, I believe him to have been right in some of his disagreements with his principal subordinate, the Jacobite icon Lord George Murray: in particular as to whether to press on to London from Derby after Prestonpans was won, which is another question about the '45 that divides historians, just as it divided the protagonists. Perhaps his boorish behaviour, then and afterward, stemmed in part from his galling knowledge that the war might have turned out differently if he had had his way. But that, as Rupert Jarvis would have said, is another story, one that is beyond the scope of this book. So is the question (historians differ over this as well) of whether a Jacobite triumph would have altered British history in the long run,[17] which is part of the broader question of whether human action can ever alter history.

1

THE RUN-UP

The Highlands were quiet in the spring and early summer of 1745. At least, that was the official line. The clans were either well affected to the government, or else rendered weaponless and impotent by the Disarming Acts of 1716 and 1725, which Parliament had passed in the aftermath of the last major Jacobite rising in 1715. The western Highlands were secured by Forts William, Augustus and George, which commanded the Great Glen from south to north; their encirclement was completed by Stirling Castle and Inversnaid Barracks in the Central Lowlands, Ruthven Barracks in Badenoch to the east, and the barracks at Bernera, near Skye, in the far west. Marshal Wade's magnificent system of roads, built in the 1730s, allowed rapid communication and troop movement from stronghold to stronghold. In the circumstances, John Hay, Marquess of Tweeddale and Chief Secretary of State for Scotland, should perhaps not be faulted too severely for ignoring rumours of a Jacobite threat. Of course he, though a Scot (from the Lowlands, not the Highlands), lived and worked in London, where the more serious rumours did not reach him.

Duncan Forbes of Culloden had no such excuse. Lord President of the Court of Session – in effect, Chief Justice of Scotland – he was also the president of the State Council, which, blurring what moderns would call separation of powers principles, constituted Scotland's highest civil authority now that the 1707 Treaty of Union had abolished not only the Scottish Parliament but Scotland's existence as an independent nation. Unlike the London-based Tweeddale, Forbes spent much of his time at his country seat, Culloden House, which would soon give its name to the famous nearby battlefield, and which stood just a few miles from Inverness, the unofficial Highland capital. By virtue of his offices, his residency, and his network of personal contacts, he would have recognised, as Tweeddale did not, that clan loyalties were uncertain, that the Disarming Acts had operated perversely because only the loyal, law-abiding clans had given up their weapons while the disaffected ones had secreted theirs, and that the forts, barracks and castles were in disrepair and their garrisons undermanned and inexperienced. Yet he too believed, and parroted, the official line.

Then, on the evening of 1 July, he learned, via a letter from one of his many informants, that there were rumours afoot of an imminent Jacobite landing somewhere on the Highland coast. The informant was sceptical, and so was Forbes, whose faith in the official line remained unshaken. Still, the Lord President took no chances. He called the next day upon his good friend General Cope, commander of His Majesty's forces in Scotland, and read him the letter in person.[1]

He was an odd duck, this Duncan Forbes. A notorious tippler, even by the standards of a bibulous age, he was as addicted to the bottle as Charles Edward later became. But he was also a respected and successful lawyer, judge and politician, as well as a serious biblical scholar whose published works on the subject attracted favourable notice in his day. He knew the Highlands intimately, and enjoyed the trust of its chiefs, whom he counted on in consequence to do his bidding; hence his confident acceptance of the official line. Historians clash over whether he was sincerely attached to their interests or whether he was a trimmer whose only driving interests were his own – a 'father' to the chiefs, gushes one,[2] a backer of 'what he supposed to be the winning side', scoffs another,[3] a 'hatchet man' for his political overlords, sneers a third[4] – although most take the former, more flattering view. On one point, however, they agree unanimously: whether for altruistic or self-serving reasons, he was completely loyal to the crown.

Ah, but whose crown? To Forbes, the answer was obvious. The crown had devolved by operation of the English Act of Settlement of 1701, as confirmed by the second article of the 1707 Treaty of Union, into the hands (or onto the brow) of George II, *de jure* as well as *de facto* King of the former nations of England and Scotland, which the treaty had welded into the unitary state of Great Britain. Thus, George owed his throne to the assent of the old English and Scottish parliaments, now one legislature. In addition to his British titles, he was Elector – that is, hereditary ruler – of the German statelet of Hanover: hence the name, Hanoverian dynasty. The Hanoverian connection is highly relevant to our story, for it was on Hanover's account, more than on Britain's, that George had committed the better part of his army – better both in numbers and in quality – to the Austrian Succession war on the continent, leaving Britain itself almost defenceless.

George had assumed personal command, in that war, over the British, Hanoverian and allied forces, against France and its allies.

The Jacobites, though, gave a different answer. Their loyalties ran, not to the Hanoverian rulers, whom they despised as interlopers and usurpers, but to the deposed and exiled Stuarts, whom they continued to regard as kings by indefeasible hereditary right – a right that derived, not from any parliament, but from God. Of ancient vintage in Scotland, where their line went back to the early fourteenth century, the Stuart dynasty had been a relative newcomer to England: hence the bifurcated titles of the aforementioned James II and VII. Whether a Jacobite should accordingly have addressed James II and VII's son James Francis (whom the Hanoverians dismissively called 'the Old Pretender', just as they called Charles Edward 'the Young Pretender') as James III and VIII is an interesting question. On the one hand, the Treaty of Union had in the meantime put an end to Scotland's separate nationhood and therefore, one would suppose, to bifurcated titles. On the other hand, however, Jacobites characteristically rejected, not only the Act of Settlement and the resulting Hanoverian succession, but also the Treaty of Union.

The Hanoverian–Jacobite conflict, then, was not just a power struggle between rival royal claimants (although there were certainly elements of that); it was a much more complex phenomenon, with many intersecting threads. It was a clash between different theories of monarchy – elective versus hereditary right – and between Scottish nationalists and those who would relegate Scotland to a subordinate place in a British union, a controversy that continues today. It also involved religious differences, social and economic class differences, and ancient clan loyalties and feuds. In addition, it was not merely a domestic phenomenon, for it was influenced by foreign events and influenced them in turn. It will be useful to examine these threads more closely.

The saga begins in 1603, when Queen Elizabeth I of England died without issue, and her throne passed to her Stuart cousin, King James VI of Scotland, making him also King James I of England and creating, between the two countries, what is known as the 'union of crowns' (to distinguish it from the later parliamentary union of 1707). James was the son of Mary Stuart, the Mary Queen of Scots of romance, who was deposed by her own nobles when James was an infant and, having taken refuge in England, was later executed at Elizabeth's order.

The son fancied himself a scholar and political thinker, and could perhaps lay serious claim to being one: he achieved fame, in his own day and in ours, as a proponent of divine right monarchy and royal absolutism. These expressions, though often conflated, are not precisely synonymous – the former goes to the source of kingly authority and the latter to what constraints, if any, inhibit its exercise[5] – but both are rooted in the same perception: the monarch receives his office from God and is answerable to him only. In matters of religion, James had long since turned his back on his mother's Roman Catholicism – detested throughout England and Scotland alike – and now, to please his new subjects, he likewise renounced the egalitarian Presbyterianism of the Scottish Kirk, adopting instead England's dominant Anglican creed, the hierarchical structure of which was more consonant with his absolutist political views.

James's son King Charles I, who succeeded to both thrones in 1625, not only shared those views but soon got into difficulties for taking them too literally, or so his parliamentary opponents perceived. In the resulting English Civil War, Charles lost both his crown and the means of wearing one: he was beheaded at Whitehall on 30 January 1649, after one of history's most dramatic trials. At that trial, Charles argued, in effect, that he had been misunderstood: his authority was certainly not 'absolute' in the sense of being limitless – on the contrary, it was limited by natural law and by custom – but he was the sole earthly arbiter of where the limits lay, and if he flouted them he was accountable, not to his parliament or even to his courts, but to God alone. To his enemies, this was a distinction without a difference, for its bottom line was the same: what Charles said went. Charles, however, saw it otherwise; indeed, he proclaimed himself a greater respecter of what moderns would call constitutional restrictions upon government than his parliamentary judges ever were, and he had a point: when he challenged the president of the court to identify a lawful basis for the proceeding, the president replied that Parliament had authorised it and Parliament's will was law.[6] Neither Charles nor his father would have made so grandiose a claim for himself – nor would his grandson or great-grandson, who are two of the central players in our story.[7]

The Civil War had a Scottish dimension; in fact, it started there. Rightly fearing that Charles was trying to force episcopacy (that is, religious governance by bishops) upon the nation – episcopacy being one of the principal features that distinguished Anglicanism from the more democratic Presbyterian creed – thousands of Scots, from all stations in life, joined together in 1638 to sign a 'National Covenant' (hence their name of 'Covenanters'), binding one another to resist.[8] Efforts at compromise failed, and by the spring of 1639 the Covenanters and the King were at war: the first of two such wars, together known as the Bishops' Wars. The first one ended bloodlessly, in a treaty that tried to paper over the disagreements between the two sides. But the second, which began just two months later, in August of the same year, was a disaster for Charles and led directly to the English Civil War that followed. Lacking funds and beaten in the field, he was forced not only to abandon his religious projects but to summon an English parliament (which he had wanted desperately to avoid), for the Scots would make no new treaty with him unless that parliament ratified it. This was the Parliament that, inspired by the Covenanters' example, rose up in arms against him in 1642.

That war dragged on for the rest of the decade, with Scotland and its people playing a chequered part. The more extreme Covenanters made common cause with kindred spirits in London, joining them in promulgating a second Covenant, styled 'the Solemn League and Covenant', that aimed at making Presbyterianism the official creed of the entire British Isles – in recognition of which undertaking Scottish troops were sent into England to bolster the parliamentary forces. But even in Scotland the reign of the Covenant did not go unchallenged: episcopacy remained entrenched in the Scottish north-east, and some of the more moderate Covenanters broke with the extremists. The most noteworthy to do so was the charismatic James Graham, Marquis of Montrose. Placing King above Covenant, he led a makeshift army into Scotland to do battle against the pro-Parliament faction. The latter was led by that fiercest of Presbyterians, the Earl of Argyll, chief of the powerful Clan Campbell, and by the veteran mercenary Alexander Leslie, whom Charles had made Earl of Leven in a futile bid for his support. Clan as well as religious attachments entered into the mix, as Montrose's ranks were swelled by MacDonalds and their Irish kinsmen the McDonnells – Catholics all – who were eager to wreak vengeance upon the Campbells for past injuries. And for a while they did: Montrose won a series of spectacular victories in 1644 and early 1645. But he came to grief at Philiphaugh later in the year, and though he himself escaped with his life for the time being (he was eventually captured and hanged in Edinburgh), his soldiers – the Catholic Irish especially – and their camp followers were massacred.

Buffeted by military reverses in England as well as Scotland, Charles concluded that he could strike a better bargain with the Scottish Covenanters than with the English Roundheads, and in 1646 he surrendered to Leven while Leven was in England besieging Newark-on-Trent. Deeming the Scots dangerous allies, Parliament bribed Leven to return with his troops to his own country, whereupon Leven, not wishing to be encumbered with his royal prisoner, gave him up to the English. They then shipped him, still a prisoner, to the Isle of Wight.

There matters took a dramatic turn. Charles, increasingly desperate, was now amenable to extending Presbyterianism to England after all if he could thereby win back his freedom and his throne. To that end, he opened secret negotiations with the more compromise-minded Scots leaders, who undertook to provide him with an army. Catastrophe awaited: a Scots army indeed crossed the border in hopes of rescuing him, but Oliver Cromwell, a religious Independent who was rapidly making himself master of England's Parliament and armed forces alike, annihilated it near Preston. Charles was sent to London for trial and execution.

The execution, which Scottish public opinion nigh-universally opposed, shattered what remained of Anglo-Scottish solidarity. The royal blood had scarcely dried on the Whitehall scaffold before Charles's son – also named Charles – and the Scots struck a bargain: Charles II (as he was thenceforward known) would embrace the Covenant, which he did most reluctantly, for his easy-going lifestyle made him the unlikeliest of candidates for it; in return the Scots would crown him their king and then regain England for him. It was in vain. Crowned he was, but not for long: Cromwell, now firmly in control of England, extended his control to Scotland by inflicting upon Charles and the Scots a pair of crushing military defeats, and afterwards tightened his grip by proclaiming a formal union between the two nations and erecting forts, at Inverlochy and Inverness, to police the fractious Highlands. Charles, for his part, slunk into exile on the continent, there to await Cromwell's demise.

That came in 1658, whereupon the unified Commonwealth sank into an anarchy that produced a stunning reversal in fortune for Scotland and for Charles. The union was dissolved, and both countries, desperate for stability, restored him in 1660 to their respective thrones. Once in power, Charles turned his back on the Covenant, which he had always detested. Freed from its shackles, he looked on complacently as episcopacy returned with a vengeance in the literal as well as figurative sense.

When 'conventicles' in the Lowlands resisted the new religious order, for instance, his high commissioner in Scotland — in effect, his viceroy there — brought down upon the countryside a 'Highland host' of some 4,500 clansmen with licence to live off the land, and perpetrate any outrage short of murder, until the dissenters submitted. This the clansmen did with such enthusiasm as to sow animosities that were still fresh when the Bonnie Prince swung through the area two generations later.

Charles died in 1685, and, as he left no legitimate issue, his younger brother James succeeded him. There had been no bifurcated titles under the two Charles, because neither England nor Scotland had had a King Charles before, but with the two James it was a different story: just as the old King James had been James I in England and James VI in Scotland, so the new one was James II and VII. There was opposition to his becoming either, because he was an avowed Roman Catholic convert, and his faith was anathema in both kingdoms. In the end, however, he was accepted as the only alternative to renewed civil war.

He soon wore out his welcome. Charles II, a consummate politician, had muted his absolutist views when dealing with his parliaments, but James II possessed the stubbornness as well as the principles of their father. He sought religious accord among his subjects, and was perhaps sincere in doing so, but his actions provoked cynicism and resentment. When he unilaterally suspended all penal laws against Roman Catholics, he was seen as arbitrary (for flouting the will of the legislature) and self-serving (inasmuch as he was Catholic himself). He tried subsequently to deflect the latter charge by extending the same indulgence to the Presbyterians, whose meetings had been suppressed by the restored Episcopalian ascendancy, and to other non-conformists, but the gesture did him no good in England, where non-conforming Protestants were almost as reviled as Catholics were. And the Presbyterians, at least the Scottish ones, were dissatisfied too: they wanted, not mere toleration, but a return to their old supremacy.

Before long, they got it. James's English subjects were willing to put up with one Catholic monarch, but not with a succession of them, and their worst fears materialised in June 1688 when James's queen gave birth to a male Catholic heir. Leading English politicians thereupon invited the Dutch Protestant Prince William of Orange and his wife Mary — James's son-in-law and daughter respectively — to come to England with an army and seize the throne. When William landed, James fled with his infant son to France: he to die there in 1701; the son, also named James, to live out his life in exile as James III and VIII (according to Jacobite loyalists) or the Old Pretender (according to their foes). England's Parliament, treating the flight as an abdication, declared the English throne vacant and offered it formally to William and Mary, who thereafter ruled jointly as William III and Mary II, although William was the managing partner. The Estates of the Scots Parliament were slower, but eventually followed suit at a 'Convention' (with the king absent, they could not assemble as a Parliament) that met in March through April of 1689.[9] When William came to Scotland, the Covenant came back with him; Presbyterianism was once more the official faith of the realm, and the Episcopalians, to say nothing of the Catholics, were out in the cold.

Some of these did not go quietly. When it became clear that the Convention's choice would fall on William, one of its members, another charismatic Graham – the staunchly Episcopalian John Graham of Claverhouse, Viscount Dundee – stormed out, vowing (in the poet Walter Scott's words, not his own) that 'Ere the king's crown shall fall there are crowns to be broke'. Finding scant support in the Lowlands, he continued northward and raised levies of MacDonalds, Camerons, Stewarts and Macleans – most of them either Episcopalian or, especially among the MacDonalds, Catholic – to fight for James.[10] Many cared little enough about James, or, if truth be told, about the underlying religious controversies, but they were hereditary enemies of the Presbyterian Clan Campbell, which, marginalised by the Stuarts, had swept back into power under William's banner. Leading his forces south again, Graham routed a Williamite army at the Pass of Killiecrankie in July 1689, but perished at the moment of victory. Bereft of their leader, his demoralised troops were soon shattered in their turn at Dunkeld by a regiment of Cameronians, an especially fanatical Presbyterian sect named for its founder Richard Cameron. So ended Scotland's first Jacobite rising.

Other risings would follow. Before they did, however, the political complexion of Britain was radically transformed.

The immediate roots of the transformation lay in the 1690s. These were harsh years for Scotland. The economic impacts of repeated famines were exacerbated by protectionist English legislation that effectively barred Scottish traders from England's domestic and overseas markets, and even at home Scottish industry suffered keenly from English competition. In the second half of the decade, the Scots Parliament floated a heady pipe dream for redressing the economic imbalance between the two countries.

Scotland would found a New World colony of her own; through it, raw materials and finished goods from Asia and the Americas would flow into Scottish ports in Scottish bottoms, and Scottish manufactures would in turn be distributed throughout the world, all unencumbered by English tariffs and other anti-competitive English practices. The scheme failed miserably. The colony, founded in 1698, was situated in Darien, in the most malaria-ridden region of the southern Panama coast. Mosquitoes quickly killed off many of the settlers, and troops from a nearby Spanish colony finished the job. After just two years, the surviving settlers surrendered to the Spaniards and slunk back home, and Scotland's leading families, which had invested heavily in the venture, were bankrupted. The collapse of this, Scotland's last hope for economic self-sufficiency, convinced many influential Scots that economic survival was attainable only through Cromwellian-style political union with the southern colossus.

The groundswell toward union gained momentum in the aftermath of the English Act of Settlement the following year. That Act, it will be recalled, had laid the foundation for the Hanoverian succession. The crown would pass from William (Mary having long since died) to Mary's sister Anne, and thence, if Anne died childless (she did), to the descendants of the Electress Sophia of Hanover, who was Anne's distant cousin. The statute thereby permanently excluded the House of Stuart from the English throne. The Scots Parliament pointedly declined to do likewise – indeed, intimated that it might invite the Stuarts back – hoping no doubt to wring economic concessions from England as the price of falling into line. The strategy backfired: the English responded instead with new and even more onerous protectionist legislation. Sentiment for union was now building on both sides: in Scotland, to stave off financial ruin; in England, to protect the political settlements of 1689 and 1701. Judicious bribes did the rest. In 1706, commissioners from the two countries hammered out a Treaty of Union, and in 1707 both parliaments ratified it even as mobs rioted against it in the streets of Edinburgh. By its terms, Scotland retained some of its old prerogatives – its own legal system, the heritable jurisdictions of the clan chiefs (which gave them powers of life and death over their clansmen), and, of course, the Presbyterian Kirk as the established church; just as importantly, the protectionist laws that had throttled Scotland's industry and commerce were wiped from the books, and investors in the ill-fated Darien venture were reimbursed, with interest, for their losses. But Scotland as a separate nation ceased to exist;

so in consequence did bifurcated royal titles, except to diehards who rejected the union; and so too did the Scots Parliament. In their place, Scotland and England became a single nation, thenceforward to be known as Great Britain; the monarch would be styled the ruler of the same; and the two parliaments were merged into one, with the Scots choosing only a minority of its membership in proportion more or less – almost certainly less rather than more – to their estimated share in the overall British population.[11]

The first post-union rising took place almost immediately, in 1708. It was mostly a French affair, albeit with promises of local support. Spain was having its own succession crisis just then; war had erupted, with France and Britain on opposite sides; and France – not for the first or last time – hoped to stir up trouble on British soil by playing 'the Jacobite card'. To that end, a French fleet set sail for the Firth of Forth with the putative James III and VIII and 6,000 French soldiers on board. The local support may well have been forthcoming – the union had stirred enough resentment to generate it – but it was never tested: the fleet unaccountably drifted 100 miles off course, and by the time it righted itself and reached the Firth a British squadron had caught up with it. To avoid being trapped in harbour, the French admiral reversed direction and headed back to France without landing either James or a single soldier. The navigation 'error' may have been deliberate and the enterprise a victim of French inter-service jealousies: there are grounds for suspecting that the French admiral purposely botched the mission in order to embarrass the army, which had advocated it whereas the navy minister and he had opposed it.[12]

The next rising, in 1715, was unique in that it had no foreign military dimension (though Spain rendered some financial assistance); France had made peace with Britain two years earlier and hence was no longer interested. Even so, it posed the most serious threat to the regime of any of the risings except, perhaps, the '45. Two factors – the death of Queen Anne and growing hostility to the union – combined to precipitate it.

The Queen had died without issue the preceding year, and, the Electress Sophia being dead also, the crown had passed to Sophia's son – George I, father of George II – in accordance with the Act of Settlement and Article II of the Treaty of Union. Towards the end of Anne's life there had been talk in government circles of amending the Act and the Treaty to allow James to succeed her, but even if the talk was serious (and that is doubtful) it foundered over James's refusal to renounce Catholicism.

George's accession was a catalyst to the union's opponents, for it brought home to them that, absent violent action, the new arrangement was likely to be perpetual. They had ample cause for aggrievement, because the union was turning out to be a largely one-sided affair. Discriminatory trade barriers had fallen, but new taxes had come instead, notionally the same as in England but in fact more onerous to the Scots: first, because the Scots were less accustomed to such taxes, and second, because they were less able to pay. Likewise, new commercial restrictions, though applicable nationwide, had a nasty way of burdening the Scots more severely. Thus, a ban on the export of raw wool throttled a thriving Scottish trade with the continent; at the same time, it was a boon to English manufacturers of finished wool products, whose European competitors would now find it harder to lay hands on the necessary raw materials. In addition, at the behest of the government the English peers in the House of Lords used their numerical superiority to tinker cynically with the process for selecting the sixteen Scots peers who would join them in the new British Parliament. These and similar indignities eroded, in most areas, whatever support the union had once enjoyed north of the border.

The leader of the Rising was John Erskine, Earl of Mar, a man who by all accounts was fitter for political intrigue than for military command. Known as 'Bobbing John', because of his penchant for switching his allegiances, he had for self-serving reasons come down finally on the Jacobite side. (He was denied appointment to George's first ministry, and convinced himself that James would reward him better.) Raising his standard at Braemar, he gathered about him between 8,000 and 10,000 men,[13] Highland and Lowland alike, mostly from north of the Forth, where anti-union and Episcopalian sentiment was strongest. After dithering too long, and thereby giving a government army time to assemble, he sent 2,000 of them south to reinforce several hundred English Jacobites who had risen in Lancashire. In the '15 as in the '45, Lancashire provided, relatively speaking, the most fertile English recruiting ground for Jacobites, due to its large Catholic population and the existence of significant industrial unrest. He then marched south himself with his main body in hopes of smashing through the smaller government army and re-joining the southern contingent.

That government army was ably led by the Duke of Argyll, who, like his ancestor in Cromwell's day, was chief of the principal branch of Clan Campbell (although Campbell support for the new dynasty was by no means monolithic and Campbells fought on the Jacobite side as well). The opposing armies met at Sheriffmuir, just above Stirling and its castle, on 13 November. The battle was tactically a draw but strategically a triumph for Argyll, because the outcome prevented Mar from continuing south as he had planned. Instead, he was trapped north of Stirling, where his soldiers, with no place to go, soon melted away. To have marched south would have been pointless in any case, for there would have been no-one to meet him: the Lancastrians and their Scots allies surrendered the next day at Preston, where Cromwell had broken another Scots army in 1648.

In a quixotic anti-climax, James III, who had not even known of the Rising until it was well underway, embarked for Peterhead on the Scottish east coast, landed in late December – five weeks after Sheriffmuir and Preston had put paid to his hopes – and proceeded to nearby Perth. Sustained, it seems, by a profound capacity for denial, he presided over a shadow court there until early in the new year. Reality set in when Argyll advanced to attack him, upon which he and Mar scurried off furtively to France. Before doing so, he ordered the torching of several Lowland towns that lay between Argyll and himself: an act which (though he tried later to make amends) did not endear him or his cause to the inhabitants and, like the 'Highland host', was bitterly remembered a generation afterward. The view from the stern of his departing ship was his last ever of Scotland.

The final rising before the '45 took place in March of 1719. As in 1708, the principal impetus came from abroad: not from France, which was still on the sidelines, but from Spain, which was at war with Austria when Britain weighed in on the Austrian side. The initial plan was ambitious: the main part of the expedition, consisting of 5,000 Spanish troops, would land in England; meanwhile another 300 Spaniards would sail to the western Scottish Highlands under the command of the veteran Jacobite soldier George Keith, join forces on shore with sympathetic clansmen, and create a diversion there. But a violent storm dispersed the larger flotilla, and the smaller one, originally intended only for diversion purposes, had to go it alone. As a further complication, Keith was joined en route by an unwelcome ally, the Marquis of Tullibardine, who had been dispossessed of his estates after the '15 and had been living in France ever since. The two men quickly fell to bickering over who was in charge, with Tullibardine being supported by some fellow exiles who had accompanied him. The Spanish nevertheless succeeded in landing and meeting up with various clan units – MacDonalds of Clanranald and Camerons, among others – and together they made for Glen Shiel, which is perhaps the most spectacular site in the western Highlands. They had little time to enjoy the scenery, however, for they soon came under mortar fire from a government troop. The Highlanders and the Jacobite leaders fled, the former bringing with them, for future use, the arms that the Spanish had given them; the Spanish themselves surrendered; and the '19 fizzled out as ingloriously as its predecessors.

On 20 December 1720 a new player appeared on the stage. Charles Edward Stuart was born to James and his wife, Maria Clementina Sobieska of Poland, at the Palazzo Muti in Rome, whence James had removed himself in 1717. The move was not voluntary: the 1713 Treaty of Utrecht, which ended the bloody, multi-nation struggle over the Spanish succession, obligated France not only to cease supporting him but to expel him from its territories. As the older son – another, Henry, would be born in 1725 – Charles Edward was heir, in Jacobite eyes, to his father's titles and kingdoms, or at least (as some Jacobites would have said) to the Scottish portions of these. For the first two decades of his life, however, his chances of gaining any part of that legacy seemed grim.

The treaty ushered in a long period of détente between Britain and France, depriving James and his followers of any realistic hope of French aid. This was the more so after King Louis XIV of France died in 1715. Louis had been genuinely attached to the Stuart family, or, if not to the family, to the dynastic principle that it represented. In contrast, both Philippe d'Orleans, who was regent during the minority of Louis's great-grandson and successor Louis XV, and Cardinal Fleury, who was France's prime minister in all but name throughout much of Louis XV's majority (his influence extended from 1726 until he died, at ninety, in 1743), were committed to keeping the peace, as was Fleury's even longer-serving British counterpart, Robert Walpole. Except for the flare-up of 1718–19, relations between Britain and Spain were also pacific. The Jacobites could accomplish nothing without help from one or both of these Catholic powers.

During the same period, the London government was tightening its grip on the Scottish Highlands by building an ambitious system of barracks, forts, and connecting roads, mostly at the suggestion and under the direction of Major-General, later Field Marshal, George Wade. Fort William, at the head of Loch Linnhe, was already in place, having gone up in William III's time, as were the great citadels at Edinburgh, Stirling and Dumbarton. To these were added Fort George, near Inverness, in 1727 (replacing an older fortification from Cromwell's era), and Fort Augustus, at the southern end of Loch Ness, in 1742. When the newer forts were finished, they would form, with Fort William, an almost perfectly straight line that bisected the Highlands north to south in a slightly westerly direction through the Great Glen, separating the north-west Highlands from the Monadhliath and Grampian mountain ranges. The barracks were erected a little earlier, before Wade entered the scene: Inversnaid, at Loch Lomond, and Kiliwhimen, on the eastern shore of Loch Ness (1720); Bernera, across from Skye (1723); and Ruthven, in Badenoch (1724).

In addition, Wade proposed the revival of 'independent companies': small, mobile units comprised of clansmen, from loyal clans, who knew the Highlands well enough to police them effectively and keep the other clans in line. They were to be 'independent' in the sense that they would not be attached to any regiment. Such companies had existed in the recent past – one, indeed, dated back to 1624 – but George I, distrusting them, ordered all of them disbanded in 1717. Wade was not the first to advise reinstating them: Simon Fraser, Lord Lovat, chief of Clan Fraser, had already sent the King a similar proposal. But Lovat's allegiances, as was well known, were even more flexible than Mar's had been, so Wade was asked for a second opinion. Once he agreed, it was done.

Initially there would be six companies of varying sizes: seventy-one apiece in the three smaller companies, and 114 apiece in the three larger ones.[14] Four more companies were added in 1739, at which time all ten were regimented as the 43rd Regiment of Foot, later changed to the 42nd. Because of the dark colour of their tartans, or perhaps because they were charged with suppressing the traditional Highland practice of 'blackmail' (viz., demanding money or goods in return for not stealing your neighbour's cattle), they were nicknamed 'the Black Watch'.[15] Five of the companies were raised from clans that were impeccably Presbyterian and dependable: three company captains were Campbells, one was a Munro, and one was a Grant.[16] The sixth captain, Lovat himself, was neither Presbyterian nor dependable – whenever the spirit moved he was a Roman Catholic, and his political undependability would bring him, in old age, to the block – but for the present he was proclaiming himself a staunch Hanoverian Protestant.[17] Besides suppressing blackmail and riots, the Watch was charged with enforcing the Disarming Acts of 1716 and 1725; the second of these, in fact, was enacted just nine days before King George issued the order that brought the companies into existence. If they failed in that mission it was not from want of trying, but from the magnitude of the territory and the task.

Between the companies, the barracks, the forts, the roads, and the reduced international tensions, it seemed that the Jacobites were finished: for instance, they were powerless to prevent George II from succeeding peacefully to the British throne in 1727. Some even cut deals with the government. Then their world changed.

In 1739, Walpole, facing mounting opposition in Parliament and the press, was forced into war with Spain over alleged atrocities perpetrated by Spanish colonial officials against captured English smugglers (who, under the Treaty of Utrecht, had no business trading with Spanish colonies in the first place). This alone was enough to re-ignite Jacobite hopes: Spain had intervened on James's behalf before, and might make a better job of it this time. Soon the war widened and the hopes soared. The following year, upstart Prussia, hitherto a minor player in European affairs, rolled into Austrian Silesia, threatening Austria's territorial integrity and demonstrating to all that she was now a force to be reckoned with. British concerns were three-fold. George II feared for the safety of his Hanoverian homeland; his ministers worried about the impact on Europe's balance of power; and the British public was chivalrously aroused by the plight of Austria's young queen, Maria Theresa, whose inheritance was in jeopardy. These concerns deepened when, in 1741, France allied herself with Prussia, and Spain – tied to France by self-interest and consanguinity (the kings of both countries were Bourbons) – swung quickly into line. Walpole's fall from power in February of 1742 and Fleury's death a year later accelerated the slide toward world war; Fleury's passing, moreover, removed a powerful opponent of French intervention on the Jacobite side. Cardinal Tencin, who was expected to succeed Fleury (but in the end did not, although he served, without portfolio, in the new ministry), was more favourably inclined: unsurprisingly, since he owed his cardinal's hat to James's influence at the Vatican.[18]

Britain responded to these events, first by slipping covert subsidies to Austria, then by paying proxies to fight for her, and next by sending troops of her own to bolster the Austrian forces. On 16 June 1743 (27 June New Style) – while Britain and France were still technically at peace – Britons, Dutch and Hanoverians, led by George II in person, faced a French army at Dettingen, in Germany. The outcome, a stunning victory for the allies, galvanised at least some French ministers into thinking once more of the Jacobite card.

The Jacobites were already stirring. As early as 1737, disaffected Highland leaders, their optimism roused by recent anti-union mob violence in Edinburgh, put out feelers to Fleury and James, asking them to support a new rising. The answers were not encouraging – Fleury stuck to his peace policy, and even James deprecated the chances for success – but the seed was planted. With the outbreak of war, the efforts intensified. A small group of Scottish activists, Highland and Lowland alike (including Lovat, who had switched sides), formed a 'concert', or 'association', the purpose of which was to seek a Stuart restoration in earnest. Once Walpole fell, influential English Jacobites organised toward the same end, though events would show that they lacked the staying power of their Scots counterparts. For the next half dozen years, spies and messengers, as well as men of substance, scurried back and forth between England, Scotland, Paris and the exiled court in Rome; there was encouragement and support, too, from an expatriate Irish community that had followed James II to France after he was driven from Ireland in 1690. The details of these activities are tangential to our narrative, have been amply reported elsewhere, and need not be reiterated here.[19] Suffice it to note that the participants were a mixed lot – some were level headed, others unstable, self-serving or both – and so the information that they disseminated ran the gamut from cold realism to intentional overstatement or wishful thinking. Thus, they might exaggerate the strength of Jacobite sentiment in their representations to the French court, hoping thereby to pry more aid out of France; or, back home, exaggerate the level of French enthusiasm in order to stiffen the backbones of their fellow Jacobites. Or they might not. But despite the conflicting information that was circulating in both directions across the Channel and the Alps, several points were becoming clear, and are even clearer in hindsight today.

Firstly, after Fleury's death, the French Council of State – which was roughly analogous to the present-day British or US cabinet – was divided, and some ministers, not to mention the King himself, changed their minds as events unfolded. There were those, like Tencin, who wanted to invade both England and Scotland (with the principal invasion effort directed to the former) in order to effectuate what in modern terms might be called 'regime change': if their scheme was successful, James Stuart would replace George II as King James III of Great Britain. In their view, a Stuart king, beholden to France and with no stake in Hanover, would become a valued ally; at the very least, he could be counted upon to withdraw British forces from the European war.[20] Others, believing that a unified Britain under any dynasty would not serve French interests, advocated invading Scotland only and helping Scottish Jacobites to break up the union so that James could reign at Holyrood Palace as King James VIII. Fleury himself seems to have been coming around to this position in his final years.[21] Still others deemed either venture too risky, and proposed an attempt on Ireland instead. This would divert Hanoverian troops from Britain and leave the Jacobites virtually unopposed. And some rejected all of these options, preferring to concentrate French military efforts on the continent. To complicate matters, King Frederick of Prussia, not wishing to see a Catholic regime displace a Protestant one – a Protestant one, moreover, with roots in Germany, which made it appealing to Frederick despite the personal and political enmity between George II and himself – threatened to withdraw from the Franco-Prussian alliance if France participated in ousting the House of Hanover from the British throne.

The Scottish Jacobites, moreover, were also at cross purposes, with some wanting James to become King James III of Great Britain and others wanting only to make him King James VIII of an independent Scotland. James and his son Charles, now a young man in his twenties, harboured no such ambivalence: they aimed at a Stuart restoration in all three kingdoms (Ireland being the third), and Charles in particular would settle for nothing less.

Thirdly, Jacobite leaders on both sides of the border were reluctant to rise, or commit to a rising, unless the French promised to support them, and some were so cautious as to insist that the French land first. The French, for their part, would do no such thing until the Jacobites had either risen or committed to a rising – especially the English Jacobites, since England was where French ministers, or at any rate the most audacious ones, intended to direct the principal invasion effort. If the objective of these ministers is explicable, in modern terms, as 'regime change', the modern expression that most aptly describes Franco-Jacobite relations is Catch-22.

In late 1743 and early 1744 the impasse was broken. With Fleury gone, Louis XV decided, to Tencin's chagrin, to become his own prime minister. While Fleury lived Louis had shared his minister's indifference to the Jacobites, but Britain's growing military presence on the continent now altered his thinking. Stung by Dettingen and related events – believing, moreover, inflated reports that English Jacobites would rise in large numbers to support a French landing – he became a vigorous proponent of regime change. To that end, he ordered a large-scale invasion of England, and assembled an army and fleet at Dunkirk to carry it out. At the same time, Charles Edward was invited or permitted – it is not clear which[22] – to come secretly to Paris, where he arrived on 28 January (8 February by continental reckoning). He went thence to Gravelines, close to where the troop transports awaited; once there, he was given nominal command of the expedition, so that the French might appear as liberators rather than foreign conquerors. The real authority, however, was vested in Maurice, Marshal Saxe, who was perhaps the most celebrated soldier of his day.

It was a formidable undertaking. The main invasion force, 12,000 to 15,000 strong,[23] was to cross in troopships to Essex once warships had opened the way. Three thousand more men from the Irish Brigade – soldiers, of Irish origin, whose forebears had come to France after James II was beaten in Ireland, and who were now incorporated, in their own distinctive units, into the regular French Army – would head for Scotland under George Keith of the '19 for the usual purpose of creating a diversion. A separate, smaller fleet would set out from Brest to lure off-station the British squadron that was guarding the Channel and thereby clear the passage for Saxe, Charles and the rest. To preserve secrecy, Louis refrained from declaring war. With England virtually empty of troops, the best of whom were off fighting on the continent, the plan seemed unlikely to fail, even if the putative English Jacobites proved supine or non-existent.

But it did fail. First, unforeseen delays destroyed the element of surprise. Then, on the night of 24–25 February, with the armada ready to sail and most of the troops, together with Charles and Saxe, on board, a powerful storm – the same 'Protestant wind' that had scattered the Spanish in Drake's time and again in 1719, and would sweep the French out of Ireland's Bantry Bay in 1796 – blew up and battered the ships, sinking several and drowning many of the men. A second storm struck four nights later, with equally devastating effects. There was now no hope of reaching England safely, and Saxe, who had never favoured the mission to begin with, gave up on it. Louis too abandoned the idea. Three weeks later, France declared war – the invasion having collapsed, there was no more reason not to (the immediate *casus belli* was Britain's insistence that France expel Charles in accordance with the Treaty of Utrecht) – and for the next year and a half Louis was guided by those of his ministers who wanted to focus exclusively on the European theatre.

Charles was left to skulk, first at Gravelines and then in Paris, where Louis tried to fob him off with a pension. But Charles had grander notions: he was now determined if necessary to go to Scotland alone,[24] rally supporters there, and start a rising on his own. He was confident that French interest would be rekindled once he did. The fact that his closest advisors warned him against this – the 'Associator' John Murray of Broughton, who became his secretary, for one; Keith, for another – did not deter him, for, as we have said, in his princely self-absorption he supposed that he could make things so by wishing them so. And on this occasion, as later at Derby, he was right.

When he came, who would fight for him, or at least welcome him and wish him well?

These are two different questions. It was one thing to drink surreptitious loyal toasts to him and his father, as the Jacobite gentry were wont to do, or to shout Jacobite slogans or sing Jacobite songs at local taverns in the manner of the 'lower orders';[25] quite another to risk life and estate for him. There were plenty, especially in England, who were willing to do the first but not the second, although we can never know how many, in that first group, might have acted differently if the circumstances had been more auspicious. One noted modern historian estimates that during the reigns of the first two Georges about a quarter of England's gentry families harboured Jacobite sympathies, perhaps up to forty per cent in Lancashire, where Catholics abounded. The same historian has also found evidence of like sympathies among significant segments of the general population, especially in industrial Lancaster, in Kent and Essex, where the projected invasion routes lay (and where there were numerous smugglers, many of whom, as we shall see, had strong Jacobite leanings), and in London, with its large Irish Catholic immigrant community, as well as in other major cities and industrial villages.[26]

Yet only a few hundred Englishmen would actually bear arms on Charles's behalf, most of them in the doomed Manchester Regiment, which was recruited from Catholic areas in Lancashire and its environs. One suspects, as to the rest, that for the majority of them the slogans and songs – perhaps the toasts too – did not reflect any profound attachment to the Stuarts but rather were mechanisms for expressing antipathy to the Hanoverian regime and its national or local agents.

On the other hand, the extent of the English commitment was never tested, for two reasons. One was that when Charles crossed into England after his triumph at Prestonpans he by-passed some of the very areas – Northumberland and the South-West – where the gentry were likeliest to rally to him.[27] The other is that his gamble was a complicated affair with many interdependent elements. He had wagered that his landing would set into motion a chain reaction whereby the Scots would rise, the French upon seeing this would send men and money to help him, and the English would rise in turn when he marched over the border with the Scots and French in train. And his judgments were prescient enough, for significant numbers of Scots did join him, and the French did indeed try to help him to a greater degree than is commonly realised. But for various reasons France was unable to supply enough troops to reassure his jittery English well-wishers, who in consequence sat on their hands.[28] Whether they would have done so if France had succeeded in dispatching a 1744-sized invasion force, or anything near it, is one of the '45's imponderables – like the question of what would have happened if Charles had persuaded his Council to press on to London even without the hoped-for English Jacobite and French assistance.

In Scotland the picture was different. There, men did turn out in abundance to fight for him: some eleven to fourteen thousand over the course of the rebellion,[29] which is an impressive figure considering that Scotland's population at the time was only one fifth of England's (1,300,000 compared to about 6,500,000 in England and Wales).[30] Moreover, the turnout came from all over the country, and not exclusively or even primarily from the Highlands.[31] One must bear in mind, though, that this may not reflect popular sentiment, because the 'heritable jurisdictions' gave Scottish chiefs and lords – Highland and Lowland alike – coercive powers over their tenantry that English squires would have envied. Some in the rank and file were no doubt there by choice, but others, on both sides of the Highland line, came because their homes would have been burnt about their ears if they had desisted. One cannot say, therefore, how many of Charles's men followed him willingly. It may be instructive that, even by the most generous estimates, he never attracted anywhere near the 20,000 or so who at one time or another flocked to Bobbing John's standard in 1715.[32]

Yet patterns emerge through the uncertainties. Often these patterns intersect like the colours of the mythical clan tartans. Thus, it is difficult to disentangle dynastic from religious loyalties, religious loyalties from clan rivalries, clan rivalries from economic exigencies, or economic exigencies (to say nothing of dynastic and religious loyalties) from Scottish nationalism, and one thread – Episcopalianism, together with its English cousin, 'non-juring' Anglicanism – seems to permeate them all.[33] I shall nevertheless try to describe each of the patterns separately. The last of them is surprising.

RELIGION

One would think that Catholics would rise in large numbers – after all, the Prince, his father and his grandfather were of their faith – but in the end they did not: in part because they were cowed by nearly two centuries of repression (which became especially severe after the '15) and in part because Charles Edward chose, for political reasons, to distance himself from them. Besides, there were not that many of them: possibly two per cent of England's population and one per cent of Scotland's.[34] But Episcopalians, or Anglicans as they were known below the border, where theirs was the Church Established, were another story.[35]

In 1689, and again in 1701, upon James III and VIII's 'accession' (though of course only Jacobites recognised it as such), England's Anglican clergy were required, as a condition of retaining their benefices, to take an oath acknowledging William, Mary and their successors as heads of state and church. Most did, but about 400 – perhaps four per cent of the whole[36] – refused. These 'non-jurants' and their spiritual descendants thereafter formed, together with their congregations, a small but committed core of Stuart loyalists.

In Scotland there was no question of requiring Episcopalian clerics to recognise William and Mary as heads of the national church, because Episcopalianism was not Scotland's national creed to begin with, but an equivalent oath was offered them via a parliamentary 'Act of Toleration' in 1712: they could keep their livelihoods by abjuring the Stuarts as monarchs.

There is disagreement over how many availed themselves of the opportunity: some say most did; some say it was only a few.[37] No matter: Scottish Episcopalians usually remained Jacobite whether their ministers took the oath or not,[38] and by the 1740s there were over 200,000 of them – about twenty per cent of Scotland's total population – with the strongest concentrations appearing in the Highlands and the north-east.[39] Moreover, purists among the clergy who declined the oath and lost their livings in consequence were far from being silenced; instead, they scattered and spread sedition throughout the countryside, and deposed Episcopalian university professors did the same, thereby providing more grist for the Jacobite mill.[40]

The Scots Episcopalians – at least, those for whom religion was the driving force – and their non-jurant Anglican cousins were the most constant, dedicated and principled devotees of the Jacobite cause. To them, allegiance to the Stuarts as God's anointed was literally an article of faith, and rebellion or resistance constituted both treason and sacrilege. To be sure, the motives of the Episcopalians may not have been altogether other-worldly. Doubtless they wanted to replace the Presbyterian Kirk as Scotland's official church, with all that that would imply in the way of earthly privilege and power, so that they might come into their own when Jamie and Charlie did.[41] And many among them mixed religion with social snobbery, by despising Presbyterianism, with its more democratic tenets and ecclesiastical structure, as a creed fit only for the masses.[42] Still, they and the non-juring Anglicans were more idealistic, and less self-seeking, than most of Charles's followers, except perhaps for the 'sentimental Jacobites' who were loyal to the exiled dynasty for its own sake – and that sort of sentimental loyalty often went hand-in-hand with Episcopalianism, and reflected its teachings. Certainly they were more idealistic by far than the clear-eyed, often hard-eyed Highland chiefs. Not all of them were militant in the sense that they would bear arms – some, indeed, retreated into mysticism and 'quietism'[43] – but enough of them were, and would, to make them the backbone of Charles's fighting strength.

It is possible, though, to overstate the impact of religion on the '45. This was no mere reprise of the Bishops' Wars. The boatmen on the River Tyne, in Newcastle, were famously Jacobite, even though they were both Scottish and Presbyterian.[44] For them, economic self interest evidently trumped religion. Presbyterian soldiers fighting on the Jacobite side reportedly liked to have their ministers accompany them on campaign and into battle, and some did.[45] The mostly Episcopalian MacKenzies were (again, mostly) a government-leaning clan in the '45,[46] and conversely the Frasers, who were mostly Presbyterian despite the wavering spiritual odyssey of their chief, sat out at first but eventually declared for Charles Edward.[47] So the correlation between religious and political allegiance was not exact. Nevertheless, it seems accurate to say that Episcopalianism, more than any other single component, was the epoxy that bound the Jacobite army together,[48] and it is certainly true that the majority of Presbyterians cast their lots with the government.

PARTY POLITICS

From the reign of Charles II onward English politics had been riven by two factions: the Whigs and the Tories. (These were uncomplimentary nicknames that each bestowed upon the other.)[49] They were not parties in the modern sense – those would await the passage of the Reform Act of 1832 – but rather were loose alignments of like-minded individuals who forged alliances with one another in order to advance common interests. The Tories traced their roots to the Cavaliers who had fought for King Charles during the English Civil War, the Whigs to the Parliamentarians who had first sought to limit his powers and then, finding him resistant, made war upon him and executed him. Thus, Tories were more likely to espouse hereditary kingship and the royal prerogative, while Whigs touted contractual theories of elective, limited monarchy. The Tories, for their part, thought the Whig commitment to limited monarchy hypocritical and self-serving: they believed (as we have seen, with some justice) that the Whigs meant to set up a dictatorial legislature, controlled of course by themselves, in the king's stead. These were not the only ideological differences between the two sides. The Tories were leery of standing armies, having suffered under one in Cromwell's time, and thus they opposed the sort of military adventurism – the War of the Spanish Succession, in the early part of the century; the War of the Austrian Succession in the middle – that made such armies necessary. And as devout Anglicans, they resented what they perceived as the cynical manipulation of the church, for political ends, by successive Whig administrations. Not surprisingly, the ideological posturing, among both factions, often masked self-interested power ploys, and many of the players were not averse to switching sides for the right price.

The Tories fared badly under the first two Georges. The 1688–89 constitutional revolution was essentially a Whig production, as was the 1701
Act of Settlement. For this reason, and also because they opposed the War
of the Spanish Succession (they had forced an early peace while briefly
in power during the closing years of Queen Anne's reign), George I
was hostile to them from the outset. Their plight worsened even more
during the two long decades that Walpole held power. A Whig himself,
he presided over a ruthless spoils system: Tories were barred, not only
from holding office, but also from the civil service, the judiciary, the
officer corps of the Army (and, to a slightly lesser extent, the Navy), and
bishoprics, as well as a host of other positions – in a word, from every
activity that might give them a voice in national or even local affairs.[50]
Consigned to political oblivion, a number of them found the Stuart
cause appealing, especially since its principles coincided with their own
conservative views. It is not clear how just many Tories were openly or
secretly pro-Jacobite. One prominent historian asserts that the Tory party
was overwhelmingly so;[51] others find Jacobitism only at its margins.[52]
Whatever the actual figures, it was with the Tories as with boys named
John: not all Tories were Jacobite, but all Jacobites were Tories, except for
a few radical Whigs who flirted with Jacobitism out of disillusionment
with the new order.[53]

The Whig-Tory divide was of English origin. How did it play out in
Scotland? Here too historians and even contemporaries appear to disagree
profoundly. Christopher Duffy and Evelyn Cruickshanks state confidently that there was 'no Tory party' in Scotland, though Cruickshanks
qualifies the statement by adding the phrase 'as such' – whatever that may
mean; and Frank McLynn quotes David Hume to the same effect.[54] Yet
Gerald Warner has authored a very creditable book entitled *The Scottish
Tory Party – a History*,[55] the first four chapters of which trace the party's
development from Charles II's day to the '45, and at one point he quotes
George Lockhart, a Jacobite leader of the period, as referring to 'the few
Scots Torys' who were elected to the Westminster parliament immedi-
ately after the union.[56] He further observes, on his own account, that in
Scotland at this time, 'Toryism and Jacobitism were the same thing'.[57]
Perhaps Warner and Lockhart are using the term 'Scottish (or Scots)
Tory', not to connote allegiance to a party 'as such', *pace* Cruickshanks,
but rather to describe a state of mind: that of being Episcopalian (or, in
some instances, Catholic), out of favour politically, and Jacobite. There

were certainly plenty of Scots who were those. And there is this much consensus: whatever the case may have been in England, in Warner's words 'there were no *Hanoverian* Tories in Scotland'.[58]

There were, however, Hanoverian Whigs in Scotland – to be a Scottish Whig was to be Hanoverian by definition – and like their English counterparts they wielded power. United they were not. On the contrary, they were divided into two warring factions: the 'Argathelians', who looked for leadership to the Argyll family, and the 'Squadrone Volante', or 'Flying Squadron', a possibly derisory nickname derived from their tendency to try to control the balance of power by switching their votes back and forth between the Whigs and Tories in the early post-union British parliaments. By the time of the '45, the Squadrones were allied to George II, the Argathelians to his ministry, from which George was alienated. Despite their mutual hostility, though, they were of one mind in rejecting the Stuarts and giving their wholehearted support to the ruling dynasty. Charles would have to seek comfort from the Tories: that is to say, from English Tories, be they few or many, who harboured Jacobite sympathies, and, if Duffy, Cruickshanks and Hume are right in maintaining that there were no Scottish Tories 'as such', from Scots with a Tory-ish state of mind.

SCOTTISH NATIONALISM

The union had provoked rioting in Edinburgh at its inception in 1707, and in most of Scotland it remained just as unpopular a generation later. Glasgow was an exception: its commercial classes had benefited greatly from the elimination of trade barriers between the two former kingdoms, and in consequence it remained adamantly Whig – in other words, pro-government – throughout the Rising, as did the surrounding areas.[59] But these commercial benefits did not percolate through to the rest of the country, and the new taxes imposed by the union parliament (where English members dominated both houses) imposed harsh burdens and triggered commensurately fierce resentments. Episcopalians also disliked the union, for while the Presbyterian establishment had originated under a Scots parliament in 1690, the treaty had perpetuated it and embedded it in constitutional granite.

In addition to economic and religious considerations, one should not underestimate the force of raw patriotic sentiment, reinforced by the fact that the Stuarts were a native dynasty. True, they had not ruled in more than fifty years, and there had been little love lost between them and their Scottish subjects when they did, especially once they deserted Holyrood Palace and moved south to Whitehall after the 1603 union of crowns. But the passage of time may have worked in their favour, by erasing unpleasant memories and making them seem, to many, an attractive alternative to the unpopular German incumbents.

For mixed economic, religious and sentimental reasons, therefore, Scottish nationalists looked to Charles to dissolve the union. Whether he would then pursue the English crown separately was (in their calculations, not his) an ambiguity to be addressed at some future date.

THE HIGHLANDS

There is a cloying mythology about the '45. It postulates that the Rising was an apocalyptic struggle between the Highland clans, as anachronistic repositories of a romantic but fey Gaelic culture, and the encroaching modern capitalism of the south: that is, of England and the Scottish Lowlands. According to the myth, each clan was almost literally a band of brothers, bound by ties of kinship to one another and to their chief, who reciprocated his clansmen's love for him. In this patriarchal, hierarchical society, the clansmen bore true allegiance to their hereditary kings, the Stuarts, as a natural extension of their allegiance – indeed their childlike submission – to their hereditary chief ('clann' means 'children' in Gaelic); the chiefs reverenced the Stuarts as well; and if any chiefs wavered in their duty Charles won them over with his personal charm. Motivated, then, by loyalty alone, the chiefs threw caution to the winds and flocked to his banner with their equally loyal clansmen in tow, regardless of personal or clan interests.

The reality was different. Of the approximately forty Highland clans that existed at this time,[60] only about half participated in the Rising at all, and at least four fought for the government, albeit with varying degrees of enthusiasm: the MacKays, the Munros, the Sutherlands, and of course the Campbells.[61] Others were pro-government (or mostly so) but did not bear arms – the MacKenzies and Grants, for instance[62] – or else were divided (MacKenzies, Grants, MacLeods, MacKintoshes);[63] and one, the MacPhersons, followed its chief in switching from the government's to the Prince's side after the conflict began, though some of the clan held back and refused to turn out for either party.[64] Still others hedged their bets cynically: the chief stayed at home, feigning neutrality, and quietly dispatched his son, or another kinsman, to lead out the clan in his place. Unsurprisingly to those who knew him, Simon Fraser of Lovat played this game,[65] and he was not the only one: so too did Alexander MacDonell of Barisdale, Ranald MacDonald of Clanranald, John MacDonell of Glengarry, and Douglas Stewart of Appin.[66]

In all instances, the choice of whom, if anyone, to support was made by the chief, or by a relative acting as his surrogate. The loyalties and preferences of rank and file clansmen did not enter into the equation. For them it was turn out or be burnt out by their 'father' the chief. Few were as able to resist his paternal ministrations as the recalcitrant MacPhersons.

Nor did the myth reflect the actual clan structure. In the first place, there was no necessary kinship between the chief and his 'children'. He would probably be related to his tacksmen, who were his immediate underlings, leasing land from him and serving as his factors in peacetime and his officers in time of war, but that was the extent of it. Kinship with the rest was unlikely in any event, given that many of the chiefs had Norman antecedents, their ancestors having imposed themselves on the native inhabitants of the area as William the Conqueror and his successors extended Anglo-Norman influence northward. This was certainly true of the Chisholms, Frasers, Colquhouns and Grants.[67] Indeed, the tradition whereby ordinary clansmen took on the surnames of their chiefs appears to date back no further than the seventeenth century, and even afterward they would move freely from one clan to another, assuming the name of whichever chief controlled the territory where they had most recently settled.[68]

There was little or no cultural affinity either. The chiefs by this time tended to be, not the rude warrior types of old (if they had ever been such), but polished, cosmopolitan gentry, comfortable in any society. James I and VI had seen to that in 1609 by promulgating the Statutes of Iona, which required the chiefs thenceforward to send their sons to be educated in England or the Lowlands. Many of the chiefs were sophisticated and calculating businessmen as well, as much so as their southern counterparts: for example, Donald Cameron of Lochiel, one of the '45's leading figures, was an eager 'improver' who utilised the latest agricultural techniques on his holdings and was heavily involved in foreign trade.[69] He was typical of the other Jacobite chiefs, not only in this, but also in the fact that – as we shall see momentarily – his decision to follow Charles was motivated as much by hard-headed economic considerations as by personal or dynastic loyalties. The more sophisticated and business oriented the chiefs became, the wider grew the gulf – social, cultural, economic – between them and ordinary clan members. This widening gulf, and the accompanying commercial mindset, led directly to the 'clearances' that depopulated the Highlands beginning in the latter part of the century.

Finally, just as the Highlands were not uniformly Jacobite, the rest of Scotland was by no means exclusively in the Hanoverian camp. Glasgow and its environs excepted, Charles was to pick up support throughout the Lowlands, with much of it coming from the Episcopalian north-east, on the far side of the River Tay. The extent of this support has perhaps been masked by Charles's practice of decking out all his Scottish troops in Highland dress, Highlanders and Lowlanders alike.[70] Clothes, however, did not make the man. In fact, only a minority of the Jacobite army was Highland – forty-three to forty-six per cent[71] – and nearly all of the generals were Lowlanders, including the two highest-ranking ones: George Murray and James Drummond, Duke of Perth. (The figures are for the entire war; they do not apply to Prestonpans, where the army was still overwhelmingly Highland, serious Lowland recruiting not yet having begun.) Forty-three per cent was a substantial minority to be sure, especially if one historian is correct in estimating that Highlanders made up less than a third of Scotland's overall population at the time.[72] But it explodes the image of the '45 as a cultural clash between retrograde – albeit achingly appealing – Gaelic clans and the rest of Britain.

Nevertheless, the Rising had a significant Highland component. The Campbell factor loomed large. Clan Campbell, based in Argyll, had long collided with its neighbours – Camerons, Frasers, Appin Stewarts and several MacDonald septs, among others – from the adjacent Great Glen. Religious differences (the Campbells were Presbyterian, the rest mostly Episcopalian or Catholic), territorial ambitions, and the Highland pastime of cattle thieving had all played a part. These ancient feuds, of which the Campbells had lately got the better, were exacerbated in the 1740s by harsh economic exigencies: overpopulation, bad weather, and tax burdens resulting from the union.

The Campbells had been more economically as well as more militarily efficient. They had taken advantage of the favour that they enjoyed with the Westminster government to secure legal land titles – hitherto unknown and unnecessary in the Highlands – that the new regime would recognise against competing claims by rival chiefs (for instance, Cameron of Lochiel, who had no land titles at all). At the same time, they had created a more profitable farming system by eliminating their tacksmen and leasing their land instead directly to tenant farmers who offered the highest bids. The practice weakened the Campbells militarily, for tacksmen served both as officers and recruiting agents in the old clan armies, but the Dukes of Argyll – who were also the hereditary clan chiefs – rightly calculated that in the coming era clan strength would be reckoned in cash rather than in fighting forces. They counted upon the union government, with its roads, forts and independent companies (half of which, be it remembered, were Campbell-officered and manned), to protect loyal clans like theirs from the depredations of lawless ones. Lastly, they used their cash superiority to build a credit system that left the surrounding chiefs indebted to them for substantial sums of money.[73]

It is easy to see why, in these circumstances, the latter found the Jacobite option attractive. Breaking the union would at one swoop eliminate their tax problems and make the land titles a non-issue. And the victorious Stuarts would surely reward them by liquidating all debts to the mutual Campbell enemy.

Even so, they were calculating and cautious. They sat on the fence as long as they could, or hedged bets, as described earlier, by sending their sons to fight instead of leading their clans themselves. Or, if they did 'come out' in person, some of them – Lochiel for one; MacPherson of Cluny for another – hedged their bets in another way: they made Charles promise to indemnify them if the Rising failed and they forfeited their estates in consequence.[74] But when push came to shove, most of the Great Glen chiefs, plus others from more distant parts, declared more or less openly for the Prince. None of them individually was an important player on the Scottish political stage – there was not a major magnate amongst them[75] – but collectively they and their 'children' made valuable contributions in manpower and fighting spirit.

DYNASTIC LOYALTY: 'SENTIMENTAL JACOBITISM'

Sentimental Jacobitism, by which is meant disinterested loyalty to Charles, to his father, or to the Stuart dynasty, appears toward the bottom of the list, because of all the motivating factors that would drive Charles's followers it was the least prevalent and least important – especially in the Highlands, despite the tartan myths. And when one does encounter this sort of loyalty, it is usually in conjunction with other factors, such as Episcopalianism (or non-juring Anglicanism), which equated obedience to the 'legitimate' dynasty with obedience to God. Thus it is no coincidence that George Murray, who would exercise day-to-day command of Charles's army (Charles retained overall command for himself), moved from Presbyterianism toward Episcopalianism as he moved toward Jacobitism.[76] And yet, there were those whose allegiance was pure: Arthur Elphinstone, Lord Balmerino, who died on the block with the Prince's praises on his lips, and the elderly Lord Forbes of Pitsligo, who called out to his new-formed cavalry troop as he led it to the Prince's side: 'O Lord, Thou knowest that our cause is just. March, gentlemen.'[77] And Murray's motives were selfless too. As he poignantly wrote to his Hanoverian older brother, the Duke of Atholl, he had chosen to join Charles because his was 'the Cause I always in my heart thought just and right', even though the choice would 'probably end in my utter ruin'.[78]

For wider incidence of the phenomenon one must look among the women, who found Jacobitism, or Charles himself, irresistible.[79] Their zeal should not be disparaged. Two raised clans, or portions of clans, behind the backs of their Hanoverian husbands: Lady Anne Farquharson, or 'Colonel Anne' as she was known, wife of clan chief Aeneas MacKintosh, mobilised the MacKintoshes while her husband was off fighting for the government; and Lady Fortrose, wife of the MacKenzie clan chief the Earl of Seaforth, did the same with at least some of his MacKenzies. But for obvious reasons most could make only limited contributions.

RADICALISM

This is the pattern that many may find surprising. Steeped as Jacobitism was in Christianity's most conservative principles – mysticism, natural hierarchy, obedience to anointed authority – one would not have expected it to appeal to what we today would call the political left. But it did. The Whig Settlement of 1689 had brought unprecedented prosperity to the manufacturing, commercial and landed classes, especially in England. However, it had also ushered in an era of ruthless profiteering and left a polarised society in its wake: one in which the underclass was worse off than before, both in absolute and relative terms. The political structure was used to reinforce the economic status quo. Dominant in Parliament (except briefly under Queen Anne), the Whig oligarchy that ruled in the interests of the more prosperous groups solidified their position, and its own, with a series of repressive statutes: a 'Black Act' against poachers who challenged landed rights in response to enclosures (the Act got its nickname from the poachers' practice of blackening their faces to avoid detection); a Riot Act against vocal protesters of all stripes; and a Septennial Act calling for parliamentary elections every seven years instead of the customary three, so as to prolong the party's control over the legislature. Plainly, the Whig rhetoric of liberty and government by consent had meaning only within the favoured circle of the oligarchy.

In this polarised atmosphere, Jacobitism easily became the currency of resentment among the poor. During the failed invasion attempt of 1744, the French had seriously considered landing in Weymouth in order to take advantage of labour unrest in the local cloth industry.[80] And the cloth-workers were not the only ones who had scores to settle with the Whig ascendancy. There were many others. Smugglers, whose natural proclivities for the business received further stimulus from high customs duties (this was especially true, one suspects, of Scottish smugglers, for whom the duties were novel). Bankrupts (there would be three of these in Charles's inner circle – his secretary of state John Murray of Broughton; the Earl of Kilmarnock, who commanded a cavalry troop; and the Earl of Cromartie, who commanded a regiment of foot – and heaven knows how many more amongst the rank and file). Apprentices. Tenant farmers. Day labourers. Artisans. Tradesmen. The unemployed.[81] All were outsiders, politically and economically, and all were known to utilise Jacobite rhetoric in the popular protests of the period. All, accordingly, had the potential to offer radical opposition to the regime. A number of volunteers from these groups did come forward when Charles sent his recruiting agents into north-east Scotland.[82] Whether their English compeers would have done likewise if the French had shown up in force is a moot point, because the French never did.

These left-wing Jacobite murmurings, by workers and the unemployed, found echoes among the intelligentsia – and from some improbable sources. During the Williamite era, the exiled James II had acquired unexpected allies in Whig radicals who were disillusioned to find William more autocratic than James had ever been.[83] Now, towards mid-century, Charles, and the Jacobites in general, were lionised by some of the leading figures of the French enlightenment. This was in part, perhaps, because his religious scepticism matched their own – in this regard, he was very different than his father – and in part because the idealised figure of the Highlander squared with Rousseau-like images of the virtuous primitive.[84] (That affinity may have been what inspired Charles to garb all his soldiers in Highland uniform.) Thus, Voltaire admired Charles[85] and even wrote one of his manifestos,[86] and Montesquieu corresponded with him.[87]

Other prominent Jacobites also had Enlightenment connections. One of them, George Keith, dreamed up the most radical vision of all. Long alienated from Charles, he confided to his good friend Rousseau that he hoped a Stuart restoration would lead eventually to an independent Scottish republic: a remarkable position for him to espouse, considering that he was Scotland's hereditary Earl Marshal.[88] But then, he was not alone in doing so; the Marquis d'Eguilles, who would become France's ambassador to Charles once the Rising was underway, would secretly hope for the same.[89]

Here lay a paradox of Jacobitism – that, rooted in divine right abso-lutism (again, the terms are not synonymous), it nevertheless attracted support from some of the most radical elements in Britain and even beyond – just as it was another paradox that Charles's political platform would incorporate some of the most cherished values of modern liberal democracy: regular parliaments, accountable ministries, religious tolera-tion, and freedom of the press.[90] There is fitting symbolism in the fact that a leading Stuart hymn, 'When the King Enjoys His Own Again' – the one that Charlie sang to Flora MacDonald as the bonnie boat sped over the sea to Skye – supplied the tune (with different title and words) that the victorious Yankees played when accepting the British surrender at Yorktown a generation later. Nor is it anomalous that some of those Yankees touted Charles, in his advanced middle age, as a candidate for what they perceived as the vacant American throne.[91]

This, then, was what present-day politicians would call Charles's 'base': Episcopalians and Catholics (the latter mostly timorous); an indetermi-nate number of Tories; Scottish nationalists; fewer than half the Highland clans (not all of them Episcopalian or Catholic); a handful of sentimental Jacobites; and – at the opposite end of the ideological spectrum from the Episcopalians, Catholics and Tories – the radicals. There was nothing paro-chial about it, because it cut across religious, philosophical, socio-economic and geographic boundaries. The questions went to breadth and depth: how many, within those constituencies, were committed enough to take risks? And here, once again, historians disagree. Bruce Lenman dismisses serious Jacobitism as 'marginal';[92] Murray Pittock argues that in Scotland, at least, it was anything but;[93] and other scholars past and present have weighed in on both sides, with those who see the accession of William and Mary as the secular equivalent of the Second Coming tending to minimise Jacobite strength.[94] The most one can say with certainty is that some members of the base were sceptical but others were ready. And none was more ready than Charles Edward Stuart.

In May of 1745, opportunity beckoned. On the 11th of the month (New Style), the French smashed a British-led allied army at Fontenoy. The Irish Brigade spearheaded the charge that sealed the victory. Only the bravery of the Black Watch, stationed overseas because it was no longer trusted on home soil after a recent mutiny, prevented a rout. It was now necessary to rush reinforcements from Britain to the continent in order literally and metaphorically to stem the bleeding. A mere 6,000 soldiers remained on the entire island, some 3,850 of whom were stationed in Scotland: 'these not the best troops in the service', as Murray of Broughton understatedly recalled them in his memoirs.[95] The kingdom had never been more vulnerable.

As Charles well knew, however, the window that had thus opened to him was a small one. If French success continued, Britain would be forced to the peace table, and, with peace concluded, all hope of French assistance would be at an end.

Duncan Forbes should therefore have been more worried in the early summer of 1745, especially after the informant's letter arrived. Despite it, though, he continued to swallow, and regurgitate, the official line: the Highlands were quiet; an invasion was improbable. But he had sense enough to know that it was not impossible either, and he knew how ill-equipped the government was to counter it. Thus his visit to Cope.[96]

See p. 18

Cope too wasted no time and took no chances. He wrote to Tweeddale the same day – 2 July – relaying Forbes's information. In the same letter, he pleaded with Tweeddale to send him more weapons. The disaffected clans, he pointed out, already had plenty of these, and would soon be given more if the rumoured landing took place; it was the loyal clans that lacked them. Such were the effects of the failed Disarming Acts of

1716 and 1725.[97]

Tweeddale, however, was not disposed to take the letter seriously, especially since the information came through Forbes. Forbes, after all, was a protégé of the Duke of Argyll, brother and successor to the victor of Sheriffmuir, who had been Forbes's patron too. Tweeddale was a Squadrone – therefore Argyll's enemy[98] – and lethargic to boot. His reply, dated 9 July, was dismissive: he had put Cope's request for weapons to the Council of Regency (George II being away in Hanover at the time); the Council had taken no action; and neither would he. The matter would have to await further developments. He counted upon Cope to keep him apprised.[99]

In a second letter, that crossed with Tweeddale's, Cope pressed the Secretary harder. He had, he reported, ordered his dragoons to be in readiness to bring their horses in from grass and to march at short notice; and he begged for permission to post announcements, in the official gazette and the regular newspapers, recalling officers who were on furlough – both measures having been approved by Forbes and other leading civil officers. Tweeddale would have none of it. He wrote back on the 18th, directing Cope to leave the horses at grass, and to refrain from any other steps that 'would have tended to have alarm'd the country too much'. Cope was to keep 'a strict Look-out' as before.[100] That was all.

Then, on 23 July 1745 – as Cope was importuning and Tweeddale still dithering – Charles Edward Stuart, accompanied by just seven companions and their retainers, landed on the tiny Outer Hebridean island of Eriskay.

2

THE ARMIES

Prince Charles Edward Stuart and Lieutenant-General Sir John Cope would spend the next two months mobilising their troops and manoeuvring towards one another in preparation for battle. Before tracing their movements further, we shall examine the forces at the disposal of each.

THE GOVERNMENT ARMY

According to Rupert Jarvis, who remains the recognised authority on the subject, Cope had almost exactly 3,850 officers and 'other ranks' under his command in the summer of 1745.[1] What manner of men were they, what was their training, and what were their tactics? For that matter, what manner of man was Sir John Cope?

There are some popular misconceptions about the mid-Georgian British army that evoke the lions-led-by-donkeys *motif* of the First World War. The rank and file, it is thought, were superbly disciplined – heroic and almost robot-like in their poise under fire and their obedience to orders – whereas the officers were fatuous, blimpish sorts who used inherited wealth to purchase their commissions and then lived effortlessly off the proceeds by skimming the pay of the rank and file. If anything, the opposite was true.

Officers purchased commissions, yes, but not all of them did, and there were powerful safeguards against abuse.[2] Purchases had to be approved by the king – and, whatever else might be said about the first two Georges, both were experienced soldiers who cared passionately about the army and paid close attention to the quality of its officer corps. As a practical matter, the local commander-in-chief and the regimental colonel (or, if the titular colonel was absent, as was frequently the case, the lieutenant-colonel) had to approve as well, with the crown mediating in event of disagreement. There was also a strict seniority system:

when an officer retired, he had to sell his commission to the officer immediately below him, unless that officer was unwilling or unable to buy, or his colonel or the king deemed him unsuitable, in which case the offer went to the next man in line.[3] So important, in fact, was seniority that during the early part of the century there was considerable jockeying for 'brevets' – temporary ranks, awarded by local commanders-in-chief, which carried no extra pay but conferred seniority so as to position the lucky holder to bid for the next available permanent vacancy, in his own regiment or another. If an officer was truly in the commander's good graces, the brevet could even be back-dated, giving him a further advantage over potential competitors. Eventually Queen Anne put a stop to the brevet system, but not before numerous young officers, including Cope himself, had benefited from it.

Commissions were not out of reach even for bidders with modest means. In Anne's day prices fluctuated with the market; thus, they rose sharply when the War of the Spanish Succession started to wind down, shortly after Cope entered the service. Beginning in 1720, however, the Hanoverian kings regulated them through a series of royal warrants, which were promulgated periodically throughout the century in an effort at once to keep pace with market forces and to control them. True, the actual purchase price was often higher than the regulation price, but not exorbitantly so; indeed, a candidate who bid too extravagantly might find himself rebuffed, by the regimental colonel, on the assumption that anyone so that desperate for a commission must lack merit. At all times, moreover, an otherwise suitable applicant with insufficient funds could borrow the money from his brother officers, as Cope did on at least one occasion.[4] After all, his creditors could expect to recoup their investment when he sold his own vacated commission in turn, both from the proceeds of the sale and from the emoluments (discussed below) that his new rank would bring him.

It appears, therefore, that deserving officers were seldom priced out of the lower grades – cornetcies, ensigncies, lieutenancies, perhaps even captaincies – although the higher ranks, being more expensive, might elude them, as might commissions at any level in the more elite and sought-after units. To be sure, whether one was deemed 'deserving' or 'suitable' depended, in part, upon one's social connections (or 'interest', as it was called) and congeniality, but experience and ability mattered too. Given these qualities, the necessary resources could be found, at least up to a point.

In addition, many promotions were not subject to the purchase system. Promotions to general never were – they were based entirely on seniority or merit – and by the end of his reign George II had succeeded in exempting full colonelcies from it as well. As importantly, about a third of the officer positions below colonel were filled by direct appointment rather than purchase, the appointments coming either from the king or from commanders-in-chief serving abroad, whenever vacancies arose because of death or the creation of new regiments – circumstances that were of course especially prevalent in wartime. It was not uncommon, in such circumstances, to promote from the ranks. The long-term prospects of these fresh-minted officers were bleak: lacking money, gentility and 'interest', they could seldom aspire to more than a subaltern's grade. But their very presence within the officer class served almost by definition to guarantee it a high degree of proved, battle-tested competence and a measure of social diversity.

Whether they acquired their commissions by appointment or by purchase, eighteenth-century British officers worked hard to master their trade. There was no formal or specialised officers' training, but the young officer would study the official drill regulations that were issued, from time to time, from the late seventeenth century onward, and would practise the exercises, alongside his men, under the watchful eyes of his seniors. He would also study military treatises, of which there were many, some of them indifferent, but others quite good. Of these, the most famous and influential was the 'Treatise of Military Discipline', by Lieutenant-Colonel, later Lieutenant-General, Humphrey Bland, which first appeared in 1727 and went through numerous subsequent editions. (Bland would command the Duke of Cumberland's advance guard at Culloden.) Many of the 1727 edition's precepts found their way into a new set of official drill regulations that was published the following year. There is every indication that the treatises and regulations alike were widely and carefully read.[5] Finally, the officer usually spent many years in each rank before progressing to the next one. J.A. Houlding, author of the leading work on eighteenth-century British military training, has shown that in 1740, five years before the Rising, foot officers from ensign to lieutenant-colonel had held their present commissions for an average of three to eight years. It would take a typical officer about eleven years to obtain a lieutenancy, another eight to obtain a captaincy, and seven more to become a major.[6] He would therefore know his business thoroughly by the time he moved on.

Did officers skim the men's pay? They surely did, or at any rate the regimental colonels and lieutenant-colonels and the company captains did, for they were the ones with access to the accounts. Be it remembered, though, that the lines between the public and private sectors were blurry in the eighteenth century, in military as in civil affairs. Parliamentary antipathy to high taxes (hated by the landed and moneyed elites who supported the Whigs at the polls) and to standing armies kept annual military appropriations below minimum levels, and regimental and company commanders frequently had to make up the differences out of their own pockets. The War and Finance offices, with skeletal, often corrupt staffs, lacked the manpower to disburse the soldiers' pay efficiently, so the colonels had to hire contractors to do it, again at their own expense. Having expended these moneys, and paid for their commissions as well, the colonels and captains should not be faulted too harshly for reimbursing themselves, and then some, from funds allocated to their regiments.[7] Since the regiments were usually vastly under strength – one source has estimated that even in wartime, when their ranks were augmented, they were lucky to muster more than half their official complement of 815 officers and men[8] – and since allocations were based on official rather than actual numbers, it was easy enough for commanders to siphon off the salaries of non-existent troops. An infantry captain might realise up to sixty pounds a year by doing so, a dragoon captain more than twice that sum. These were accepted perquisites of office and were reflected in the commission's purchase price.[9]

The purchase and pay systems did not function perfectly. Some commanders no doubt stinted their men and lined their own pockets inordinately; some colonels accepted illegal bribes to facilitate non-purchase promotions;[10] commissions were occasionally granted to minor children of influential families.[11] Yet British officers on the whole were dedicated, studious, career-minded, and – for the period – remarkably diverse socially, especially in comparison to European armies; wealth neither predominated nor guaranteed success. For all of these reasons, most of them were very good at their jobs.

Not so the men.

Murray of Broughton's characterisation of the troops under Cope's command – 'not the best' – was equally applicable to most British private soldiers of the era. Perennially undermanned even in wartime despite emergency measures such as bounties and short enlistments, the army was qualitatively as well as quantitatively deficient. Recruitment standards were not rigorous: all that was necessary was that the candidate be Protestant, at least 5 feet 6 inches of height (both requirements were ignored when manpower shortages were especially severe), and free from obvious disabilities such as lameness, fits or a rupture.[12] The under-aged, the elderly and idiots were unwelcome also.[13] Demographically, the pool seems to have been narrower than for officers: recruits consisted largely of the under-employed, the seasonally employed (the most fruitful recruiting drives, or 'beatings-up', as they were called, occurred in the countryside just after the harvests),[14] or the unemployed, who were often prodded into enlisting by local magistrates as an alternative to being jailed for vagrancy, or else forced to serve under 'Press Acts' that were enacted in periods of crisis. (One such Act was in effect from 1745 to 1746, the duration of the Jacobite emergency.)[15] So common was the practice of coercing vagabonds into service that these unwilling warriors acquired a nickname: 'vestry men', from the fact that the government paid bounties to the magistrate and the local parish vestry for producing them.[16] It was not only the unemployed who entered the army in this manner: debtors and the criminal classes could sometimes avoid prison, or even the gallows, by doing the same.[17] Lacking, despite these measures, anywhere near the 780 'other ranks' who were necessary to fill a foot regiment,[18] the army took to augmenting regiments assigned to war zones by 'drafting' men from the ones serving at home, thereby depleting the latter even further. Since the men selected for the drafts tended to be among the most experienced available, those who remained in Britain were especially likely to be fresh from the plough or the parish jail.[19]

It would be romantic to imagine that the army took this unprepossessing raw material and whipped it rapidly into shape through an invigorating basic training program, as armies are thought to do today. But that did not happen, because the training too was 'not the best'. The home regiments spent most of their time dispersed, in small detachments, throughout the kingdom (except northern Scotland, the preserve of the independent companies), either doing garrison duty or acting 'in aid of the civil power', the first for the purpose of deterring, the second for the purpose of suppressing, riots and other unlawful activity by the under-employed, the seasonally employed, the unemployed and the criminal classes.

Thus pre-occupied and dispersed, it was not easy to bring them together for the large-scale manoeuvres that they needed to learn and to practise in order to prepare for the massive, set-piece battles that characterised European warfare at this period. And even when it was possible to assemble them in the necessary numbers, it was no simple task to find a large enough field to accommodate the exercises. A brigadier or colonel could not just march his men to a suitable open area and start training them: British respect for law and for private property rights – the same constraints that would inhibit the raising of a militia after Charles Edward landed – entitled the land-owner to charge rent, and the rent might be more than the War Office was willing to pay or the brigadier or colonel could afford. In these circumstances, it was a challenge to progress beyond the most basic drill.[20]

That drill was simple, and easy enough to master, at least for parade purposes. During the 1740s it was still conducted in accordance with the 1728 Regulations. Those, it will be recalled, were promulgated a year from the first appearance of Bland's treatise, and incorporated many of its principles: principles that were based in turn on older regulations and practices, many of which had been in effect since Charles II's day. The actual implementation of these principles, however, varied from regiment to regiment, and perhaps even within each regiment, depending upon time, opportunity and the tastes of the officer in charge.[21]

The most important cog in the mid-Georgian military machine was the infantry. Its training did not prepare it adequately for its role.

The neophyte foot soldier was first given a uniform – a double-breasted red woollen coat with blue, yellow or buff facings on the lapels and distinctive white-braided patterns on the lapels, cuffs and button loops (the function of the facings and patterns was to tell the regiments apart); a skirted waist coat and breeches, also red; stockings, shoes and thigh-length white canvas gaiters; a white linen neck cloth; and a black tricorne hat laced with white (hence the nickname, 'hatmen') or, in the grenadier companies, a mitre[22] – and then taught to march. Marching was a more casual business, during the first half of the century, than it subsequently became. Music for marching, as opposed to signalling, was not introduced until 1747, after the '45 had ended (except in the Guards regiments, where it was first used in 1745), and neither, therefore, was the stylised, cadenced step that one associates with the British Army of later periods, because the maintenance of that step required the accompaniment of a steady, musical beat. Indeed, cadenced marching was actually disparaged, by some officers, as too suggestive of dancing. Instead, the pace of the march was left to the discretion of individual commanders, rather than being standardised as it was by the century's conclusion. Other than distinguishing 'long' from 'short' paces, and 'quick' ones from 'slow' ones, more attention was given to posture and turns than to speed and rhythm.[23]

The marching instruction, such as it was, once over with, the soldier was issued his weapons. Principal among these was the standard muzzle-loading musket of the period, the 'Long Land Pattern' flint firelock, colloquially known as 'Brown Bess'. It fired a soft, seventy-five-calibre bullet, weighing about one and a half ounces, from its forty-six-inch barrel. With the musket came a bayonet: a nasty, triangular seventeen-inch blade connected to a metal tube that – in theory, anyway – fitted tightly around the outside of the barrel, next to the muzzle, so as to allow simultaneous slashing and firing.[24] In fact, however, the fit was often imperfect, and one source has suggested that, on the relatively rare occasions when hand-to-hand fighting occurred, the infantryman might prefer clubbing with the butt of the musket to stabbing.[25] In theory, too, the equipment included a short, slightly curved sword, called a hanger, but this was of little use in combat, and some soldiers chose not to carry one at all, deeming it a nuisance;[26] thus, Henry Hawley, who would command the government forces at the battle of Falkirk, once wrote plaintively that ''Tis soldierlike and graceful for the men to have swords, especially in garrison, but too many inconveniences attend them… and when are they ever used in the field or in action?'[27] What mattered most was massed firepower from the musket, and even the bayonet was secondary to that.

The staple of basic training was the so-called 'manual exercise', in which the soldier was taught how to carry, load, and fire his musket, and thrust with the bayonet.[28] The thrusting technique was different than in the present day: instead of slashing upwards, as in modern armies, you would raise your musket to your chest with the barrel resting in your left hand and the back of the butt against your right; then, upon command, you would use the right hand to push the weapon forward and downward, all of this being done in unison with your fellows.[29] The musket drill included some marksmanship training, but not much: for one thing, there was never enough ammunition for productive target shooting;[30] for another, such training was of limited use anyway because even the most skilled marksmen found the Brown Bess inaccurate at distances of more than fifty yards.[31] Hence, the emphasis on mass volleys, rather than aimed fire.[32]

The next step was the platoon exercise, which, like the manual one, was popular because it was only necessary to assemble a few men in order to teach and practise it.[33] Here, the recruits were taught to keep up a sustained, rapid, synchronised fire in three-deep ranks: the first rank kneeling, the second rank crouching over it, the third rank standing. The most critical component of this exercise was known as 'locking', whereby the second rank would move slightly to the right and the third rank a half step to the right, so that each soldier in the two rear ranks would have an open field of fire and thus be less likely to kill the man in front of him by accident.[34]

The manual and platoon exercises were surely useful, even necessary, at the outset of the training process. The problem was that they were repeated over and over again, long after the basic skills were mastered, for the simple reason that – with the home regiments broken down into small detachments and then dispersed over wide areas – it was not possible to bring together units large enough for more sophisticated manoeuvres. Discerning officers recognised the futility of putting experienced soldiers through these basic drills: for instance, Hawley sneered that discipline and conditioning would be better maintained by having the men work on building and repairing roads.[35] But habits die hard, and the manual exercises persisted, *faute de mieux*, on a once- or twice-weekly basis,[36] despite the fact that everyone involved was probably as weary of them as Hawley was. The more serious training would have to await assignment to war zones, where, brigaded at last with thousands of comrades, the British soldier would learn – literally under fire – the advanced skills that he would need in order to conquer and to survive.[37]

Battle tactics were far more complex than the exercises, and were conducted on a vastly larger scale. In order to explain them, it is first necessary to address how the infantry was organised.

Its basic administrative unit was the regiment. Foot regiments at the time were named for their proprietary colonel – Sempill's, Loudon's, Battereau's, etc. – even though the colonel, who was often a general in his own right, might be stationed elsewhere and the regiment run on a day-to-day basis by its lieutenant-colonel or major. (The practice of numbering regiments in order of seniority did not begin until 1751.)[38] There were two types of foot regiments: 'marching regiments', which were moved from place to place as need required, and guards regiments, which were usually attached to the king's person.[39] At the beginning of

1745 there were fifty-six marching regiments and five guards regiments, and the former had risen to eighty by the time the rebellion was over.[40]

In theory, a foot regiment, as already noted, numbered 815 including officers. It was separated into ten companies, one of which was a grenadier company.[41] Each company carried a captain, a lieutenant, an ensign, three sergeants, three corporals, two drummers, and seventy privates.[42] There were also, at the regimental level, three field officers – the colonel, lieutenant-colonel and major – and four staff officers: an adjutant, a quarter-master, a surgeon and a chaplain.[43] That does not add up exactly to 815, but is surely close enough, especially since the numbers never added up in any event, for the regiments (again, as already noted) tended to be woefully under strength.

What is confusing, and must have been equally so to the men, is that the battlefield dispositions replicated the regimental structure only loosely. In battle the regiment was reconstituted into one or two battalions: two, if it was at or near full strength, but, since this was almost never the case, usually one, to the point where contemporaries and modern historians alike have used the terms 'regiment' and 'battalion' interchangeably.[44] The battalion was then separated into four 'grand-divisions', and each grand-division was separated in turn into platoons, which were supposed to contain at least thirty men apiece. Thus, if a regiment was only half full, and could therefore support just one 400-man battalion, there might be three platoons per grand-division. If it was fortunate enough to have 600 men (an unusually large complement), it could still support just the one battalion, but now each grand-division would contain four platoons.[45]

Importantly, the composition of the 'hatmen's' platoons bore no relationship to the composition of the companies. The company was an administrative unit: its men were billeted together, but that was all. When it came to fighting, or marching for that matter, the platoon system took over, and the members of each platoon came from different companies, except for the grenadier company, the two platoons of which were always the same. A hatman, therefore, might find himself marching and fighting alongside virtual strangers.[46]

In combat, the platoons, having advanced to within thirty to sixty yards of the enemy,[47] would halt there in three even ranks, except again for the grenadier companies, which operated independently on the battalion's flanks, and one regular company that was held in reserve. Each platoon then arranged itself and 'locked' as hitherto described:

the first rank kneeling, the second rank crouching, the third rank standing; the second rank positioned slightly to the right of the first, the rear
rank somewhat more so, in order to give each soldier an unobstructed
field of fire.[48] They were now ready to commence the complicated process of staggered 'platoon firing'.

In theory this worked as follows. The right-hand platoon in each grand-
division would fire first, at the same instant as its counterparts in the other
grand-divisions, with all three of its ranks firing at once. The platoon to
its left would fire next, then the one to the left of that, and so forth.
Meanwhile, the platoons that had already fired would re-load. When the
platoons at the grand-divisions' furthest left had discharged their muskets,
the sequence would begin again.[49] The platoons that were supposed to
fire simultaneously with one another were known collectively as a 'firing',
which meant that a platoon would belong to both a grand-division and a
'firing', and the two would not be the same.[50] Sometimes the commander
would alter the sequence: the two platoons on each grand-division's flanks
would fire first, and the platoon or platoons in the centre would take over
after they had finished.[51] Since the average infantryman could fire two to
three volleys a minute,[52] and the effective range of the musket was well
over fifty yards,[53] simple arithmetic will show that when the firing system worked properly it could wreak havoc even without careful aiming,
especially upon a conventional enemy that was drawn up, like the British
themselves, in stationary solid ranks only thirty or so yards away.

That was the theory. Translating theory into practice, however, posed
at least three problems.

First, it took exquisite discipline – the product of meticulous training
– for troops to deliver such carefully synchronised, staggered fire when
they were under fire themselves. As we have seen, training of this kind
was hard to come by: for one thing, it was seldom possible, in peacetime,
to assemble enough men, in one place, to form the necessary number of
grand-divisions.[54]

Second, even the best-trained troops probably found it difficult to follow
the proper sequence for long. Sooner rather than later, the shooting must
have become chaotic, with each man obeying the law of self-preservation
– sterner still than the 1728 Regulations – by firing as fast as he could.[55]

Third, the firings, while they lasted, may have worked well against
European armies which, fighting as the British did, advanced at a stately
pace, then stood obligingly in line and discharged their muskets in more

or less the same stylised manner. They were unlikely to work nearly as well against irregulars – Highlanders, say – who, as we shall discover, had their own notions of how to advance.[56]

The focus thus far has been on the infantry, because they were the army's backbone, with the other services operating mainly in their support. A brief overview of those is nevertheless in order.

CAVALRY

The cavalry consisted of horse regiments and dragoons, of whom the latter figure more prominently in our story. Unlike the horse, who fought only from the saddle, the dragoons were expected to fight either mounted or on foot, and their training reflected this: they had to master the same exercises as the foot soldier, while also learning how to care for and exercise their horses. Once they had acquired these skills, they were taught to ride, and then progressed to more advanced manoeuvres such as opening and closing ranks and wheeling.[57] Because their training and duties were more complicated than the foot's, they were thought to attract a higher-type soldier,[58] although not as measured from the ground: whereas the minimum height in the infantry was 5 feet 6 inches, a cavalryman could not be taller than 5 feet 8 inches.[59]

The dragoon's dress, like his training, was similar to the foot soldier's, except that he wore knee-length boots instead of gaiters and his coat had no lapels. His firearm was also similar: it was a Short Land Pattern musket, with a forty-two-inch barrel – just four inches less than the barrel of the infantry musket – which he carried strapped to his saddle.[60] He was equipped, in addition, with a basket-hilted broadsword, the blade of which was straight and thirty-five inches long,[61] and what some say were two pistols[62] and others one.[63]

As with the foot, the basic cavalry unit, for the dragoons and horse alike, was the regiment, but the cavalry regiment was smaller, and was separated into troops instead of companies. There were six such troops in a dragoon regiment, containing fifty-nine men apiece; the total strength of the regiment (including officers) was 435. In action, the troops were usually paired to make three squadrons per regiment – two in front, one in reserve – though the number and positioning of the squadrons might vary according to how many men were available and the strength and dispositions of the enemy.[64]

There was another important difference between infantry and cavalry tactics: the former fought in closely-packed, 'locked' ranks for maximum fire-power, but the cavalry squadrons were taught to keep their distance from one another, as were the individual troopers within each squadron, so as to leave room for the horses to manoeuvre.[65] The advance was at a trot, and the weapon of choice was the broadsword, with the pistols (or pistol) used mainly in pursuit.[66]

ARTILLERY

Technically the Royal Regiment of Artillery was not part of the army at all, but rather was organised under a separate establishment that answered to its own Master-General, not to the regular army generals, and its training regimen emphasised different, highly specialised skills: mathematics and the physical sciences in lieu of marching and arms drill.[67] There were four artillery companies in 1739, and twelve by the time the War of the Austrian Succession ended in 1748;[68] each consisted of seven officers, three sergeants, three corporals, eight bombardiers, twenty gunners, sixty-two matrosses (gunners' assistants), and two drummers, or 105 officers and men in all.[69] Their preferred weapon was a smooth bore muzzle loader that fired either a three-pound ball or grape-shot – metal fragments, packed in a canister, that scattered on impact and inflicted horrific damage on tightly-packed enemy infantry – for a distance of about 500 yards.[70] They also made imaginative use of the coehorn, a small, highly mobile mortar, named for a Dutch military engineer who had invented it.[71] Originally designed for sieges (it fired bombs, rather than solid shot), it was readily adaptable to ground warfare in mountainous countries such as Scotland, where its diminutive size made it relatively easy to carry over rough terrain.[72] As we shall see, Cope was not favoured with three-pound cannon at Prestonpans – he had to make do with one-and-one-half-pounders instead – and, while he did have coehorns, as well as larger mortars, we shall also see how little use he was able to make of them.

MILITIA

The raising of militia was delayed by legal barriers and political squabbles, the latter bordering on farce, until long after Prestonpans. The main problem was that militia were summoned by county, the Lord Lieutenant of the county was the only official with the authority to summon them, and several Scottish and northern English counties had no Lord Lieutenant in the summer of 1745. These, of course, were the very counties that were most in harm's way. The reason the Scottish lieutenancies were vacant, cynics believed, was that the warring Whig factions – the Squadrones, in the person of Tweeddale and his local proxies, and the Argathelians, led by the Duke of Argyll, who was at loggerheads with the King but allied with the ministry, which in turn was hostile to both Tweeddale and the King – could not bury their differences long enough to agree on suitable candidates.[73]

The appointment of a Lord Lieutenant would not have resolved things, however, because in counties that had them the recruitment process was impeded by legal uncertainties. To reduce the matter to its essentials: the immediate responsibility for providing militia in each county fell upon local men of property, acting under the Lord Lieutenant's direction. They were not expected to serve themselves, but were expected to muster, pay and equip those who did. They would then recoup their expenses from the central government. Only Parliament, though, could authorise the expenditure of public funds, and it was not clear whether the existing militia laws sufficed as authority or whether a new enabling act was necessary each time the militia was mobilised. Ordinarily, the easy solution would have been for Parliament simply to pass such an act, thereby dispelling the uncertainties. But Parliament was not in session when Charles Edward landed; King George, who alone was empowered to convene it, was abroad, and he had refused to delegate this power to the Council of Regency, which governed the country in his absence. He returned at last, on the final day of August, but it took Parliament a while longer to come together. And when it finally passed the necessary legislation – which did not occur until early November, when Charles was already poised to invade England – the text contained an ambiguity that kept the uncertainties alive. In the circumstances, the county gentry, from the Lord Lieutenant down, were understandably reluctant to hazard their pocketbooks on a venture that might be illegal and for which reimbursement might not be obtainable.[74]

In the Highlands, there was yet another legal wrinkle: the Disarming Acts, it was feared, might prohibit militiamen from obeying an otherwise lawful summons unless, once again, Parliament intervened, which Parliament, for the reasons stated, was not initially able to do. The Duke of Argyll, in particular – hereditary chief of Clan Campbell,

Lord Lieutenant of Argyll, and the most powerful Highland magnate of all – declared that he would neither bear arms nor distribute them to his clansmen until Parliament either repealed or suspended these Acts or created exceptions for Highlanders defending the government during the emergency. Whether he was expressing genuine legal scruples (he was a lawyer himself), or merely playing the passive aggressive in order to tweak his adversary Tweeddale, was and is uncertain. In either case the authorities were hamstrung.[75]

They tried to circumvent these restrictions in various ways. In late summer, the government entrusted Duncan Forbes with eighteen blank commissions for the raising of new independent companies (the Black Watch having been regimented six years earlier), which he began doing on 13 September, although he did not receive money to pay them until 11 October.[76] Soon afterwards, Major-General John Campbell of Mamore, cousin and eventual successor to the Duke of Argyll, was given eight commissions more and told to do the same in Argyll, and to raise a militia regiment there as well.[77] (This regiment, the Argyll Militia, is not to be confused with the militia that were to be mustered under the auspices of the Lord Lieutenants.) But none of these units was operational in time for Prestonpans, and none played a significant role in the remainder of the war, except for Campbell's Argyll Militia at Culloden. Likewise, the cities of Edinburgh and Glasgow (among others) would produce, in time, their own volunteer regiments, but they too were never a factor: perhaps fortunately so for their own side.

What of the forces under Cope's command? How did they compare, in training and experience, with British troops as a whole?

There is no reason not to trust the account that Cope himself gave to the military board that investigated his conduct the following year. He was speaking from memory, it is true, because his papers had been captured at Prestonpans, but he had taken steps to verify his recollections before he testified.[78] He had, he declared, three and a half regiments of foot – Guise's, Thomas Murray's, Lascelles's (the latter, surprisingly, at almost full strength)[79] and five companies of Lee's – and two dragoon regiments: Gardiner's and Hamilton's. The foot regiments were of English origin, although they had probably been in Scotland long enough to have picked up a number of local volunteers; the dragoons had been raised in Ireland. (The Irish army was theoretically separate from the British, but its units were dispatched across the Irish Sea as needed to serve Britain's needs.) In addition, there were nine detached Scottish companies: three from the Black Watch regiment, which was commanded by Colonel John Murray, and two each from the Royal Regiment of Foot, alternatively styled the Royal Scots or simply 'the Royals' (St Clair's), the Scottish Fusiliers (Campbell's), and Sempill's. Sempill's has been described as about two-thirds Scottish. All were in Scotland on recruiting assignment for their parent regiments, which were stationed overseas. To bring those regiments to fighting strength, the Royals, Fusiliers and Sempill's companies had been badly depleted by drafts to the point where they mustered barely twenty-five men apiece: about a third of their notional strength. Finally, another regiment, Loudon's – also Scottish, and known as the 'New' Highland Regiment in order to distinguish it from the Watch, which was sometimes called the 'Old' Highland Regiment – was still in the process of forming; its officers' commissions had only been issued in April and June of that year, and none of its companies was available yet for service.[80]

These units were dispersed throughout Scotland. Lascelles's companies, for instance, were divided between Edinburgh and Leith; Lee's were in Dumfries, Stranraer, Glasgow and Stirling; and Thomas Murray's were spread out among the Highland barracks. They would shortly be switched with Guise's companies, which were stationed for the moment at Aberdeen and various points along the coast. The dragoons, too, were scattered: Gardiner's over Stirling, Linlithgow, Musselburgh, Kelso and Coldstream; Hamilton's over Haddington and its environs.[81] The dispersals cannot have helped with the training.[82]

In his testimony, Cope did not supply numbers, except to note the depleted state of the Scottish detachments, and historians are in hopeless disagreement on the subject. Jarvis, however, has done a heroic job of reconstruction. His conclusion, which is generally accepted today, is that Cope had about 3,850 officers and men under his command when Charles Edward landed.[83]

Their quality was appalling, as Prestonpans was to prove; Murray of Broughton's dismissive 'not the best' seems to have been understated. Except for a handful of Guise's men, none had ever been in combat.[84] The foot consisted of 'some of the youngest regiments in the British Army'.[85] Guise's again was an exception – it dated back to 1674 – but the others had only been raised in 1741.[86] The two dragoon regiments were older, having been formed in 1715. Besides lacking experience, however, they were Irish; worse, many were rumoured to be Catholic. (Catholics were in theory barred from military service, in Ireland as in Britain, but this was probably a difficult requirement to enforce in that Catholic nation.)[87] Hence, they were deemed unreliable.[88] The Scottish units, especially the Watch, were suspect as well, and with good reason, as later events would show. Another difficulty with the dragoons was that their horses were at grass during the summer, and the dragoons themselves, lacking their mounts, would have been doing manual rather than mounted drills at the time. This meant that the animals were out of condition and the riders out of practice.[89]

Cope did not lack artillery, for there were cannon and coehorns available from Edinburgh Castle, but here too there was a problem: he had no-one to serve them. In all of his far-flung command, there was not a single trained artilleryman, except for a super-annuated veteran who had performed that function in the old Scottish army prior to the union.[90] There were gunners of a sort in the Castle garrison; there was even an unsuccessful attempt to smuggle some of them out to Cope on the day before Prestonpans, after the city of Edinburgh had fallen to the Jacobites, and the Castle's 'Master-Gunner', a Mr Eaglesfield Griffith, was with Cope during the battle (as was the old veteran – though not for long). None, however, belonged to the Royal Artillery.[91]

As for Cope himself: his contemporary Sir John Clerk of Penicuik – a Scottish Court of Exchequer judge and staunch Hanoverian – described him as 'a dressy, finical little man', though acknowledging him to be 'easy, well-bred and affable'.[92] But more than that, he was an unusually successful product of the purchase system. He owed his success in part to his affability, which he used to cultivate 'interest', and in part to luck: he gained his early promotions just before the old brevet system was phased out and commission prices soared. In largest part, though, he owed it to merit, without which the affability and luck would not have availed him.

The backbone of the British officer class – by no means its only component, but surely its largest – consisted of gentry of modest means.[93] Cope seems to have been a prototype of this genre. Born in 1690, and christened Jonathan, he was the only son of Henry Cope and Dorothy Waller, who had married the year before. She was previously married to an exciseman, from whom she was widowed. The Cope family, originally from the south of England, had re-located to Ireland in the sixteenth century and become prominent among the gentry there, but William Cope – Henry's father, John's grandfather – returned to England about 100 years later, married an Earl's daughter, and settled on a Gloucestershire estate. Henry attended Oxford and became a captain in the Coldstream Guards, which meant that he was carried on the Army List as a lieutenant-colonel; Guards captains were 'bumped up' in this manner in recognition of the Guards' elite status. Then, for unknown reasons, he resigned from the Guards in the fateful year 1688. William apparently disapproved of Henry's marriage, for although he left Henry a life estate he disinherited the infant John shortly before dying in 1691, when John was about a year old. John nevertheless received a good education, at Westminster School, but in his reduced circumstances the army now offered him the best prospects for advancement.[94]

That advancement was astonishingly rapid, especially by the standards of the day. It began when Cope was appointed page to Lord Raby, Britain's ambassador in Berlin, who was also the absentee colonel of the Royal Regiment of Dragoons. Taking a liking to Cope, Raby procured for him a cornet's commission with the regiment in July 1707. Cope was just seventeen. He promptly ingratiated himself with Lieutenant-Colonel James St. Pierre, the regimental commander in Raby's absence. A few months later, St. Pierre was writing to Raby: 'Mr. Cope will make a very good officer if I am not mistaken, and I do not see that he is given to any manner of vice'. For his part, Cope was assiduous in cultivating his patron, sending Raby numerous letters thanking him and soliciting his continued advice and support.

The cultivation paid off, as Cope rose from rank to rank and regiment to regiment: at one point borrowing from other officers to pay for his next commission; at another winning a coveted back-dated brevet. In 1708 he accepted an assignment as aide-de-camp to General Stanhope, commander of British forces in Spain, who, like Raby, esteemed and sponsored him. By July of the following year he was a captain in a foot regiment, but only briefly: in October he transferred, still a captain, to a different dragoon regiment and resumed his former duties as aide-de-camp to General Stanhope. Then, a year later, he became a captain in the Foot Guards, so that he, like his father before him, was now listed as a lieutenant-colonel. After some further moves – and after suffering a brief setback in 1713 by being forced to retire at half pay when his regiment was disbanded at the end of the Spanish Succession war – he received his first full colonelcy that same year. True, it was only a brevet colonelcy. But this was the promotion that was back-dated, by nearly two years, giving him the necessary seniority to rise even further, over the heads of competitors: to brigadier-general in 1735, major-general in 1739 and finally lieutenant-general in 1743. It had taken him just six years to advance from cornet to colonel. On 18 February 1744 he was named commander-in-chief of the government forces in Scotland.

He acquired combat experience along the way. He took part in the battle of Almenara in 1710, and in much of that year's campaign. Perhaps the apogee of his career, though, was Dettingen, where, fighting along-side George II – who seems to have retained a lifelong regard for him in consequence – he earned, for his bravery, the ribbon and title of a Knight of the Bath. The Scottish appointment followed in short order.[95]

It did not pass without controversy, for others had aspired to the post, notably Lord Mark Ker, who would exact a measure of revenge after Prestonpans. And Cope's celebrated affability cut no ice with Argyll and Tweeddale. Those two, agreeing with one another for once, are said to have disliked him, and to have instructed their Scottish dependents to keep him at arm's length.[96] On the other hand, he got on famously with Forbes, an Argyll dependent if ever there was one. The two men corresponded warmly and prolifically,[97] and Forbes deemed him 'one of the best of the English officers'.[98]

His resistance to vice deserted him north of the border. His amorous conquests exceeded his military ones, and one of them cost him dear: he came down with venereal disease. Medical confidentiality must not have been, in those days, what it is today, for his physician commemorated the event with verses more ribald than Skirving's.[99]

While mounting the promotion ladder, Cope achieved civic distinction as well. He was a Member of Parliament anywhere from one to three times. Cadell places him there in 1741, representing Orford,[100] and the Dictionary of National Biography has him serving on three occasions: from 1722–1727 (for Queenborough), 1727–1734 (Liskeard), and 1738–1741 (Orford).[101]

The word 'finical' has vanished from everyday English usage. But it still appears in present-day dictionaries, which continue to assign it its eighteenth-century meaning: 'foppish'.[102] Foppish Cope may have been.

But foppishness can be a symptom of an overall attentiveness to detail; indeed, at least one modern dictionary suggests, as a synonym for 'finical', the word 'meticulous'.[103] That is not a bad quality in a general.

THE JACOBITE ARMY[104]

There are two important facts about the Jacobite army. The first is that it strove at all times to operate along conventional lines, both for tactical reasons and more importantly for propaganda ones: it wanted to present itself, to the British people and to the rest of the world, as the military arm of a legitimate sovereign state, and not as an armed rabble. The second is that it was only partly successful.

Conventional it was in its organisation and appearance. At Prestonpans it was still an almost exclusively Highland force (that would change later, as it moved southward and Lowlanders, French regulars and even a few Englishmen signed on), and each clan fought separately from the others. But they fought as regiments, albeit of vastly different sizes; the regiments were separated into companies; and all were commanded by officers with familiar titles – colonels, captains, lieutenants and so forth – who kept orderly books, issued orders of the day, received and dispensed pay commensurate to rank, and conducted at least rudimentary drill to the extent that this was possible with troops who were freshly raised and always on the move.[105] Officers and men alike wore uniforms of sorts, of which we have already spoken: tartan in one form or another, except for the French, who were not at Prestonpans, and the cavalry, who were not there either apart from one small troop of horse. Highlanders displayed the tartan on their plaids: long, cloak-like garments which, clasped at the shoulder and belted or folded around the waist, covered the body from the shoulders to the knees. Lowlanders (few of whom were at Prestonpans) were likelier to wear tartan breeches, or 'trews', and the more genteel clansmen, especially the officers, might prefer them as well.

Where the Jacobite army fell short of its aspirations was at the company officer level. These officers were the tacksmen of the clan: that is, the factors, usually relatives of the clan chief, who managed the chief's estates, and collected his rents, in peacetime. While they were brave enough, most were inexperienced, in contrast to the Hanoverian army, where the officers were long-serving, often combat-hardened, professionals. To some extent their inexperience was offset by the fact that, because they were authority figures in each clan's social hierarchy, the rank-and-file clansmen found it natural to obey them in war. But there was a downside: though the clansmen found it natural to obey their own tacksmen-turned-officers, they would not obey the officers of any unit but their own. For these reasons, the Jacobite army lacked the discipline, cohesion and staying power of its opponents. This deficiency, well known to its leaders, dictated its tactics in the field.

Hanoverian and Jacobite military operations were a study in contrasts. The former relied on discipline, the latter on speed, as befitted an army that knew it had to win quickly or not at all. The difference manifested itself in marching formations, weaponry and methods of fighting.

On the march, the government forces, already divided into grand-divisions and platoons, usually proceeded in three lines along a wide front. This made it easier for officers to dress the men and keep them together. Rapid movement, though, was impossible unless the country-side was flat and completely open; any uneven terrain or obstacles would impede the rate of advance. The troops were also encumbered by large baggage trains, because, legally bound to respect private property, they could not forage as the Jacobites did, and by artillery, which the Jacobites did not acquire until they carried off General Cope's guns from the Prestonpans battlefield. Even the hatman's uniform slowed him: in particular, his long canvas gaiters, which protected his feet and legs in wet conditions, but at the same time weighed him down.

The Jacobites, on the other hand, were not hampered with a baggage train, for they lived off the land, nor by artillery, for in the early stages of the war they had none, nor by gaiters, for they had none of those either; many, indeed, did not have shoes. They marched – loped would be a better word, because they often moved at a dog trot – in long columns, three abreast, wheeling to form a wide front only when they approached the enemy. Thus they could keep to narrow tracks, manoeuvre quickly, and avoid obstacles. The only drawback was that their lines, being longer, might stretch out to the point where the men became separated. This was especially so later on, when their ranks had been swelled by Lowlanders and others who lacked the Highlander's hardiness and his familiarity with rough terrain.

As for weapons, the Highlander too carried a musket – at least the better-equipped ones did – but his weapon of choice was a broadsword, which was more suited to the close-up fighting that he preferred. This was sharp edged and single-handed (the traditional two-handed claymore having long since gone out of fashion) and was used to hack rather than to thrust. His other weapons were also designed for hand-to-hand combat. These were his shield, or target as it was known; a sickle-handled, short, straight dirk; and a fishtail-handled pistol of Scottish manufacture. The target was circular and roughly twenty inches in diameter, with a spoke protruding from its middle; accordingly, it could be employed both offensively and defensively – to thrust, as well as to parry. The dirk, which was concealed under the plaid, made the Highland soldier a double threat, for he could hack right-handed at the enemy in front of him while slipping his dirk left-handed into the victim's neighbour.

Only the regiment's front rank, consisting of the clan gentry, possessed all of these weapons. The rear ranks, unable to afford them, had to make do with 'Lochaber axes', which were halberd-like contrivances with a blade on one side and a hook on the other for unseating and disembowelling cavalry, or even with scythes affixed to long poles. Both were crude devices, yet capable of producing severed limbs and spilled entrails, and of sowing panic among regular soldiers – especially untrained, inexperienced regular soldiers – who had never encountered them before. After Prestonpans many of the rear rankers would also acquire muskets, either captured on the battlefield or provided by the French. But they did not acquire the broadswords, dirks or targets, because neither the government troops nor the French used them. Nor did they acquire hangers, for Cope, sharing Hawley's disdain for them, made his men leave theirs behind, and the men would probably have done the same had he given them the option.

The difference in weapons between the two armies was directly related to their different fighting methods. The government forces, it will be recalled, relied on mass concentrations of firepower with no great concern for accuracy. These they would deliver from fixed positions, in tightly-packed, 'locked' formations, at a distance of as little as thirty yards, against an enemy which – on European battlefields, anyway – was trying to do the same thing to them. Battles were decided when one side or the other wilted under the barrage; despite the availability of the bayonet, infantry charges culminating in hand-to-hand combat were rare. At any rate, that was the British practice against European armies, which played the game by the rules. The Highlanders had different rules.

Their stock in trade was their patented Highland charge: a phenomenon that Julius Caesar had observed, in more primitive form, among their Gallic ancestors. To conduct it properly, it was they who now needed flat, dry, open ground, for broken terrain meant delay, and delay would expose them to the withering fire of the Hanoverians. There would be no drawn-out exchanges of musketry at measured distances for them; they lacked the discipline, cohesion and staying power for that – the training and the weapons too. Instead, their game plan was simple: close rapidly and do rapid execution. A mere quarter-turn, in either direction, transformed what had been their marching column moments earlier into a three-deep line of battle,[106] with the better-armed men in front. This was an uncomplicated manoeuvre that even untrained soldiers could carry out without confusion. Then, casting aside their plaids, and knotting their long shirts, which they wore underneath, high at the groin for greater mobility, they surged forward. As they approached the government lines the men in the front rank fired their muskets once – aimed shots, in contrast to the synchronised but un-aimed volleys from the Hanoverian side – before discarding them and closing in. Upon coming up to the enemy, they dropped to one knee, beneath the probing bayonets, and covered themselves with their targets. From this position, they could bring both broadswords and dirks into play, while their comrades slashed or hacked away with an odd yet terrifying medley of weapons from behind them.

Against raw, impressionable troops, the charge was a devastating tactic, guaranteed to produce terror, carnage and victory within minutes. That, of course, is what the Jacobite commanders desperately wanted, for they knew that their forces lacked the discipline, cohesion and staying power for a longer affair. But if the enemy stood its ground, as would occur later at Culloden, well, it was (again, as Rupert Jarvis might put it) another story.

Of the cavalry there is little to say. At Prestonpans the Jacobites possessed but a single unit, Strathallan's Horse, raised in Perthshire and comprising just thirty-six troopers and their servants. They were useful for show (a virtue not to be minimised in an army that aspired to legitimacy), scouting, collecting taxes and guarding prisoners. As a fighting force, however, they were worthless, and they played no part in the battle. Of the artillery, there is nothing to say at all, for at this stage of the war the Jacobites had none. The reason will become apparent in the next chapter.

Artillery, moreover, was best suited for siege warfare, the drawn-out nature of which did not comport with the Highlanders' preferred fighting methods – as their futile, almost farcical sieges of Stirling Castle and Fort William would demonstrate later on. Lacking familiarity with artillery, they also feared it in the hands of an enemy.[107]

Despite their differences, the two armies had one characteristic in common: most of the rank and file did not serve willingly. The coercion occurred in varying forms and degrees. The Hanoverians had their 'vestry men', pressed men, and men driven by economic necessity into notionally voluntary enlistments. On the Jacobite side, the propellant was usually naked force. The ancient Highland custom of sending a messenger bearing a burning cross from village to village, as a primitive conscription notice, had fallen out of use,[108] so recruiters employed more direct methods: calling in person, they kidnapped or beat recalcitrants, and burned down their homes and drove off their cattle. The phenomenon was not confined to the Highlands. By statute, Lowland landlords had the power – long lost to their English counterparts – and indeed the duty to provide, from among their tenants, a fully equipped soldier for every 100 pounds of rental value at the behest of the authorities. The Jacobite commanders, deeming themselves the lawful authorities, enforced this duty rigorously in occupied areas, and landlords who resisted risked having their property burnt. The landlords in turn were not gentle, using similar techniques on their tenants to fill their quotas – although some hired mercenaries, or paid a cash substitute, rather than displace a tenant and lose his rent.

Only in the cavalry was one likely to find a preponderance of true volunteers, for they, being of a higher social class (they had to provide their own horses), were not as easily coerced. But the cavalry were not a factor at Prestonpans.

The self-appointed commander-in-chief of the Jacobite army was Charles Edward Stuart himself. At twenty-four years of age, his qualifications were dubious; his sole previous experience of war had been as a fourteen-year-old observer with Spanish forces laying siege to Gaeta, in southern Italy, during the War of the Polish Succession ten years earlier. Yet he was a serious student of military science, and events would prove him a sound tactician when his narcissism and paranoia didn't get in the way. I shall describe his principal subordinates as they enter our story.

3

To Edinburgh

It was the Irish who came to Charles's rescue when his French, English and even Scottish supporters held back. Large numbers of Irish had accompanied or followed James II and VII into exile, creating the nucleus of what became a flourishing Franco-Irish community. Some of its members entered military service as the famed 'wild geese' of the Irish Brigade: a consortium of six regiments that at first fought independently but was later incorporated into the French army. Others settled into France's North Atlantic seaports – Nantes, Brest, St Malo – where they established themselves as international traders, slavers, and privateers: that is, owners or skippers of armed private vessels that were for practical purposes pirate ships, except that they carried official papers authorising them to attack enemy shipping in times of war. The papers, known as 'letters of marque', insulated their captains and crews from being hanged as true pirates in event of capture. Like the wild geese, many of these Franco-Irish entrepreneurs adhered to the Stuart cause, either out of political and religious affinity or with a view towards improving their fortunes.

Three émigré Irishmen figured especially prominently in the '45. One was Charles O'Brien, Viscount Clare, commander of the Irish Brigade. A second was Antoine Walsh, a shrewd, successful and not overly-scrupulous shipper and trader headquartered in Nantes, who worked on Charles's behalf in concert with two other Franco-Irishmen in the same business: Walter Ruttlidge and Dominique O'Heguerty. The third, John William O'Sullivan, was a sometime seminarian turned soldier. The transformation occurred when, assigned as a tutor to the children of French marshal Jean Baptiste de Maillebois, he discovered a military vocation, obtained a commission from his patron, and, owing to the marshal's habit of drinking himself into a stupor on most afternoons, often wound up directing the latter's military operations as well as his large household.[1] Dispatched to Charles's side by James Francis Stuart in January of 1745, he quickly insinuated himself into Charles's inner circle, and would eventually become quartermaster-general – in other words, chief of staff – of the rebel army. Some historians, disparaging his capabilities, deem him to have been Charles's undoing, but the verdict is not unanimous.[2]

These three appeared, as *dei ex machina*, when Charles's fortunes were at a low ebb following the failed invasion attempt of February 1744. For the balance of the year, the Prince had lived obscurely in a succession of French country houses, subsisting on a small, grudging pension that Louis XV – fearful of alienating France's Protestant Prussian ally – granted him on strict conditions that he remain incognito and avoid Paris. Charles took petulant pleasure in flouting these conditions when he could, but by doing so he further alienated the King. Then, early in 1745, Clare introduced him to Ruttlidge, who introduced him in turn to Walsh. Events moved rapidly from there.

Ruttlidge and Walsh each lent Charles a ship: Ruttlidge, a captured British warship re-named the *Elisabeth*; Walsh, a small frigate ingratiatingly called *Du Teillay* (or *Doutelle*) after the French Commissioner of Marine at Nantes. Some sources describe *Elisabeth* as carrying sixty-eight guns, while others give her sixty-seven, or sixty-four, or sixty, and *Du Teillay* is said to have had anywhere from fourteen to twenty.[3] Such are the certitudes of history. *Elisabeth* was commanded by a Captain D'O, or D'Eau, or D'Oe, or Dau, or Douaud (among other recorded variations), seconded by his brother. *Du Teillay*'s commander was Walsh himself; although a Captain Durbe, or Darbe, was her titular master, it is clear from later events that her owner was literally and figuratively calling the shots.

Aeneas MacDonald, a Scottish banker resident in Paris and, at this stage, the only significant Scottish player in the venture, lent Charles money to purchase arms, as did the Paris banking house of Waters and Son. Charles secured the loans by pledging his mother's crown jewels: collateral with which he was remarkably prodigal, as we shall soon discover. He used the money productively, accumulating an arsenal of twenty small field pieces, 11,000 muskets, 2,000 broadswords, and powder, all of which was stored, for a time, in a Nantes warehouse.[4] In addition, Walsh and Ruttlidge advanced him a large sum for his personal use: some say 4,000 louis d'or, others 3,800.[5] Eventually, 1,500 of the muskets, 600 of the broadswords and the field pieces were smuggled on board *Elisabeth*.[6] Accompanying them were 700 'volunteers' from the Irish Brigade –

they probably had as little actual choice as the 'forced' Highlanders – whom
Clare had raised from his own regiment. Another 1,500 guns and 1,800
broadswords, along with the money, found their way onto *Du Teillay*.

Finally, Charles disingenuously procured, from French Navy Minister
Jean Baptiste de Maurepas, letters of marque that authorised *Elisabeth* to
sail on an intelligence-gathering mission in Scottish waters. The enterprise was underway.

Who would be privy to the secret, and who would make the journey
with the Prince? Those in the know were remarkably few. James Francis
Stuart was totally ignorant of the project, and would have thwarted it
if he could, for he deemed it folly to initiate a rising without substantial French support. The numerous agents whom he had attached to
Charles's person were hoodwinked also. So, in all likelihood, were Louis
XV and his ministry, although that is less certain.[7] Even Lord Clare may
have been deceived about the destination of the ships and the volunteers: he may have supposed that they were intended for a privateering
scheme that Walsh and O'Heguerty were pursuing in the West Indies.[8]

In the end, the plan was confided only to a handful, of whom just
seven, plus their servants, sailed to Scotland with Charles. They are
immortalised in Jacobite legend as the 'Seven Men of Moidart', after
the remote region in the western Highlands where the military campaign would begin in earnest, but they were not the romantic characters
that the soubriquet suggests. Most of them seem also to have been Irish,
though there is doubt even about that. The seminarian *manqué* O'Sullivan
certainly was: born in Kerry, around 1700, he was the only one in the
group with significant military experience. He left behind him a valuable
(though self-serving and not always accurate) account of his adventures.[9]
Thomas Sheridan was Irish as well – at least, partly so, for his mother is
thought to have been an illegitimate daughter of James II. Formerly the
Prince's tutor, he was an old man by 1745, and had little to offer except
devotion to his former pupil. The Irish non-jurant Protestant minister
George Kelly had even less: an elderly intriguer, of no judgment, he is
described by one source as Charles's 'evil genius'.[10]

Francis Strickland's origins are less certain. Christopher Duffy and
Alistair and Henrietta Tayler thought him English, as did his contemporary John Home,[11] but Frank McLynn – taking his lead, perhaps, from
the memoirs of George Murray's aide-de-camp James Johnstone[12] – calls
him the expedition's fourth Irishman.[13] There is general agreement,

however, that his principal qualification for the mission was his personal friendship with the Prince, and he is said to have been ill besides.[14] So too with Sir John MacDonald, whom McLynn (here parting company with Johnstone) describes as a 'bibulous' Scot, but whom the Taylers, Duffy and Johnstone include among the Irish, or Franco-Irish, in the group.[15] He had been a cavalry officer in his youth – hence his appointment as Charles's 'Instructor of Cavalry' – but that had been a very long time ago, and Charles in any case had scant cavalry to instruct. Like Strickland, he appears to have been selected primarily on the basis of friendship, although he may also have had some useful connections with his Franco-Irish compatriots in the shipping trade. Johnstone was probably speaking of him in particular when he scoffed that, except for O'Sullivan, the Irish in Charles's entourage 'possessed no other knowledge than that which usually forms the whole stock of subalterns; namely, the knowing how to mount and quit guard'.[16] MacDonald too left memoirs; unpublished, portions of them nevertheless found their way into the Taylers' book as footnotes to O'Sullivan's tale.[17]

To these Irishmen, or putative Irishmen, should be added the name of Antoine Walsh. Even though he is not numbered among the legendary Seven, he not only owned *Du Teillay* but commanded her on her voyage to the Outer Isles.

If the Taylers, Duffy and Johnstone are right, then, there were just two Scots in the party. One was the aforementioned Aeneas MacDonald, who, in addition to being a banker, was related to some of the Highland chiefs whose support Charles hoped to win. His presence was deemed necessary to exploit these ties. We are indebted to him for a description of the voyage to Scotland, which he dictated to a fellow-prisoner while both were incarcerated together after the Rising was over.[18] The other Scot was the anti-hero of the '19: William, Marquis of Tullibardine and, in Jacobite eyes, Duke of Atholl. However, he did not control the latter estate, having forfeited it, to his Whiggish younger brother James, as punishment for participating in that failed Rising. He had lived in France ever since. Elderly and gout-ridden, he was of no military use, but Charles hoped that he could bring Atholl's numerous and well-armed tenants into the Jacobite camp. And in fact they did turn out – perhaps as many as a thousand of them over the course of the war[19] – although it was probably George Murray, yet another younger brother, rather than William who seduced them from their allegiance to brother James.

In France these seven had formed, around Charles, a *de facto* exile court, rival to that of James Francis, who disliked and distrusted many of them: Strickland, Kelly and Sheridan most of all. For good or for ill (and the consensus is for ill), they, and especially O'Sullivan, were to be Charles's principal advisors before and during the Rising, to the chagrin of his Scottish followers. In this unlikely company, he set out to conquer three kingdoms.

From Navarre – where, using a hunting trip as cover, he had tarried while events unfolded – Charles set out in early June for Nantes, perhaps detouring through Paris and stopping there briefly.[20] Before departing, he sent a letter to his father, in which he outlined and explained his plans, taking care, however, that the letter would arrive too late for James to interfere. The Seven also made for Nantes, travelling by different routes, arriving at different times, and lodging, upon arrival, at separate hotels. Like Charles himself, they went incognito, with Charles, the life-long religious sceptic, incongruously dressed as an abbé in a frock that Walsh had procured for him. After a short stay in Nantes, the entire party proceeded together in a pair of river boats to Saint Nazaire at the mouth of the Loire, where *Du Teillay* was berthed. They reached Saint Nazaire on the evening of 21 June and boarded the frigate the next morning. As soon as her illustrious passenger crossed the gangplank, still wearing his religious costume (which he retained throughout the voyage), *Du Teillay* set sail for Belle Isle, off the southern coast of Brittany, and dropped anchor there the following day to await *Elisabeth*.

Elisabeth, though, was a long time coming, for she was held up in the harbour at Brest by a French bureaucratic snafu that took judicious bribes to unravel. Released at last, she joined *Du Teillay* at Belle Isle on 4 July. A day later – on the 5th – the two ships left together for Scotland.

Their destination had been a matter for much debate within Charles's inner circle (which included, besides the Seven, various correspondents on the Scottish mainland). The first choice had been the Inner Hebridean island of Mull, where the dominant Macleans were attached to the Stuart interest, but the untimely arrest of the Maclean chief put paid to that notion. So the entourage settled, instead, upon the Outer Hebrides, the southern islands of which – Eriskay, Barra, South Uist – had the advantages of being remote, Catholic, and under the control of the MacDonald of Clanranald family, which Charles assumed would be friendly: an assumption that proved only partly correct.

The first four days at sea were uneventful. But on the fifth day, the 9th, the Rising almost ended before it had fairly begun. Charles had wanted to transfer, that day, to *Elisabeth*, in order to enjoy her roomier quarters.[21] Fortunately for him, for his mission, and for the present-day Scottish tourist industry, he was thwarted. Before he could change ships, the British warship *Lion*, an approximate match for *Elisabeth* in size and armament, hove into view. Her captain had no notion of who was on board the two French vessels, or of where they were headed and why. But they were French, and that was enough for him. He pressed forward to attack. For his part, Captain D'O of *Elisabeth* feared (mistakenly, as it turned out) that *Lion* would shortly be joined by another warship, and that the two together would overwhelm *Elisabeth* and her tiny consort. So, rejecting Walsh's advice to avoid battle, he opened fire first, hoping to dispose of *Lion* quickly and then confront his next adversary on equal terms. The two behemoths pounded each other relentlessly for several hours. Charles, by most accounts, wanted *Du Teillay* to go to the larger ship's aid. However, Walsh, solicitous of Charles's safety, would have none of it, and threatened to exercise his authority as captain by ordering Charles below if he persisted. Instead of joining in, therefore, *Du Teillay* sheltered ingloriously behind *Elisabeth* throughout the engagement. When it was over, *Lion* was so badly damaged that she had to withdraw and return to port. *Elisabeth*, though, was in even worse state: Captain D'O and his brother dead, along with at least 140 of her crew, and she herself dismasted and listing badly. So crippled was she that she could neither continue the journey nor transfer the weapons and Franco-Irish volunteers she was carrying onto *Du Teillay*. All she could do, and that barely, was limp back to Brest, taking her cargo and passengers with her. Charles, still on the smaller craft, was spared to fight another day, but the cannon, the volunteers, and a substantial portion of the expedition's muskets and broadswords were gone.

Some of the Prince's companions – it is not clear which ones – were disheartened enough at this point to suggest aborting the venture and following *Elisabeth* home.[22] Charles, however, would not be deflected. *Du Teillay* pressed on alone.

It is difficult to reconstruct exactly what took place during her remaining days at sea. The participants' accounts conflict, and so, in consequence, do those of modern historians. It appears that she was pursued by yet another warship on 11 July, escaped, and thereafter travelled with her lights out to avoid detection. In this manner she proceeded more or less without incident until 22 July, when, after passing Berneray at the southern tip of the Outer Hebrides, she reached the harbour of Barra, immediately to the north. There Aeneas MacDonald, accompanied by Parson Kelly and Duncan Cameron – the latter a pilot who had guided *Du Teillay* on her perilous journey from Saint Nazaire (and who, like MacDonald himself, later dictated an account of the voyage)[23] – rowed ashore in quest of one of his many important kinsmen. The relative in question, his brother-in-law Roderick MacNeil, was chief of the island and, it was supposed, a likely ally. Whether he was an ally or not was never determined, for he was not to be found. The excursion ashore was not wasted, however, for Cameron stumbled across MacNeil's piper, an old acquaintance and a local pilot himself, who offered to guide *Du Teillay* to a safe anchorage off the adjacent isle of Eriskay. Or perhaps the obliging pilot was one whom Walsh, still on the mother ship, had spirited off a passing cattle boat: the sources differ on this point too.[24] Through the good offices of one pilot or the other, *Du Teillay* made her way by the 23rd to a safe mooring in the Sound of Eriskay, between Eriskay and its larger northern neighbour South Uist.

But the Prince and his party did not stay on board her for long. Alarmed by what looked like a large warship that lurked outside the Sound, trying to beat its way in against the wind, he and the others – all, that is, except Tullibardine, who was too ill to be moved – evacuated the frigate and landed, together with their stores, on a western Eriskay beach known ever since as Coilleag a Phrionnsa: Prince's Strand. He spent the night in a humble crofter's cottage, of the sort that is styled a 'black house', with only a hole in the roof for a chimney. The host had no notion of his guest's identity, for Charles was still wearing his priest's garb, and, to enhance the disguise, had not shaved since leaving Saint Nazaire. He could not decide which made him more uncomfortable, the trapped smoke inside the cottage or the cold wet wind outside it, and for much of the night he paced in and out. There is an amusing tale, reported by Aeneas MacDonald, of how the crofter eventually cried out in exasperation (in Gaelic, a language that Charles fortunately did not understand): 'What a plague is the matter with that fellow, that he can neither sit nor stand still, and neither keep within nor without doors?'[25]

The next morning brought more serious business, and a crushing disappointment that took the heart out of all but the most intrepid of the group. Charles had vested high hopes in the loyalty of the Clanranald MacDonalds, who controlled most of the southern islands of the archipelago as well as important territory on the western mainland. He also expected support from the two principal chiefs on nearby Skye: Alexander MacDonald of Sleat and Norman MacLeod of Dunvegan. Accordingly, he summoned the nearest Clanranald dignitary – Alexander MacDonald of Boisdale, on South Uist, half-brother to the Clanranald chief and an important magnate in his own right – for what he assumed would be a kissing of hands. Their meeting, begun inside the cottage and continued on *Du Teillay*, was nothing of the kind. In blunt language, Boisdale informed Charles that, without French military support, he would not assist him; that he would advise his kin not to assist him either; and that the two Skye chiefs had recently told him personally that they would sit out also. (Had Charles but known it, Duncan Forbes held both of those worthies firmly in his grip: as President of the Court of Session, he had declined to press charges against them after they had attempted to sell about 100 of their 'children' into slavery, and he had been blackmailing them ever since; indeed, MacLeod was the informant who had warned Forbes on 1 July that the Jacobites might be on their way.)[26] 'Go home', Boisdale counselled the interloper. To which Charles simply, and famously, replied: 'I am come home'.[27] Boisdale was unmoved.

Boisdale's resistance demoralised most of the Prince's followers. 'Every body was strock as with a thunder boult', recalled O'Sullivan.[28] All except Walsh and O'Sullivan – perhaps Sheridan too – wanted to give up then and there and return to France.[29] But Charles persisted, and as was usual in the early stages of the Rebellion his view prevailed.

He faced, however an even more immediate problem: that suspicious vessel, apparently a warship, was still nosing in and out of the bay, and Walsh was eager to give her the slip. Charles was agreeable, for he hoped for a better reception from other Clanranalds on the mainland. *Du Teillay*, therefore, stole away from Eriskay the same evening (Wednesday the 24th), entered Loch nan Uamh, off the rugged Arisaig coast, the following afternoon, and anchored. Charles – shaven at last, but still dressed as a priest – disembarked and took up residence at Borrodale, a Clanranald farmstead near the shore, which he would make his headquarters for the next two weeks, although he sometimes stayed on *Du Teillay* instead. More bad news awaited him there.

Upon arriving, Charles had dispatched Aeneas MacDonald in a small boat to fetch Aeneas's eldest brother, Donald MacDonald of Kinlochmoidart, who lived at the head of a smaller loch that emptied into Loch nan Uamh. When Aeneas returned, on that day or the next, he brought with him not only Kinlochmoidart but three others: their younger brother, Ranald MacDonald; the oldest son of the Clanranald chief – also named, confusingly, Ranald MacDonald, and known as 'Young Clanranald' (he was not quite twenty) – who had happened to be in the vicinity; and Young Clanranald's aide Alexander MacDonald of Glenaladale.[30] Discussions with the Prince commenced, immediately, aboard *Du Teillay*. The visitors, echoing Boisdale, were of one mind: Charles's mission was hopeless and he should abandon it. The most they would undertake was that Clanranald would relay a final appeal from Charles to the two Skye chiefs; Kinlochmoidart would carry letters to presumed sympathisers, advising them of the Prince's arrival; and Glenaladale would assemble a small Clanranald bodyguard to protect Charles until his situation was resolved.

Charles did not have to wait long for his answer from Skye. Within days, Young Clanranald brought back a definitive rejection of his plea. A 'Don Quiksot's expedition', scoffed the Skye duo, who, far from being rude warrior-savages, had learned the classics well at their southern universities.[31] At about the same time, Murray of Broughton – one of the presumed sympathisers to whom Kinlochmoidart had carried letters – responded with a letter of his own. Its message was the same that Charles was receiving from all quarters: go home. From Murray, this was especially disheartening, for he had hitherto been encouraging, as Sheridan reminded him in an acrid rejoinder. Meanwhile, more MacDonald leaders – some in person, at meetings that took place either at Borrodale or on *Du Teillay* (which was periodically shifting anchorages), others through correspondence – added their voices to Murray's and the rest.

These combined disappointments sapped the spirits of the remaining holdouts in Charles's small party. Without dissent, they urged Charles to cut his losses and quit the country.

Charles, single-minded as ever, would not listen. As early as 27 July, two days after reaching Arisaig, he ordered *Du Teillay* to be unloaded and her stores, weapons and ammunition secreted in caves and on islets throughout the area.[32] By this theatrical gesture, which has been aptly compared to Cortes's burning of his boats,[33] Charles let it be known that he had come to stay. Then, when his prospects seemed bleakest, they suddenly began to change.

Just as it is impossible to discern, from the conflicting contemporary accounts, exactly when and where the preliminary sparring with the Clanranalds and other MacDonalds took place – at Borrodale? on *Du Teillay*? – or even who attended, so too it is uncertain who first cast his lot with the Prince. Sir John MacDonald assigns the honour to his kinsman Young Clanranald (the interlocking relationships are too complex to explore here). His memory, though, may have been self-serving, inasmuch as he credits himself with having persuaded the Clanranald heir to change his mind.[34] On the other hand, Hugh MacDonald, another of the Clanranald gentry and a Roman Catholic bishop to boot, met up with Kinlochmoidart as the latter was delivering Charles's letters, and quotes him as saying, at the time, that he was 'engaged already' in the Prince's cause.[35] This would have been before anyone else had committed himself, and would make Kinlochmoidart the first to do so. The Taylers, dismissing Sir John's account, adopt this view.[36] But the most common, and surely the most dramatic, tale – one, moreover, that modern historians accept – is John Home's. According to Home, Charles, despairing of convincing either Young Clanranald or Kinlochmoidart during their discussions on *Du Teillay*, thought he detected sympathetic body language from Kinlochmoidart's (and Aeneas MacDonald's) younger brother Ranald MacDonald, who was standing silently nearby. As Home tells the story, 'Charles, observing his demeanour, and turning briefly towards him, called out, Will you not assist me? I will, I will, said Ranald, though no other man in the Highlands should draw a sword, I am ready to die for you.'[37] Once this domino collapsed, others toppled swiftly. Ranald's histrionic declamation, says Home, shamed Young Clanranald and Kinlochmoidart into following suit, and two other MacDonald chiefs – MacDonald of Keppoch and MacDonald of Glencoe – fell into line soon afterward.

Charles then set his sights on the most important domino at all: Donald Cameron of Lochiel, named 'the gentle Lochiel' by the romantic historians of the next century, but known in his own time simply as 'Lochiel'.[38] His prestige, and the strategic location of his territories – astride the southern end of the Great Glen, close by the Campbells – made him not only a prize catch but also a necessary one. He was predisposed to the Stuart cause, for his father and grandfather had figured prominently in earlier risings; indeed, the father had suffered exile for backing the losing side in 1715 and again in 1719.

But he did not come easily. His first response to Charles's missive
– borne to him, as to so many others, by Kinlochmoidart – was a firm
refusal, which, as if not trusting his own resolve, he conveyed to Charles
through his brothers Archibald and John. Charles persisted. If Lochiel
was to stand aloof, he told the brothers, let him at least have the courage
to say so in person. Against their advice (for they too, it seems, mistrusted
his resolve), Lochiel made the pilgrimage from his home at Achnacarry
to Borrodale, arriving on 30 July.

Nobody even knows where Charles and Lochiel met – some say at
Borrodale,[39] others on *Du Teillay*[40] – and thus it is not surprising that
nobody knows or is ever likely to know what transpired between
them.[41] Like the Ranald MacDonald story, the most romantic version of
events was disseminated by Home, who purported to have heard it from
Lochiel's brother John many years later: namely that Charles, employing
the same emotional blackmail that had served him so well with Ranald
and the other Clanranalds, announced to Lochiel, 'In a few days, with
the few friends that I have, I will erect the royal standard, and proclaim
to the people of Britain, that Charles Stuart is come over to claim the
crown of his ancestors, to win it, or to perish in the attempt: Lochiel,
who, my father has often told me, was our firmest friend, may stay at
home, and learn from the newspapers the fate of his prince'. Whereupon
Lochiel, his defences swept away by this impassioned appeal, threw caution to the winds and succumbed.[42] But this time Home is probably off
the mark. Lochiel, the hard-headed businessman, would not have been
manipulated so easily. It is more likely that Charles, knowing his man,
played successfully on Lochiel's personal and clan interests. A Stuart triumph would be bad for the Campbells, hence good for the Camerons,
on whose territories (to which Lochiel lacked clear title) the Argyllmen
were poaching. With Lochiel on board, that triumph was attainable,
especially since the French would surely come off the sidelines once
the Jacobites had achieved some initial success. And then (this is the one
near-certitude) Charles threw in the clincher: a promise to indemnify
Lochiel if the rebellion failed and the Cameron estates were in consequence forfeited. The promise was secured by Charles's mother's crown
jewels: the very ones that had been pledged earlier to guarantee the loans
from Waters and Son and Aeneas MacDonald.[43]

Whatever inducements Charles held out to Lochiel – sentimental,
practical, or a combination of the two – the outcome of their discussions

is beyond cavil. Lochiel declared unequivocally for the Prince, and, once he did, others, previously sceptical or even hostile, did the same: Stewart of Ardshiel for one, Glengarry's chief for another. (Lochiel had supposedly made Glengarry's accession a condition of his own.)[44] Almost overnight, a forlorn hope had become a viable, expanding enterprise.

Buoyed at having reeled in Lochiel, Charles and his counsellors now launched their military operations. *Du Teillay*, already emptied of her stores, was ordered home on 6 August with Walsh at her helm.[45] On her way, she sent back a parting gift: three barges, laden with barley and oatmeal. Walsh, invoking his letters of marque, had captured and then released them upon their promise to deliver their cargo to Charles, a condition they appear to have kept.[46] This allowed Charles and his party to stop purchasing food, through intermediaries, at nearby Fort William, the garrison of which had been blissfully unaware of where the provisions were going.[47] Even more importantly, Charles arranged to rendezvous with his new clan army for a standard-raising ceremony at Glenfinnan, at the far – that is, the north-east – end of Loch Shiel, at 1p.m. on 19 August. To reach it he would have to travel three days over land and water.

On 11 August, Charles, with his entourage, cut a day from the journey by crossing the Sound of Arisaig and taking up new lodging at Kinlochmoidart, home of Aeneas MacDonald's brother Donald, in Moidart, at the head of the loch which bears that name. He seems to have had mixed motives for the move. One, no doubt, was to shorten the trip to Glenfinnan. Another was to communicate more easily with his growing clan following.[48] A third, suggested by O'Sullivan, may have been to escape the attentions of an inquisitive smuggler.[49] The party remained at Kinlochmoidart for a week. During their stay, there was one untoward incident. Hearing, incorrectly, that Aeneas MacDonald had been playing a double game, Charles tried to insist that the Moidart Seven sign a bond, pledging their loyalty. Tullibardine, insulted, refused, but the others acceded more or less reluctantly, except for Sir John MacDonald, who claims that he was never asked.[50]

On 18 August, just before the departure for Glenfinnan, another newcomer presented himself: Murray of Broughton. He had overcome his qualms, and evidently been forgiven, for Charles appointed him as his secretary a week later, and afterward also named him Colonel of Hussars, although his duties in the latter capacity were nominal.

Also joining Charles at Kinlochmoidart was a lesser known figure: John Maclean from Mull, who had been a lieutenant with the Independent Companies of the Black Watch, later the 43rd/42nd Foot, until he was cashiered in 1744 for fighting a duel. Arriving on the 16th, Maclean stopped at Kinlochmoidart only long enough to 'Get a kiss of his royall Highness his hand',[51] receive from that hand a captain's commission, and eat dinner. He then returned to Mull on a recruiting assignment. He met up with the army again just in time to fight at Prestonpans, and continued to serve until he perished at Culloden. Unlike Murray of Broughton, he did not hobnob with the Rising's movers and shakers. But he too was a diarist, and his diary – retrieved from his dead body by a fellow clansman – provides an interesting sidebar to the Prestonpans campaign.

Almost immediately after welcoming Murray, Charles, accompanied by a bodyguard of fifty Clanranalds, set off for Glenfinnan. He proceeded on foot until he reached Dalelia, on the north shore of Loch Shiel, close by its western end. He and his escort then travelled by boat down the long, narrow loch, stopping overnight at Glenaladale, about halfway to their destination. There they met a recently-arrived Aberdeenshire laird, John Gordon of Glenbucket, who had come to offer his services. Glenbucket was elderly (some say he was fifty-eight,[52] others put him in his seventies[53]), and had had a chequered career; a rebel in the '15, he had afterward changed sides and become a government agent.[54] But now he was a Jacobite again, and his accession was significant, for he was the first leader to join from outside the Highlands. Meanwhile, the other Clanranalds in Charles's train were on their way to Glenfinnan also, bearing with them the expedition's weapons and supplies, which had been unloaded from *Du Teillay* three weeks earlier. It is uncertain how they got there. Christopher Duffy argues that they too went by water, for he does not believe that Highlanders would have been willing to function as 'pack animals' by carrying the baggage on their shoulders,[55] but the consensus has them portaging along the loch's northern side.[56]

On the 19th, a Monday, Charles left Glenaladale at 7 in the morning, again by boat, and arrived at Glenfinnan a few hours later: some think before noon,[57] others after,[58] but in any event by 1p.m., the time appointed for the rendezvous. The various Clanranald units, numbering three to four hundred in all, were present as well, whatever route they may have taken; perhaps some of Glenbucket's Gordons too.

(Most of the latter were raised subsequently, by the familiar technique of burning out recalcitrants.)[59] But nobody else was. For the next two to three hours, Glenfinnan – an isolated, open expanse, rising gently from the loch and enclosed, except on the loch side, by high hills – was silent and empty. Lochiel and his Camerons, upon whose promised support so much depended, were nowhere in view. Neither were Keppoch and his MacDonalds, who were likewise supposed to attend. With nothing to do but wait, Charles passed the time in a shepherd's hut, reportedly much agitated by the non-appearances.[60]

Then, between three and four in the afternoon, the silence was shattered by the skirling of pipes, at first distant, then coming closer, sounding a Cameron war rant. Next the Camerons themselves – anywhere from 700 to 900 of them[61] – emerged from the far side of the hills and scrambled down the near face. The gentle Lochiel had kept his word. He had not been gentle about it, for some of his men would testify later that like Glenbucket he had threatened to torch their homes if they held back.[62] But he had got them there. As Sir John MacDonald understatedly wrote, 'Never have I seen anything so quaintly pleasing as the march of this troop of Highlanders as they descended a steep mountain by a zigzag path'.[63]

What followed was short, simple and moving. Once all of the Camerons had reached the bottom of the hills, they and the rest assembled somewhere in the glen; the exact location is unknown. The decrepit Marquis of Tullibardine (with two attendants supporting him to keep him from falling) then carried the new Jacobite standard, furled, across the narrow River Finnan, which extends northward from the loch's eastern extremity. Upon reaching the far side, he stopped and held it while the Catholic bishop Hugh MacDonald blessed it. Next, he passed it to Charles, who immediately handed it back to him with orders to loosen its red and white colours[64] and flourish them aloft.

After doing so, Tullibardine read out two documents – a Commission of Regency and a Manifesto – which James Francis had given Charles prior to the failed invasion attempt of 1744, and which the Prince had kept about him ever since. The Commission vested Charles with authority to act in his father's name. The Manifesto was a statement of the Jacobite political program. There were, in fact, two Manifestos: one earmarked for Scottish audiences – this, of course, was the one that Tullibardine read at Glenfinnan – and the other for use in England.[65]

Both displayed shrewd knowledge of the respective constituencies. The Scottish document announced that James would dissolve the union and repudiate the hated taxes imposed upon Scotland by the English-dominated post-union Parliament. Its English counterpart tactfully made no reference to dissolution; instead it dwelled on issues that were of concern south of the border, promising, in particular, religious toleration and parliamentary government. When Tullibardine had finished, Charles himself made 'a short but very Pathetick speech'[66] – pathetic in those days meant 'passionate', not 'pitiable' as in ours[67] – in which he vowed to place his subjects' welfare above all other considerations.

The bemused Highlanders, Gaelic speakers all, listened uncomprehendingly as Charles declaimed to them in his Italian-accented English. To paraphrase Churchill's famous remark to Stalin, they might not have known what he was saying, but they evidently liked the way he said it, for they responded by giving three cheers and tossing their bonnets into the air. Afterward, he cemented their loyalty by distributing casks of brandy, together with cows, cheese and butter.[68]

Keppoch and 300 to 350 of his MacDonalds followed Lochiel's Camerons over the hills and down into Glenfinnan. The question is when they did: before or after the standard-raising. Murray of Broughton places them at the scene, as does Sir John MacDonald,[69] but others maintain that they did not arrive until evening.[70] Whatever the truth of the matter, by day's end the rebel force had swelled to well over a thousand, with pledges of more to come.

It is risky to guess at the unrecorded thoughts of the dead. In Charles's case, though, no guesswork is necessary. He found the afternoon's events more than just 'quaintly pleasing'; he was euphoric. In the words of one eyewitness, never was 'the Prince more cheerful at any time, and in higher spirits...'.[71] He could not then have foreseen that the road from Glenfinnan would lead to the abattoir at Culloden. Nor could he anticipate the sequel: more than four unbroken decades of exile, alcoholism, failed relationships, humiliation and despair. Here in the glen he basked in the unconditional love of his subjects. Today he was Prince, and his father King, and his dreams knew no boundaries.

There were some reluctant guests at the standard-raising ceremony. From 9 to 11 August, one Edward Wilson, in charge of the barracks at Bernera, opposite Skye (not to be confused with the Outer Hebridean island of the same name), sent Major Hu Wentworth, governor of Fort Augustus, three letters – one each day – with news of Charles's presence in the area.[72] The letters, increasingly frantic in tone, made the threat seem even greater than it was: for instance, *Du Teillay* was transmogrified from a small frigate into a large French man-of-war, and Charles's strength was put at 6,000, including French troops. (On the other hand, Wilson accurately reported the capture of the three meal ships.)

Wentworth dutifully passed these letters along to Cope. In addition, he took action on his own authority. The two reduced Royal Scots companies that remained in Scotland – the rest of the regiment, it will be recalled, was fighting abroad – had been stationed in Perth through July. Together they numbered fifty men at most. They were assigned mainly to recruitment duties, because, freshly raised themselves, they were not ready for combat. Toward the end of the month, they were transferred to Fort Augustus, which, it was supposed, would provide a better base for recruiting in the Highlands. But Fort William, being closer to where Charles had landed, was the needier of the two strongholds, so Wentworth dispatched them there, untrained though they were, to reinforce its undermanned garrison.[73]

At about the same time, Cope, having received Wentworth's correspondence (and having had confirmation of Charles's arrival from other sources, including Tweeddale), ordered an engineer, Captain John Sweetenham of Guise's 6th Foot, to go to Fort William also. His instructions were to take command of the Fort and use his engineering expertise to improve its defences. To reach it from Ruthven Barracks, his former posting, Sweetenham would have to follow the military road over the Corrieyairack Mountain pass, soon to figure even more prominently in our story. He was assigned an escort of approximately sixty men.

Both expeditions came to grief. Sweetenham and his escort were intercepted and captured without a fight on 14 August as they crested the Corrieyairack: by a party of Glengarry Kennedys, according to one source;[74] by Keppoch and his MacDonalds, on their way to Glenfinnan, according to others.[75] Two days later, on Charles's instructions, a detachment of Keppoch's, seconded by a few Glengarrys, ambushed, chased, and defeated the Royal Scots in a running fight that began at Highbridge, above the River Spean. About six Royals were killed and the rest forced to surrender, giving first blood, literally, to the Jacobites.[76]

Sweetenham was handed over to old Gordon of Glenbucket, who brought him, under parole, first to Glenaladale and then to Glenfinnan, where he witnessed the standard-raising. Many of the surrendered Royal Scots were there as well, delivered, it seems, by the Keppochs, who in that case would have been present themselves. (While under guard, these captives irked O'Sullivan by rejecting his invitation to change sides; he also complained about the expense and difficulty of housing them.)[77] Still other prisoners, including the more seriously wounded, wound up at Achnacarry, Lochiel's home, where they were treated with exquisite care.

Released on parole two days after the ceremony, Sweetenham – almost alone of the many captured Hanoverian officers who were paroled throughout the war – kept his word and took no further part in the fighting. Unwittingly, he also did Charles great service by disseminating exaggerated accounts of Jacobite prowess to the government side.

On the very day that Charles was haranguing his clansmen across the language barrier at Glenfinnan, Lieutenant-General Sir John Cope was making his way from Edinburgh to Stirling, where his army awaited him.

Reports of Charles's arrival had been pouring in to the Hanoverian authorities – to Cope, to Forbes, and to Cope's London masters – so rapidly and from so many quarters that even the complacent Tweeddale could not ignore them. On 30 July, the day that Charles was wooing and winning Lochiel, the Secretary advised Cope by express letter of disturbing news that he and the Council of Regency had received that morning from an informant in France. The informant averred that Charles had sailed from 'Nantz' on 15 July New Style and had landed in Scotland. Tweeddale professed himself sceptical, but at least there would be no more nonsense about not alarming the country. He directed Cope to bring the dragoons' horses in from grass – which he had only recently forbidden the general to do – and to 'make such a Disposition of the Forces now in *Scotland*, as you shall judge most convenient for drawing them together in case of Necessity'.[78]

The express reached Cope on 3 August. He too was sceptical. Nevertheless, he immediately called in the horses, sent express letters of his own to military posts throughout Scotland with orders to stay alert and in readiness, and reminded Tweeddale – in two separate replies that he wrote and posted that same day – that he desperately needed arms, trained gunners, and, as importantly, credit, so that he could draw money rapidly should need arise.[79]

Meanwhile, on 1 August, Tweeddale wrote to Cope again. He had by then received 'several other Accounts', likewise, it seems, from French sources, confirming the 15 July embarkation date, and identifying Mull as the probable landing spot. The sources were close to the mark. True, Charles had left 'Nantz', that is, Nantes, by mid-June, but 15 July New Style would have been 4 July Old Style, just one day before *Du Teillay* and *Elisabeth* set out for Scotland together from Belle Isle. And Mull, of course, was where Charles had hoped to land before the arrest of the island's chief forced a change of plan. His scepticism evidently shaken, Tweeddale enjoined Cope to 'make a strict Enquiry' into whether the accounts were true. He also told Cope that he was sending to Scotland, at once, 5,000 stand of weapons, to be stored in the castles of Edinburgh, Stirling and Inverness. Perhaps, he suggested to the general, some of these arms could be quietly channelled to the Duke of Argyll – but it was important to do this discreetly, lest other clans, less trustworthy than the Campbells, learn of it and demand to be armed as well.[80]

Tweeddale was not the only Hanoverian official who was reluctantly facing reality. Others, even more exalted, were doing the same. On 2 August, the Duke of Newcastle, England's principal secretary of state and brother to the prime minister, wrote to George II, beseeching him to return from the Continent. In the event, His Majesty did not arrive until the 31st, leaving the Council in charge for the rest of August.

Cope answered Tweeddale's 1 August letter on the 6th. He stated that upon receiving it, or maybe even sooner – he is not clear on this point – he had begun casting for information far and wide, offering rewards to those who provided any. He urged Tweeddale to earmark as many of the weapons as possible for Inverness, where Forbes, who would shortly be heading north to his Culloden country estate, could distribute them to loyal chiefs. He himself was trying to prevail upon the Provost of Edinburgh to lend him a sloop to transport them there. (Because of the law's solicitude for property rights, he lacked power simply to requisition one.) And he had transmitted Tweeddale's suggestion to Argyll.

News of the unwelcome visitor was also reaching Edinburgh and London from nearer to home. Towards the end of July the Presbyterian minister of Ardnamurchan, in Arisaig, noticed that the Jacobites amongst his parishioners had been in unusually high spirits since a purported smuggler's vessel had anchored off the coast a short while before. Questioning them, he discovered that the ship was *Du Teillay*, and that Charles Edward was aboard her. He scurried at once to alert the Duke of Argyll's local factor, who relayed the message by letter to his master the Duke of Argyll. The letter, after passing through several intermediaries, reached the Duke on the 7th. A prominent guest was in attendance: Andrew Fletcher, Lord Milton, Lord Justice-Clerk of Scotland and a colleague of Forbes's on the Scottish State Council. Argyll showed Milton the letter and Milton thereupon forwarded it to Cope, with a copy to Tweeddale. Cope had it in hand the very next day, and he too sent a copy to Tweeddale. One or both of the copies arrived in London on the 13th.[81]

Then, on the morning of the 9th, as Duncan Forbes was setting off for Culloden House – where he planned by threats and persuasion to keep the chiefs of the vicinity in the government's corner – he received a letter also. Dated the 3rd, it contained definitive confirmation of Charles's presence, by one who was especially well positioned to know of it. The informant was none other than the ever-obliging Norman MacLeod of Dunvegan, whom Charles had courted so assiduously from Eriskay. The Prince had not realised that he was announcing himself, through MacLeod, to the Lord President. MacLeod deprecated the interloper's prospects, predicting confidently that 'no man of any consequence benorth of the Grampians' would join him.[82] But Forbes was no longer wedded to the official line, and took the warning seriously. He did, accordingly, what he had done upon first hearing from MacLeod at the beginning of July: he interrupted his northward journey long enough to call upon Cope – 'in his Boots', as Cope described the visit afterwards – in order to show him the letter and tell him solemnly that he credited its content. Cope was in considerable physical discomfort, having had his right hand bled that day in consequence of some unknown ailment, but he promptly wrote, or dictated, an express to Tweeddale, conveying the latest tidings.[83]

All was now in motion, as Cope prepared to execute a plan that he, Forbes and other members of the Council – Robert Craigie, the Lord Advocate, and Robert Dundas, the Solicitor-General – had devised together while Forbes was still in Edinburgh. The plan was that Cope

would march his troops as expeditiously as possible to the chain of forts
that bestrode the Great Glen – Fort William to the south, Fort George
to the north, and Fort Augustus, the centrepiece of the three – leaving
behind only the dragoons, whose mounts would be useless on the rough
Highland terrain, and enough infantry to guard the Lowlands. The tactic
of responding rapidly to rebellion – of quelling it before the contagion
spread – was not new: it was a standard technique of the Romans,[84] and
had worked well for the Hanoverian regime in suppressing the Rising of
1719. Present-day Americans would recognise it as a variant of Iraq-style
'shock and awe'.

The march would commence at Stirling, the natural assembly point
for Cope's dispersed units. It was to have four purposes. One was simply
to secure the forts and beef up their depleted garrisons, which were in
desperate straits: for instance, Fort William's consisted of just 130 private
soldiers,[85] and the governor of the fort, his tenure extended by Captain
Sweetenham's discomfiture, was so infirm that his daughter had to write
his letters for him.[86] A second was to make a show of strength that would
dissuade the wavering clans from joining the rebellion. A third was to pick
up reinforcements from the loyal clans whom Cope would meet along the
way. This objective was especially important to him, for he well knew that
his own forces were pathetically inadequate, both in numbers and quality, and he had high hopes of recruiting successfully from the likes of the
Hanoverian Duke of Atholl's Murrays, the Breadalbane Campbells, and,
further north, the Grants, MacPhersons, MacKintoshes, Sutherlands and
even the Frasers of Simon Lovat. (The day Cope was laying his proposal
before Tweeddale, that wily old trimmer was penning a fawning note
to Lieutenant-General Joshua Guest, commander of Edinburgh Castle,
pledging fidelity to the Hanovers and regretting that age prevented him
from bearing arms for them in exchange for 'a moderate reward'.)[87] In
these hopes Cope was encouraged by Forbes, who, though he was no
longer wedded to the official line (which had ceased to be the official line
in any case), still overestimated his influence among the chiefs. Finally, if
Cope's route brought him anywhere close to the Jacobite army, he would
intercept and destroy it before its ranks could swell.

Cope could make some of his preparations without awaiting permission from London, and he did: he set ovens to work in Leith, Perth and
Stirling, 'Day and Night, *Sunday* not excepted', baking three weeks' supply
of bread, for he knew that there was no bread to be had on the march;[88]

he arranged to purchase biscuit at Leith and Edinburgh (though in Edinburgh, it turned out, there was none available); he hired a ship to deliver oat, meal and the biscuit to Stirling; and he sent field pieces to Stirling 'in proper Artillery Trumbrils and Waggons' so they would be ready to bring with him when he took to the road.[89] He thought it essential to carry artillery, despite the logistical difficulties of transporting it: even if he had no opportunity to deploy it, it was conventional wisdom that Highlanders were terrified of cannon, and that displaying some would therefore enhance the 'shock and awe'.[90] He did not, however, let his men take their swords; deeming these an encumbrance, he left them at Stirling.[91]

While Cope could do this and that on his own authority, the overall scheme required Tweeddale's imprimatur. Accordingly, he sketched out the plan to the Secretary in a pair of letters: one of them the 9 August letter that reported the visit from Forbes; the second – the more important of the two – dated the following day. In that one, Cope laid out in detail the nature and purposes of the march, and stated that he intended to undertake it 'unless I hear anything to alter my present Design…'.[92]

It would be confusing to trace the precise sequence of the correspondence that followed, between Cope and Tweeddale (whose letters often crossed), and between them and the many individuals who were providing intelligence. Suffice it to say that, in the ensuing days, Cope did hear things to make him 'alter [his] design': in particular, reports, from Edward Wilson of Bernera, from Fort William's governor, and from others, that Charles was accompanied by anywhere from two to ten thousand French troops. It was even reported that a second French landing was imminent.[93] The reports were wildly inaccurate – the sort of hysterical rumours that commonly circulate during crises – but Cope did not know this, and they changed his perception of the military odds. In particular, they made him reconsider the wisdom of dividing his tiny force and leaving Edinburgh and its environs with reduced garrisons; to do so, he feared, would jeopardise the security of the capital. He resolved instead to send just 300 men to the forts – enough, in his opinion, 'to support the Garrisons in the north, and to awe the People in their Neighbourhood' – and concentrate the rest in the Lowlands.[94]

But Tweeddale demurred. He was all for the march, gave it his blessing, and became more committed to it over time. By the 13th, the

Secretary had received Cope's letter of the 9th (the one written on the 10th had not yet arrived). At this point, he knew nothing of any purported French invasion. He wrote back gushingly – the italics are mine – that 'the Lord Justices [i.e., the Council]…entirely approve of your Conduct; *and are particularly pleas'd with your Resolution to march…*'. If Cope came across the enemy, he was to attack, for, said Tweeddale, 'I am hopeful that even the small Number of Troops you have, will be able to give a thorough Check to any sudden Insurrection that may happen, as we do not hear, that any foreign Troops are yet landed to support the Disaffected'. Since Cope was on the scene, and Tweeddale and the rest of the Council far from it, Cope was to exercise discretion, but the discretion, in Cope's understanding, only let him decide *how* to conduct the march, not *whether* to conduct it: in other words, it did not extend to altering the design.

Tweeddale also had good news for the general. He would get his letters of credit (they were delivered, in fact, on the 17th; Cope, remember, had first solicited them on the 3rd), and a Royal Navy vessel, *The Happy Janet*, would be placed at his disposal for transporting arms to Inverness. 'Allow me to add,' Tweeddale concluded, 'that it will be much for your Honour, and highly to my Satisfaction, that I be able to tell his Majesty on his Arrival, that you have dissipated a Rebellion in Scotland before the News of it had reached the Continent.'[95]

By 15 August, Tweeddale could no longer plead ignorance of a possible French military presence. On the 11th – as Charles was transferring his headquarters from Borrodale to Kinlochmoidart – Cope forwarded to him the first alarm: an anxious communication from Fort William's governor, based on hearsay, to be sure, but disquieting nevertheless. Tweeddale, however, would not budge. He now had in hand Cope's detailed proposal of 10 August, and had laid it before the Lord Justices. He must also have got wind, though, that his man on the scene was having second thoughts, for his reply was stern. 'Their Excellencies,' he wrote,

entirely approve of the Disposition of the Troops, and the Measures you did design to pursue, as mentioned in yours of the 10th, but they are surprised to find, that the Execution of so prudent a Disposition should have been in the least suspended on such slight Intelligence as that contain'd in your Letter of the 11th. [Cope was] *to march forthwith, and to*

execute the Plan laid down in your Letter of the 10th, notwithstanding the Report
of the landing of Troops, and even notwithstanding any actual Debarkation of
Troops; and I am very hopeful you will already have begun to execute the
said plan, upon your receiving my letter of the 13th Instant by the last
Express.[96]

Cope backed down at once. On the 17th, he acknowledged to Tweeddale
that he had indeed determined to downsize the march to a token force
of 300, but insisted that he had abandoned the notion as soon as he read
Tweeddale's 13 August letter. And by the next day he seemed to have
forgotten that he had ever contemplated altering the design at all. 'I am,'
he protested, 'very sorry I am so unhappy as to be misunderstood, as I
find my Letter is of the 11th. Your Lordship will find by my Letters, both
before and since, that providing Bread has been the only Stop to the
Troops marching…'.[97]

Taking no chances, Tweeddale wrote to Cope four times more over the
next several days. On the 17th, it was to say that he hoped Cope was
already on the move; that, even if the French had arrived, they could be
resisted more effectively from the forts than in the Lowlands; and that in
any case one ought not to act on the basis of unsubstantiated rumours.
On the 20th, the message was terse and faintly menacing: 'I have nothing by this Post to add to what I formerly wrote to you'. On the 22nd,
Tweeddale reiterated, again succinctly, that 'All Accounts hitherto received,
confirm the Opinion, that your advancing towards *Fort Augustus* [emphasis
in original] is the most probable Method of disconcerting the Designs of
the Enemies to his Majesty's Government…'. And on the 24th Cope was
reminded that the march was 'not to be neglected from any Consideration
of what might afterwards happen in other more distant Parts'.[98]

All four of these admonitions were superfluous. On 19 August, before
any of them had reached him, Cope cashed in his letters of credit and
departed at night for Stirling. The next day, he left Stirling with his troops
and headed toward the Highlands.

Charles too was on the march. After the standard raising, he ordered
that the muskets from *Du Teillay* be counted and distributed to clansmen
who did not have their own. Then, in the evening, he conducted his
first war council, probably at the bothy where he had waited earlier, and
where he would spend the night.

One order of business was to name a second-in-command. Lochiel, who was the most obvious choice, demurred, citing his lack of military experience, and Sir John MacDonald urged Charles to name O'Sullivan instead. Charles agreed, although he wavered for two or three days before he actually made the appointment.[99]

Even more important was the question of where the army would go next. Some of the chiefs advocated pressing north toward Inverness: perhaps because they feared for the safety of their estates in the area, or hoped, as Cope did, to win the undecided local clans to their side.[100] But the consensus adopted Charles's plan, which was supported by Murray of Broughton, Tullibardine – who was impatient to recover his ancestral holdings in the Lowlands from his Whiggish brother James – and, in all likelihood, the rest of the Moidart Seven.[101] This was to engage and destroy Cope's forces, and then swoop down on the capital.[102]

With that end in mind, the Jacobites, now about 1,400 strong, left Glenfinnan on 21 August[103] – some say the 20th[104] – and set out east in the general direction of Fort William. Before departing, they freed Captain Sweetenham, a good deed that would shortly be rewarded. They stopped that night at Kinlocheil, on the northern shore of Loch Eil, just five or so miles from their starting point.

The journey had not been easy. O'Sullivan, in his new capacity, was discovering the differences between a Highland army and the continental one of Marechal Maillebois. He tried to organise the clansmen into companies of uniform size – fifty men apiece was his preference – but they insisted on remaining with what he called their 'tribes': in other words, their clans. This meant that he found himself commanding units of vastly differing sizes, according to whether the clan was large or small. In addition, the smaller clans demanded the same number of officers – two captains and two lieutenants apiece – as the larger ones. As a result, they were absurdly, and expensively, over-officered.[105]

Another problem concerned the stores that Charles had taken off *Du Teillay*. These included some twenty swivel guns – possibly *Du Teillay's* own (though how, in that case, could she later have captured those meal ships?) – which, though poor substitutes for the cannon that the battered *Elisabeth* had carried back to Brest, would at least have given Charles a credible artillery arm. Slogging heavy equipment over rough country, however, was not to the Highlanders' liking, so they buried twelve of the guns not far from Glenfinnan.[106] Many of the remaining stores –

'pouder & bal, picaxes, Shouvels, hatcheds &ca.'[107] – suffered the same fate, but not for long: jettisoned at or close to Kinlocheil, they were recovered in short order by the garrison from nearby Fort William.

At Kinlocheil Charles learned that Tweeddale had placed a 30,000-pound reward on his head. It is said that he inveighed bitterly against the savagery of the gesture, and then, with grim humour, disseminated a proclamation offering a mere thirty pounds for the head of the 'Elector of Hanover'– the only title of George II's that the Jacobites recognised.[108] The chiefs, deeming the jest unseemly, persuaded him to raise the figure to 30,000 pounds also.[109] At the same time, he received his first intelligence that Cope had quitted Stirling and was advancing toward him.[110]

Charles spent two days and nights at Kinlocheil. He used his time there productively, collecting carriages to transport the weapons and provisions that his followers had not abandoned, and firing off expresses to the likes of Stewart of Ardshiel and MacDonald of Glencoe, summoning them to join him.[111] On the 23rd, he took to the road again, this time to Fassifern, home of Lochiel's younger brother John Cameron. Buoyant after Glenfinnan, he 'alwaise marched a foot at the head of the men', who, O'Sullivan tells us, were 'incouradged prodigiously' by this practice.[112] Despite his vigorous example, and despite having discarded most of its baggage, the army continued to move slowly; Kinlocheil and Fassifern were only four miles apart. John was not in residence: despairing of the Rising's success, he had decamped and sought refuge at Fort William. But the womenfolk stayed on, and made Charles and his staff welcome.

On the morning of the 24th, Charles undertook his longest march yet: a twelve-mile trek that brought him and his men into the Great Glen and thence to Moy, on the north shore of the River Lochy. Their progress was rendered more difficult by the need 'to crosse a cursed montaigne, where the horses cou'd hardly passe', rather than follow the main road, which would have taken them within cannon shot of Fort William.[113] Indeed, they could actually see the fort on the far side of Loch Linnhe, and at one point they had to alter their route slightly to avoid being sighted in turn by a warship lying at anchor just below it.[114]

The army spent two nights at Moy. O'Sullivan says it was partly because Charles fell ill – perhaps the vigorous marching had taken its toll – and partly because he was expecting more troops to join him there.[115] But Murray of Broughton makes no mention of any illness, and ascribes the delay solely to the anticipated arrival of the troops. In fact, some additional Clanranald MacDonalds, Keppoch MacDonnells and Camerons did trickle in, although the more important accessions – Stewart of Ardshiel's and his Appin Stewarts, for one – were still to come. One other event occurred at Moy: Murray of Broughton was formally named Charles's secretary.

On Monday, 26 August, Charles was underway once more. The achingly slow progress of the early stages was a memory: he would cover twice as much ground this day as he had done en route from Fassifern to Moy. His twenty-five-mile forced march through heavy rains culminated at Invergarry Castle, on Loch Oich, where he would spend the night. The Castle lay in close proximity to the Corrieyairack Mountain, and he planned in short order to cross it, via the Wade military road, which passed over its peak and then descended, in a series of dizzying zigzags, to Garva Bridge on the other side.

He had good reason for haste. He now knew that General Cope was approaching the Corrieyairack also, along the same road, from the opposite direction. Both men were seeking a battle.

Cope was not having an easy time either. His affairs had begun to unravel before he left Edinburgh, when the Duke of Argyll, citing the Disarming Acts, told him to his face on 16 August that the Campbells would accept no weapons. They worsened on the road.

Leaving about half his total force to guard Edinburgh and other strategic places in the south, he started out from Stirling with just under 1,200 men. These consisted of all ten companies of Thomas Murray's 46th Foot Regiment; two Black Watch companies from John Murray's 'Old Highland Regiment', now officially styled the 43rd Foot; and five companies of Lee's. (The other five were stationed at Berwick, just below the English border; Cope had begged Tweeddale to send them to him, but the request was ignored.)[116] All were at full strength or close to it. Eight companies of Lascelles, which had stayed behind at Stirling to wait for the bread – the regiment's two remaining companies had been posted to Edinburgh Castle – caught up with the main body at Crieff after the first day's march, and forty or fifty men from the Earl of Loudon's 'New Highland Regiment', which was still being raised, joined it at Taybridge on the 23rd. This meant that the expedition was now between 1,900 and 2,000 strong: a figure that does not include either its artillery train, which was of indeterminate size, or the civilians who drove the baggage horses.[117]

Cope also brought with him four one-and-a-half-pound cannon and four mortars, plus 1,500 stand of arms that he planned on distributing to the loyal clans whom he hoped, optimistically, to recruit along the way.[118]

He did not keep his 1,900-odd men for long, for the Highlanders, from the very first, deserted in large numbers:'mouldered away', as Cope himself picturesquely described the process.[119] The bread and the horses, to borrow his phrase, mouldered away also. A large portion of the bread was held up at Stirling, causing him to waste a day at Crieff awaiting it; when it finally arrived – at Amulrie, on the night of the 22nd – it had been depleted by pilferage and spillage. So too with the horses: some were stolen by country folk, or by their own drivers, despite his best efforts to guard them, while others simply wandered off in the night because there were no enclosures in the open countryside to contain them. Precious time was lost each morning rounding up as many of the stragglers as possible – and it was never possible to round up all.

The problems with the bread and the horses fed one another, so to speak. The daily round-up delayed Cope badly: the longer it took, the later the march began – sometimes not till noon – and the less distance he could cover that day.[120] The fewer the horses, the less bread he could carry and the more bread he was forced in consequence to abandon on the road.[121] The less bread he had left, of course, the less he could afford the delays, for fear he would run out of food – and he could not afford them in any event, because for reasons of geography it was of utmost importance that he reach the Corrieyairack before Charles did. He'd had the happy foresight to bring a herd of lumbering black cattle with him, even though he'd been ridiculed for doing so, and this to some degree alleviated the risk of starvation. But it cannot have quickened the pace of the march.[122]

He received little or no succour from the local population, whose attitude ranged from indifferent to hostile. A local sheriff deputy was particularly obstructive: he promised to bring Cope more horses, but came up 100 shy; entrusted with bread and other provisions that Cope, lacking horses, had left in his safe keeping, he contrived to mislay the bet-ter part of them.[123] The obstructionism appears in a different light when one realises that the passive-aggressive official was probably Lord George Murray, brother both to Tullibardine and the Whig Duke of Atholl, who soon afterward emerged as the most important military leader on the Jacobite side.[124]

Then there was the matter of recruitment from the well-affected clans: the expedition's principal purpose. Chastened by Argyll's rejection, Cope had found a way around the Disarming Acts, or so he supposed. Instead of distributing weapons to the clans or the chiefs directly, he would incorporate willing clansmen into his existing regiments. As an inducement, he offered short-term enlistments: three months or the duration of the conflict, whichever was less. Now, all that was necessary was to prevail upon friendly chiefs to produce 'volunteers'.

To this end he wrote, before leaving Edinburgh, to the Duke of Atholl and Lord Glenorchy (whose father headed another branch of the Campbells), both of whose territories lay along his route, and to other putatively receptive clan leaders in the area. Some of the replies were lost at Prestonpans, along with the rest of Cope's baggage, but he recalled them as encouraging, and those he managed to preserve were that and more. Thus, Atholl wrote back, long-windedly but reassuringly, 'I find it will be the duty of all his Majesty's faithful Subjects, at this Juncture more especially, to exert themselves, not only in discovering, but to suppress, as far as in them lies, any Commotions that may arise, in all which, you may be sure, for my part, I shall be as diligent as possible'.[125] And this from Glenorchy: 'You'll always find me ready to give all the Assistance in my Power, to carrying on any thing for his Majesty's service'. Glenorchy, it is true, also expressed concerns about the effects of the Disarming Acts, but insisted that they in no way diminished his 'zeal' for the government.[126] Buoyed by these responses, Cope invited both men to meet him at Crieff on the 21st.

They did, Atholl arriving in the morning and Glenorchy later in the day – and sang a different tune. Cope describes Atholl's visit as follows:

I acquainted the Duke, that I had brought one thousand Stand of spare Arms, and hoped to be joined by a Body of his Men. The Duke told me, he could not supply the Troops with any Men, and express'd great Concern about it. I ask'd his Grace, if he did not keep some Men in Arms, as a Guard to protect his Country from Thefts; the Duke said, he had about twenty or thirty Men so employed, who were dispersed at great Distance from one another. I begged that his Grace would order these to join us, to be a Beginning, and to set somewhat of an Example to the other well-affected Clans. The Duke said he would do what he could. Of these, twelve or fifteen did join us; and after marching a Day or two with the Army, went home again.[127]

So much for Atholl's exertions, diligence and duty. As for Glenorchy, he protested 'that the Notice he had received was so short, he could not get his Men together'. [128] So much for his readiness and zeal.

Neither Atholl nor Glenorchy came to Crieff alone, and the identities of their companions tell us much about the protean state of clan loyalties. Atholl was accompanied on the journey by his brother George Murray and by 'Glengary [sic] the Father' – that is, the chief of the Glengarry clan. Murray, as already noted, would shortly turn up in Jacobite uniform; indeed he was to become the most famous Jacobite soldier of all. At this point, however, he was either undecided or playing a double game, though given the integrity of the man the latter is unlikely. In any event, he seems not to have attended the actual conference with Cope, which may mitigate any duplicity on his part. Of Glengarry's duplicity, in contrast, there can be no doubt: not only was he already pledged to Charles, but Lochiel, it will be recalled, had committed himself only upon being assured that this was the case. Glengarry's younger son, moreover, uninhibited by having recently accepted a commission in Loudon's New Highland Regiment, had assisted in the capture of the Royal Scots at Highbridge five days earlier. [129] And Glenorchy's second, according to Cope, was a 'Lord Menzie' (Menzies). Suffice it to say that the Menzies clan later fought for the Jacobites, although the clan's principal factor, rather than its chief, may have been responsible for this. [130]

If Charles's mood at Glenfinnan – euphoria – can be deduced without undue guesswork, so can Cope's after Crieff. It was utter dejection. He had failed to gain a single adherent from any of the clans in the vicinity of the capital (except the twelve to fifteen Atholls – MacGregors, actually, the Duke apparently being unwilling to risk any of his own people – who promptly deserted), and it was beginning to dawn on him that he might fare no better with the more distant ones. Now he truly wanted to alter the design: to stop, or even to turn back. Lord Loudon, who was with him, agreed. [131] But there were the orders, the cursed orders, which as Cope read them were 'so positive, that I could not disobey them, but at my utmost Peril'. [132] He had received, at Crieff, Tweeddale's letter of 17th August, confirming them: he was to march 'towards *Fort-Augustus*' no matter what, and, if the French had really landed, he was to fight them from the forts. Cope was no Nelson, to turn a blind eye to senseless commands. He plodded on.

From Crieff, he marched on the 22nd to Amulrie, after first sending 700 stand of arms back to Stirling. These he deemed useless (since the clans were unwilling to accept them), and an impediment to progress (since the horses he needed to carry them were already, as he might have put it, mouldering away). On the 23rd, from Amulrie to Taybridge, where Loudon's new levies caught up with him. On the 24th, to Trinifuir. On the 25th, to Dalnacardoch. He covered, on the average, perhaps ten miles a day, taking precautions against surprise attack by having his Highlanders – those, that is, who had not mouldered away – advance ahead of him on his right and left, under the command of trustworthy officers, to warn him with signals if the enemy showed up suddenly. By this means, he believed, he could be ready to fight upon three minutes' notice.[133] Such precautions were commendable and even necessary, but they too cannot have quickened the pace of the march.

On the 25th Glenorchy, belatedly having second thoughts, sent Cope a letter stating that if Cope could rush 300 stand of arms to him at Taybridge, he would find men to use them. But the general could not do this, for he could spare neither horses nor an escort. The messengers back and forth must have ridden post-haste, because upon reading Cope's answer Glenorchy travelled to Dalnacardoch in person, arriving either that day or early the next, with a new offer: if Cope could wait where he was just two or three more days (the witnesses differ over whether it was two or three), the men would join him there. But Cope could not do this either, for his orders, as he understood them, enjoined him to lose no time, and he had lost time enough already.[134]

Another important visitor stopped in at Dalnacardoch on the 25th: someone of less exalted station than Glenorchy, heir to a Campbell chief, but who would have a greater impact on the immediate course of the war. This was Captain John Sweetenham of Guise's, who, released from captivity with a safe-conduct signed by Charles himself, came calling upon his general. Sweetenham had applied his eyes and his ears in the king's service both at Glenfinnan and on his way to Cope's camp, and his intelligence-gathering was facilitated by the loquacity of his Jacobite captors, as well as of other Jacobites whom he encountered on the road as they flocked to Charles's colours. Some of the information that they fed him, or that he observed for himself, was accurate. For instance, he had Charles's numbers right at Glenfinnan – about 1,400 – and he was more or less correctly informed as to how many swivel guns Charles's party had unloaded from *Du Teillay*.

(This was before the Highlanders deep-sixed the better part of them on the first day's march from Glenfinnan to Kinlocheil.) Purposely or not, however, he was egregiously misled about the number of recruits Charles had picked up subsequently. He himself had passed several groups of these newcomers as they travelled in the opposite direction to join the Prince, but they had amounted to no more than 400 in all. One of them, though – a 'Boreland MacIntosh' (probably MacKintosh of Borlum) – assured him that Charles's strength had by that time grown to 3,000. This was a gross exaggeration: the actual figure was perhaps half of that. (As with almost everything else about the '45, there is no consensus regarding the true size of the Jacobite army at this juncture: estimates range from 1,400 – approximately the same number as at Glenfinnan, the later accessions having been cancelled out by desertions – to, at most, 1,800.)[135] But Sweetenham, taken in, relayed the misinformation, or disinformation, to Cope, along with the outdated and inflated accounts of the swivel guns.

He also passed along to Cope an additional detail that 'MacIntosh' had revealed to him earlier that day. This was that Charles, with his 3,000 men and his swivel guns, was making haste to seize the Corrieyairack pass, and might already be there.[136]

One has only to see the Corrieyairack in order to recognise its tactical importance to both armies. The mountain, which is part of the Monadhliath mountain range, climbs to a height of 2,500 feet. The Wade military road that crosses its peak provided (and still provides, for ambitious hikers), the only direct access to Fort Augustus from the range's eastern side. The road has a remarkable feature: a series of steeply ascending traverses just below the summit on that eastern side – the side, that is, from which Cope was approaching – which carry the traveller over the top. There were seventeen in Cope's day, thirteen of which remain. They were not built with the automobile in mind, so their angles are sharper than one would encounter on any modern Alpine highway. A few determined men, especially men with swivel guns, could easily have held them even against a large and experienced army attacking from below. A child with a popgun might have held them against Cope's. And now Cope had reason to fear that the Jacobites, with their twenty-one swivel guns (the number given him by Sweetenham), had occupied those traverses and were waiting for him there. What was he to do?

Monday and Tuesday, the 26 and 27 August, were fateful days for both armies.

We left Charles dashing twenty-five miles through the rain on the Monday en route from Moy to Invergarry Castle. He had started the march late, at around noon, because he had intended initially to cover only a short distance. But when he came to Spean Gorge, at Highbridge – where the Royal Scots had been beaten on the 16th – he received intelligence, probably from Black Watch deserters, that caused him to alter his plans. The intelligence consisted of the earliest reports to reach him that Cope, too, was nearing the Corrieyairack and meant to get there before he did. This was what precipitated the twenty-five-mile forced march to Invergarry.[137]

At Invergarry, he made another important decision: not, this time, to alter his plans, but to persist in his present ones. He found upon arrival that the Inverness option was beckoning again, in the person of a messenger from Lord Lovat: one Fraser of Gortuleg, who was Lovat's cousin. Lovat, through his factotum, had three matters to place before his Prince. First, he sought a warrant authorising him to seize Duncan Forbes dead or alive: this at a time when he was corresponding warmly with Forbes and assuring the Lord President of his loyalty.[138] Forbes, he warned, posed the greatest single threat to Jacobite success. Second, he wanted Charles to hand over to him commissions naming him lieutenant-general and lord lieutenant of his county. The exiled King James had signed these commissions and entrusted them to Charles for delivery before Charles departed for Scotland. Most importantly of all, Lovat urged Charles to change direction and come instead through Inverness – Fraser country – where the Frasers and neighbouring clans would surely join him. He regretted that age and infirmity prevented him from 'coming out' in person (the same excuse he'd recently given the Hanoverian general Joshua Guest) but would answer for his clan.

Although Lovat was clever enough not to put any of this in writing, in other respects his habitual caution deserted him. It is very likely that, despite their kinship, Fraser of Gortuleg was a double agent who was also working for Duncan Forbes. And it was unfortunate, to say the least, that the discussion took place in the presence of Murray of Broughton, who would later help to send Lovat to the gallows by recalling it, at Lovat's trial, after the Rising was over.

Gortuleg's mission was for the most part a failure. Charles issued the warrant (indeed, Murray drafted it) but toned it down considerably –

it merely called for detaining Forbes in safe custody until further orders – and in any case it was never executed: Forbes, as wily as Lovat, and no doubt forewarned by Gortuleg, remained at liberty. Lovat also received his commissions. The originals that Charles had brought with him from France had been left behind with the baggage, so George Kelly drew up new ones. But the effort was wasted, for Lovat, acting in character, kept his head down throughout the war and therefore never used them. Finally, and most significantly, the Inverness option was rejected. Charles, thirsting for battle, would continue his march over the Corrieyairack, where he hoped to meet and defeat Cope and then sweep into the Lowlands.[139]

The next day, Tuesday the 27th, the army inched forward just three miles, to Aberchalder, gateway to the Corrieyairack. There seem to have been two reasons for the slow pace: to rest the troops on the eve of the anticipated battle, and to give new levies – Glengarry MacDonalds, Glencoe MacDonalds, Appin Stewarts and some Grants who had risen in defiance of their chief – time to catch up with the main body.[140] It was they, presumably, whom Captain Sweetenham had met on the road. These accessions, though, were partly offset by the desertion of many Keppoch MacDonnells, who were miffed because their Protestant chief would not allow them the company of a Catholic priest.[141] At Aberchalder Charles encountered more Black Watch deserters, who confirmed that Cope was on the way.[142]

The Prince broke camp at 3a.m. on the 28th. After sending Murray of Broughton and another clan officer, MacDonald of Lochgarry, ahead of him as scouts, he and his men proceeded up the Corrieyairack's relatively gentle western slope, via the Wade road, which they picked up about two miles east of Aberchalder. By all accounts his heart was light, his step also; his clansmen even complained that he walked ahead of them too rapidly for them to keep pace, and they were delighted when he broke the heel of one of his boots, because they hoped it would slow him down.[143] Based on his intelligence reports, he expected to encounter Cope around noon,[144] at which time he would be firmly in control of the pass and the traverses. But by then Cope had other ideas.

Cope was meanwhile receiving his own intelligence. It was not reassuring. Sweetenham had issued his alert on the night of the 25th. In spite of it, Cope advanced the next day another dozen or so miles to Dalwhinnie, just below where the Wade road forks off in two directions: the lower branch – the one he was planning on taking – climbing to the left over the Corrieyairack; the upper, right-hand branch leading to Inverness and Fort George in the north. At Dalwhinnie, he received an urgent letter from the Lord President. The letter has not been preserved, but both men testified to its content at the board inquiry. That content was grim. Forbes too had learned of the Jacobite design to seize the Corrieyairack before Cope got there, and he warned the general against trying to force a passage. He couched the warning 'in the most decent Manner that [he] could think of', as he himself described it afterward: that is, he did not try to tell Cope what to do, but merely spelled out the dangers and expressed the earnest hope that Cope 'had foreseen, and found Means to obviate the Difficulties…'. But Cope was no fool, and understood the import of the advice.[145]

So well did he understand it, and Sweetenham's too, that he sent some of his remaining Highlanders into the hills to see whether the reports were true. Their discoveries were more harrowing still. The rebels were indeed on top of the Corrieyairack, and their numbers had grown wondrously: instead of Sweetenham's 3,000 men they now had 3,800, and the eight swivel guns that had survived the march from Glenfinnan had multiplied to twenty-four. What is more, they had not contented themselves with merely occupying the pass and the traverses; they also intended to swarm around the slopes as he ascended the mountain and encircle him from the rear. For good measure, they had broken down a bridge over a steep ravine on the far side of the mountain and 500 of them were waiting for him there in case he somehow cut his way across the top. (The place, which Wade's soldiers had nicknamed 'Snugborough', was where Charles's men would join the road after leaving Aberchalder the next morning. There was, in fact, a bridge – but it had not been broken.) These tales were corroborated by several Royal Scots officers who, like Sweetenham, had been captured and then released after Glenfinnan.[146]

Shaken, Cope summoned a council of war on the morning of the 27th. Such councils were not common in the eighteenth-century British army, but they were not unheard of either,[147] and Cope had good reason for seeking one: if he altered his design, as he was now contemplating, he would need all the support he could muster when facing an angry Tweeddale. Ten of his highest-ranking officers attended. One of them, Major William Caulfield, the Quartermaster-General, was especially familiar with the terrain and with the road, for he had helped to build it, and his duties required him to inspect it annually.

Cope opened the meeting by familiarising his audience with Tweeddale's letter of 17 August: the one that reached him at Crieff, in which the Secretary expressed the hope that the army was already on its way to the forts. (Whether he read this letter aloud or merely summarised it is not clear.)[148] Then, he suggested to the council four options, without revealing his own preference. He could try to force his way across the Corrieyairack – traverses, broken bridges, swivel guns and all – with his 1,400 remaining effectives.[149] He could retreat to Stirling. He could stay at Dalwhinnie and hope that the rebels would descend and offer him battle on level ground. Or he could turn right instead of left at the fork and proceed to Inverness and Fort George.

He left the council to ponder these choices out of his hearing.[150] None of the four was appealing. The first would get all of them butchered; Major Caulfield attested to that. The second – retreat – would display the white feather to Charles's white cockade. It would also demoralise the loyal clans, hearten the disloyal, tilt the wavering ones in Charles's direction, and give Charles a free hand to recruit throughout the Highlands. Besides, Cope and his tiny troop might not make it to Stirling: the Jacobites, with their greater mobility and closer knowledge of the terrain, might slip in front of him, surround him, and destroy him. Alternatively, once having surrounded him they could starve him into submission, the more readily so because they would have known, from the Black Watch deserters, that his bread supply was running low and would be exhausted in less than three days, with no means of replenishing it, since the laws forbade him to forage. Finally, a retreat would be squarely against orders.

So too with staying put at Dalwhinnie: he could hardly expect the Jacobites to oblige him by coming down from their mountaintop and fighting him on his own terms. They would simply bypass him and occupy the Lowlands, or remain aloft and watch him starve. And staying put was also squarely against orders.

1 Caricature of Lieutenant-General Sir John Cope, by George, 1st Marquess of Townshend.

2 Lord President Duncan Forbes, by Jeremiah Davison.

3 John Hay, 4th Marquess of Tweeddale, by William Aikman.

4 Engraving of Charles Edward Stuart at Holyrood, by Robert Strange. Strange was later commissioned to design Jacobite currency, but Culloden put paid to that.

5 Lord George Murray in civilian attire, by unknown artist.

6 Posthumous portrait of 'the gentle Lochiel', by Sir George Chalmers.

7 James Drummond, titular 3rd
Duke of Perth, by unknown artist.

8 David, Lord Elcho, by Domenico
Dupra.

9 South-facing view of Prestonpans battlefield, as it appeared in the mid-nineteenth century. Tranent kirk is visible in the background.

10 Colt Bridge, site of the dragoons' discomfiture, c. 1831, by James Skene.

11 Bankton House, home of Colonel Gardiner.

12 Prestonpans kirk and tower. The south is to the left, so Alexander Carlyle would have been facing in that direction when he was acting as lookout the night before the battle.

13 Original wing of Cockenzie House, Cockenzie, where Cope stored his baggage and left the Highland regiments to defend it until Peter Halkett persuaded them to surrender.

14 No. 8, The Causeway, Duddingston, where Charles held his war council the night before he marched out of the capital to meet Cope.

Above: 15 Pinkie House, Musselburgh, Scottish residence of the Marquess of Tweeddale, where Charles stayed on the night after the battle, and where wounded enemy prisoners were sheltered once he had departed.

Left: 16 Memorial cairn, Prestonpans battlefield. It stands near the extreme right of the government line, on ground occupied – not for long – by the artillery guard.

17 Trooper, 13th dragoons, c. 1742. It lacks verisimilitude only in that the mounted figure appears to be standing his ground.

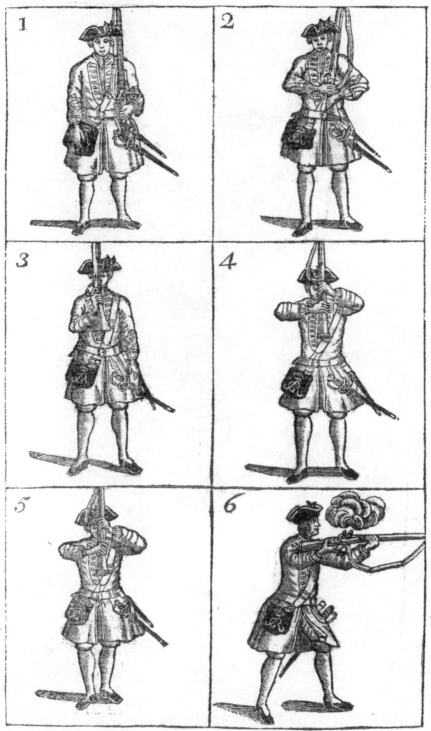

1 Take Care.   2 Join your Right-Hand to your Firelock.   3 Poise your Firelock.
4 Join your Left-Hand to your Firelock.   5 Cock your Firelock,   6 Present, Fire.

Opposite: 18 Manual exercises, British army, 1745.

Right: 19 Private soldier, Clan Cameron, by R.R. MacIan.

Below: 20 Map, Prestonpans and vicinity, with routes and dispositions of armies, from Forrest's Map of Haddingtonshire, 1799.

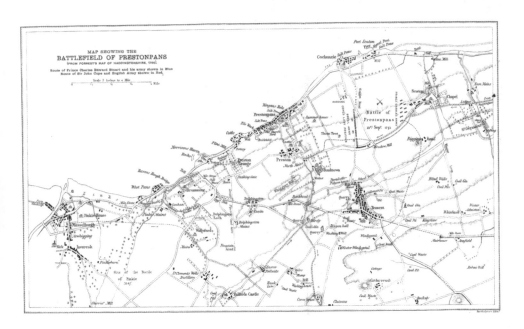

MAP SHOWING THE
BATTLEFIELD OF PRESTONPANS
(FROM FORREST'S MAP OF HADDINGTONSHIRE, 1799.)

Route of Prince Charles Edward Stuart and his army shown in Blue
Route of Sir John Cope and English Army shown in Red.

Scale 3 Inches to a Mile

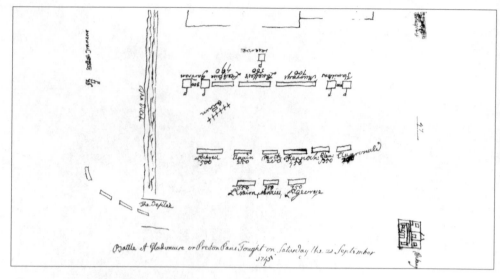

Above: 21 Lord Elcho's map of the Prestonpans battlefield.

Below: 22 John Home's map of the Prestonpans battlefield. Both the Home and the Elcho maps err in important particulars. Each depicts the Jacobite front line as a coherent entity – left, right and centre – when in fact there was no centre, and neither reveals that the Jacobite right outflanked the government left, and trailed behind its own left, by a considerable distance.

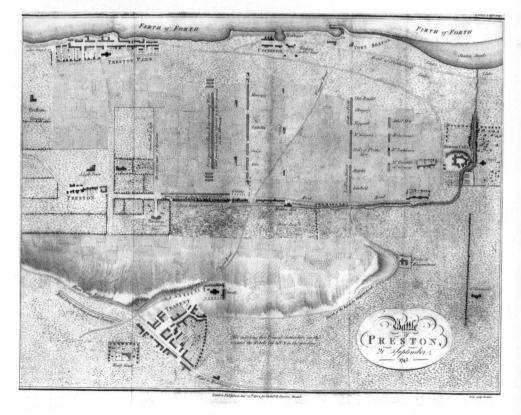

In all, therefore, the Fort George option seemed, *faute de mieux*, the most promising of the four. Cope still hoped for the support of the puta-tively well-disposed Presbyterian clans in the Inverness vicinity; these included, in his wishful thinking, the Frasers. One of the officers at the council, Major Hugh MacKay, even produced a written statement from two of the northern chiefs, Lord Sutherland and Lord Reay – the latter the head of MacKay's own clan – which suggested that in their cases, anyway, the thinking was not just wishful: in the statement, their lordships vowed to support the government, and MacKay predicted con-fidently that he personally could recruit 500 experienced soldiers from amongst their clansmen. True, if Cope headed north the lightly-defended Lowlands would be open to the Jacobites, but with his augmented forces he could follow and defeat them, and Edinburgh, with its walls and cas-tle, should be able to hold out until he came. Additionally, going to Fort George was at least arguably consistent with Tweeddale's positive orders. It was not Fort Augustus, where Tweeddale had wanted him to go, but it was part of the chain.

This, then, was the option that the council adopted – unanimously except, initially, for one dissenter, Colonel Peregrine Lascelles. He origi-nally advocated a retreat to Stirling but changed his mind when he saw all of the others aligned against him.[151] The group's view – which it expressed in writing, as Cope had requested – coincided with Cope's own.

As soon as the council gave its assent, Cope marched another nine miles in the same direction, almost to the base of the Corrieyairack, near the hamlet of Garvamore. The march was a feint: he expected that the Jacobites – who he supposed were ensconced on the top – would see him coming and dig in to await his expected attack, thus giving him time to sneak away. Then he and his troops turned their backs to the mountain and headed for the north.[152]

And so, when first Murray of Broughton and MacDonald of Lochgarry, and later the rest of the rebels, peered down from the top of the Corrieyairack on the 28th, they found the far side empty except for a few more deserters who were walking toward them.

All of them assumed, upon beholding the spectacle, that they had won the race to the Corrieyairack. Murray and O'Sullivan thought so,[153] and some modern historians have replicated their error.[154] But they didn't win it, of course. The intelligence, on both sides, had been wrong;

each mistook the whereabouts of the other. Cope's council took place on the morning of 27 August. Charles and his army did not cross the Corrieyairack until midday on the 28th. Cope, in consequence, could have passed over it unmolested on the 27th. Had he done that, this book – if written at all – would have been called 'Snugborough 1745' or 'Aberchalder 1745' instead of 'Prestonpans 1745'. We shall never know whether it would have had the same ending.

Cope fairly flew north on 27 August in response to another piece of alarming intelligence, from a spy in the Jacobite camp. The spy told him that the rebels had devised a fallback plan in case he chose to bypass the Corrieyairack. This was to ambush him at a place called Slochd Mor, twenty-one miles south of Inverness. It was not an appetising prospect. Slochd Mor, in Gaelic, means a large pit or cavity, and the location in question was just that – a deep gully where a small army like his could easily be trapped and annihilated. Thus his haste: he needed to pass it before the Jacobites got to it. [155]

He paused long enough, however, to have a brief and inconclusive meeting with Ewen MacPherson of Cluny, eldest son of the MacPherson clan chief, whose territories lay close by. Young Ewen MacPherson – or Cluny MacPherson, as he is better known – was the captain of one of Loudon's new Highland companies, and Cope looked to him for succour. Dissatisfied with the results of the discussion, Cope ordered him to return to his home at Cluny Castle and await further instructions. This order would shortly have consequences. [156]

Succour did come, or appear to come, that same day, in the form of a letter, from Grant of Moriston, which reached Cope on the march. Grant's territories, like MacPherson's, were on Cope's projected route, and also abutted Slochd Mor. His message seemed to vindicate the selection of the northern option and to bode well for the success of the mission. He was eager, he said, to place his clan at the general's disposal, and he could make 300 men available immediately. In reply, Cope 'intreated' Grant, 'in the strongest Terms', to have the men secure Slochd Mor at once and then meet him there. The messenger promised faithfully that this would be done. [157]

Somewhat reassured, Cope continued on to Ruthven Barracks, just across the River Spey, where he and his men spent the night. He departed the next morning, after first snatching up a full company of Guise's, which had been stationed at Ruthven, and ordering it to accompany him.[158] All that remained to guard the Barracks were sergeant Terence Molloy, a corporal, twelve privates and a handful of invalids. This decision too would shortly have consequences.

When Cope entered Grant country, he received a foretaste of what to expect during the rest of his stay in the north: a second message from Grant, this time sending regrets. The rebels were threatening his house, he explained, and he needed all of his men to protect it. He had none to spare for Cope.

Cope was nevertheless able to shepherd his troops through Slochd Mor without incident. Charles had indeed contemplated setting up an ambush at that very spot – whether the idea occurred to him before or after he learned that Cope had abandoned the Corrieyairack is not certain – but changed his mind upon concluding, correctly, that the general had too much of a head start. Evidently the feint to Garvamore had been productive. Still proceeding by forced marches, Cope reached Dalrachny that night and Inverness the following day, the 29th. His first order of business at Inverness was to set all of the town's ovens to work baking bread. His existing supply had run out that morning.[159]

Wade's engineering marvel across the Corrieyairack, built to contain the Jacobites, had just been put to military use for the only time in its history – by the Jacobites. One would expect Charles to have been exultant. Yet Murray of Broughton tells us that after the Prince had negotiated its seventeen-mile length successfully, and learned that Cope had gone north, his earlier high spirits gave way to 'chagrin', which he tried to conceal from the rank and file.[160] The chagrin was understandable: he faced a quandary. With Cope out of the way, the road to the Lowlands was open, and he was eager to take it – but not without first fighting a battle. It had never been part of his strategy to leave an army in being at his back, even so poor an excuse for one as Cope's. Again in Murray's words, 'nothing on earth was further from his thoughts than marching South before a battle', and most of the chiefs were of the same mind.[161] Only Tullibardine and a few others, anxious to recover lost legacies or to protect their existing Lowland holdings, argued otherwise.

Arriving at Garvamore at 2p.m., Charles ordered dinner for himself and his men. Then it was his turn to summon a council, which was to meet when the dinner was over. The question he meant to put to

the council was whether to pursue Cope and seek a battle, or continue in his present direction. But his men almost wrested the decision
from his hands. Hearing, from deserters, exaggerated tales of booty in
Cope's baggage, they wanted to chase after him at once, even if it meant
marching through the night, and they clamoured almost to the point
of mutiny.[162] The dinner was postponed, the council convened instead.
Most in attendance agreed with Charles: the army had marched some
twenty miles already, and to catch up with Cope it would have to cover
at least twenty more. Not even Highlanders could travel that sort of
distance without rest.[163] The battle would have to wait. It was now that
someone proposed sending 500 picked men on a shortcut through the
hills to intercept Cope at Slochd Mor and 'amuse' him there until the
main body could come and finish him off.[164] (Although this is the first
recorded mention of Slochd Mor in any of the Jacobite sources, Cope,
it will be recalled, had learned the previous evening that something of
the kind was in the works, so the plan was probably mooted earlier.) But
Charles, reluctantly, rejected this scheme too as impractical, and he was
right: it called for the advance party to reach Slochd Mor on the following morning – that is, the 29th – and by that time Cope was already
north of it at Dalrachny. Convinced by his logic, the chiefs contrived
with difficulty to quell the incipient revolt among the men.

On the 29th, the Jacobites sustained their first setback: a minor one, but
nevertheless embarrassing, as well as heartening to the enemy. Although
Ruthven Barracks was not on their route, and at this point in the war
was of no strategic value to them, old Gordon of Glenbucket advocated
sending a raiding party to attack it, in order, he said, to seize its supplies
of arms and oatmeal. He may also have had an ulterior motive: to get it
destroyed, so that it would no longer threaten his own territories in the
neighbourhood.[165] O'Sullivan demurred, or so he later claimed, thinking
the place too strong to attack without cannon. (It is not clear whether
the army still had *Du Teillay's* eight remaining swivel guns, and, even if it
did, they could not have been hauled overland in time.) But Glenbucket
and some of the other chiefs persisted, and Charles, who like O'Sullivan
was sceptical, gave in against his better judgment. O'Sullivan, despite his
doubts, was placed in charge of the mission, seconded by Lochiel's brother
Archibald. They brought with them perhaps ninety men, though as usual
different sources give different figures. The attack took place at night. The
attackers had not reckoned with the architectural features of the building,

which – as O'Sullivan and Charles had foreseen – made the assault difficult to begin with, or with the grit and leadership qualities of Sergeant Molloy, who mounted an exceptionally spirited defence. When it was over, the raiding party had nothing to show for its efforts except two dead and three wounded. The tiny band of defenders had erased, to some extent, the indignities of Highbridge and the Corrieyairack, and Cope recommended to Tweeddale that Molloy receive a commission for his pluck.[166]

Also on the 29th, Cluny MacPherson re-entered the picture, as the Jacobites offset the Ruthven debacle by winning him to their side. Like so many others, his story is a microcosm of the Highlands' convoluted and ambivalent politics. Cousin to Lochiel, and son-in-law and neighbour to Lovat, he was a blackmailer: that is, he extracted money in return for promising to refrain from stealing other people's cattle and to prevent anyone else from stealing them either. He was remarkable in his day, not for the nature but for the scope of this activity, which extended from his ancestral base in Badenoch all the way into the Lowlands. The Westminster government and its Edinburgh proxies winked at his practices, because they imposed a crude sort of order upon the region, thereby sparing the government the trouble and expense of imposing order directly. Cluny was even entrusted with a warrant (which he never executed) to arrest Glengarry's eldest son (who later became a government spy himself) for recruiting Highlanders into the French army while Britain and France were at war. He accepted a captaincy under Loudon, not out of patriotic spirit, but for its income and because his troops could serve him as enforcers in his blackmailing operations. Placed under house arrest by Cope after he showed insufficient enthusiasm for the colours at their 27 August meeting, he was kidnapped from his home soon afterwards by raiders under the command of his cousin Archibald Cameron. On 29 August he declared himself a Jacobite, won over by what he called Charles's 'soothing, close application' – and also by Charles's offer of the much-encumbered Sobieska jewels, the ones that had belonged to Charles's mother, as security for any estates he might forfeit if his former side prevailed.[167] Whether he had been kidnapped against his will, or his capture was collusive, remains a mystery.

Meanwhile, Charles stayed the night of the 28th at Garvamore. Then, reversing his adversary's route, he marched to Dalwhinnie on the 29th and Dalnacardoch on the 30th. With Cope out of the way, the road to the Lowlands was open. He took it.

At Inverness Cope added three under-strength 'New Highland' companies to his desertion-depleted numbers – a fourth would sign on at Aberdeen[168] – and replenished his bread supply. But he accomplished little else.[169] One by one, the chiefs whom he had counted upon for assistance answered his urgent summonses with excuses: some by letter, others in person or by proxy. Lords Sutherland's and Reay's assurances evaporated, and Major MacKay was in consequence unable to raise his 500 kinsmen. Lord Lovat, through his son and heir the Master of Lovat, conveyed only the 'ambiguous Expressions' that were his stock in trade.[170] Eventually the Frasers did turn up in arms, under the Master's command – but on the Prince's side, not the government's. Lord Fortrose said he could provide 400 men, but explained that it would take time to assemble them. This was unacceptable: with Charles roaming loose in the Lowlands, Cope could not stay at Inverness awaiting his lordship's convenience. The Earl of Cromartie and the equivocating Grant chief also held back. The one chief who did produce was the Presbyterian Sir Harry Munro, who offered Cope 200 men. But he offered them for two weeks only, on the ground that they would afterward be needed at home for the harvest. On Duncan Forbes's advice, Cope accepted this grudging support. It was becoming increasingly apparent to both men that it was the most they would get.

There were other matters Cope needed to address. One was re-establishing his links with Forbes, who had long since arrived at nearby Culloden House. He'd fallen in with interesting company on his way north: a fellow passenger on the Forth ferry was David Wemyss, Lord Elcho, an active Jacobite who would join the Prince in time to fight at Prestonpans (and would later come to despise him). Unaware of Elcho's sympathies, Forbes told him confidently that Cope would make short work of the rebels.[171] The President was less confident now. He met with Cope on at least three occasions – on the 29th, while Cope was still in transit, and again on the 30th and 31st – and did everything he could to help him win over the recalcitrant chiefs.

Another matter that required attention, of less moment militarily but important to Cope personally, was explaining his movements to Tweeddale. He had hesitated to write from the road, lest his letters be intercepted, but from Inverness he could post them in safety by sea. He made up assiduously for lost time, sending long missives on the 29th and 31st. In large measure the contents replicated what has already been

said about the deliberations at Dalwhinnie (he enclosed, with the second letter, a copy of the council's report), the army's progress during
the remainder of the march, and his fruitless approaches to the chiefs.
In addition, he reiterated his understanding that the Secretary's 'strict
repeated Orders'[172] left him no choice but to proceed northward from
Crieff, and then continue on from Dalwhinnie to one of the forts, when
he himself would have preferred to turn back. He ended the 31 August
letter on a note that was at once plaintive – even self-pitying – and as
reproachful as he dared to be toward his superior:

> From the first I treated this as a serious Affair; I thought it so, I am sorry I was
> not mistaken; my fears were for the Publick, and for the Publick only they
> still continue the same. I came to engage the Rebels, they would not let me,
> but in Passes, as has been describ'd. I'll still engage them if I can; I'll do my
> best for his Majesty's Service.[173]

Before writing this peroration, however, he interrupted his letter to meet
again with Forbes; Loudon also attended. The gist of their talk was that
since there was to be no help from the clans, Cope's best course now was
to go south as quickly as possible and prevent Charles from advancing
further. He would leave when the bread was ready.

He laid detailed plans, keeping his options as open as he could. His
preferred route was by sea, which he deemed quickest and safest. To that
end, he posted orders to General Guest, at Edinburgh Castle, to ship
transports from Leith to the north-eastern seaport of Aberdeen, where
his men would board them after marching overland to meet them. In
case the orders or the transports miscarried, he sent Lieutenant-Colonel
Charles Whitefoord first to Aberdeen and then to Montrose, thirty-eight
miles south of Aberdeen on the east coast, to secure back-up transports
in both places – a task that Whitefoord was somehow able to accomplish
'without any additional Expence to Government'.[174] Whitefoord was
further charged with obtaining shoes and more bread, on the chance
that Cope might later decide to make the entire journey by land, and,
on the same contingency, to procure small boats at Dundee so that the
men could cross the River Tay. Finally, Cope hired a coastal vessel to
follow the army to Aberdeen, carrying stores and some cannon that he
had taken from Fort George. He also took with him, from Fort George,
another of Guise's companies, and left in its place a company of Loudon's,

which was still forming, and one of the depleted Black Watch companies. His reasoning was that, since both companies had originated in the Highlands, they would recruit more successfully if they stayed there.

The bread was ready on 3 September. Cope thereupon composed a final letter to Tweeddale, in which he asserted once more that he had deemed himself bound by the Secretary's instructions. 'I have not found any body here yet,' he wrote, 'either Civil or Military, who thought I could do otherwise than I have done, consistent with the repeated Orders your Lordship did the Honour to send me.'[175] The letter dispatched, he left Inverness on the 4th, after a frustrating week in that city, relieved to see the last of it, and looking forward to his delayed rendezvous with Charles.

The Bonnie One had not yet come into his own again, although his prospects had brightened remarkably. But on 31 August Tullibardine did, for the Prince and his army arrived that day at Blair Castle, ancestral seat of the Murrays of Atholl.[176] The place was unoccupied, Whig brother James being elsewhere, and the Murray 'vassals' are said to have welcomed their rightful master with 'the strongest affection'.[177] The affection notwithstanding, they were slow at first to volunteer for military service, but recruitment improved when rumours circulated – accurate ones, it turned out – that Tullibardine's younger brother George would soon declare for the Jacobite side.[178]

Charles spent three days at Blair, where his clansmen enjoyed their most luxurious accommodations yet: warm beds in the houses of local villages, and fresh bread to supplement the all-meat diet that had sustained them on the road.[179] The unaccustomed comfort did not prevent them from deserting in large numbers – indeed may have encouraged them – but 'officers were sent to the Contry, & brought the most part of them back'.[180] He also acquired the services of John Roy Stewart, an experienced officer who had served in both the British and French armies. Stewart would command what was to be called the Edinburgh Regiment, which was raised in that city after Prestonpans.[181] Joining the colours as well was Alexander Robertson of Struan, whose territories abutted the Lowlands. Struan brought with him about 200 of his clansmen; these were incorporated, together with the Atholl 'vassals' and others, into what became the Atholl Brigade.[182]

The Blair idyll ended on the 3rd, when the army left Atholl and marched south-east through the historic Pass of Killiecrankie. Charles and the main body halted at Dunkeld, while an advance party under Lochiel's command pushed ahead to Perth and proclaimed James Francis Stuart King in a ceremony at the market cross.[183] The Prince and the rest of the men entered Perth the following day. They remained there for a week.

During that week, the army's size increased, and its complexion changed, as new volunteers, many of them Lowlanders, poured into the city. They included Viscount William Drummond of Strathallan, who commanded the only Jacobite cavalry unit at Prestonpans (where it took no part in the action) and later governed northern Scotland while Charles was in England. Lawrence Oliphant of Gask, Strathallan's second-in-command in both capacities, who came with his son. James Johnstone of Edinburgh, the self-styled Chevalier de Johnstone, who served as aide-de-camp to George Murray and left memoirs that are not always reliable. David Ogilvy, heir to the Earl of Airlie, who would lead the Forfarshire foot regiment, which he recruited soon after the battle; its surviving orderly book yields valuable insights into army administration and routine.[184]

The most important newcomers, though, were the fifty-one-year-old George Murray and James Drummond, Duke of Perth, who was nineteen years his junior. In theory these two shared operational command of the army as co-lieutenants-general, under a cockamamie system that had each in sole charge on alternating days. Thus they outranked O'Sullivan, who remained a major-general only. (O'Sullivan, in pique, claims that initially Murray was appointed a major-general also but complained until Charles promoted him.)[185] In practice, however, Perth deferred to Murray because Murray was older and had more military experience, and because Perth knew that, as a Catholic, he would be a propaganda liability to the cause.

Murray's ascendancy was a mixed blessing. He was an inspirational leader. He had a stronger military background than most Jacobites, for he had served as an ensign in the British army during the War of the Spanish Succession, and had later switched sides to take up arms for the Stuarts: as a colonel during the 1715 Rising, and as a major-general in 1719. He enjoyed tremendous credit among the Atholl tenantry, and this was no inconsequential matter, inasmuch as these 'vassals' – thanks mainly to him – eventually comprised one of the two largest units on the Jacobite side, the other being Lochiel's Camerons. He also seems to have been a supremely decent human being: compassionate to the weak, devoted to his wife and children (even though he left them in parlous circumstances to follow Charlie), and highly principled – perhaps too much so for his own good and the good of his relations with his fellows.

On the other hand, when you scratched the surface his military experience was less impressive than it appeared. His only taste of combat had come in the '19 Rising, at Glen Shiel (he had been away on a tax collecting assignment during Sheriffmuir), and that had been more of a skirmish than a full-blown battle. Afterwards he had toured the continent in an unsuccessful quest for a foreign commission, then accepted a pardon from the Hanoverian regime and lived peacefully as manager of his brother James's estate.[186] There were gaps in his tactical and strategic vision – as Derby would reveal. Finally, he could be petulant, hot-tempered, stubborn, and intolerant of other opinions. In other words, his personality failings were the same as Charles'. No wonder the two clashed.

They clashed for another reason as well. O'Sullivan, Sir John MacDonald and Murray of Broughton had been jealous of George Murray from the beginning ('his carracter,' clucked O'Sullivan, 'was not of the best'),[187] and warned Charles repeatedly that he was a government mole.[188] The charge is preposterous: no evidence has emerged to support it, and no-one who reads Murray's poignant letter to his Whig brother James – in which he explained his decision and predicted, correctly, that it would ruin him – could ever credit it.[189] But Charles was only too willing to do so. His suspicions of his leading general poisoned their relationship and impeded their pursuit of common goals.

Perth was a more substantial figure than some of his contemporaries, and most historians, have recognised.[190] One of the former famously dismissed him as 'a silly horse-racing boy'.[191] There is an episode in his life that suggests the contrary. Shortly before the Rising began, he was duped into inviting to his home, as dinner guests, a pair of Hanoverian agents: captains Campbell of Inverawe and Patrick Murray of Auchertyre, each of whom commanded one of the new-forming Highland companies. They carried with them a warrant to arrest Perth for his activities as an 'Associator'. Midway through the meal, Inverawe drew Perth into an adjacent room and there tried to execute the warrant. As calmly as you please,

Perth asked if he could first say farewell to his other guest, who was still at the dinner table. The permission given, he snuck out of the house instead by a private door, slipped past Inverawe's company, which the captain had brought along and stationed behind the building, and made his way through the woods to safety. No mere horse-racing boy he.[192] His qualifications for command were never really tested, because he had scant opportunity to display them. What he did, he did ably.

Once in control, Murray conducted as much drill as the army's mostly peripatetic existence allowed. He also set up a commissary, in order to reduce reliance upon foraging, for foraging, he knew, would alienate the local population and slow the pace of the march. He even persuaded the private soldiers to carry knapsacks, so that their food would last.[193] It is no small testament to his leadership that he was able to impose this sort of discipline upon men who in peacetime had lived by cattle reiving.

On Wednesday, 11 September, Charles left Perth with his troops and headed south-west, after a council of war had rejected an alternative proposal to go north and intercept Cope on his way to Aberdeen.[194] The chiefs were glad to be off: they thought that the men had grown soft in urban billets,[195] although the long stay had also provided the first opportunity for serious training.[196]

The next halt was at Dunblane. Charles slept there on the 11th, but many of the men – 'leasy', says O'Sullivan, from their long sojourn at Perth[197] – didn't trickle in until the 12th. Their tardiness kept Charles at Dunblane an additional night. Dunblane, however, was merely a convenient stopping point for the Prince and his army. They were on their way to Edinburgh.

Cope knew it, and made all haste to save the city. Covering the entire distance by forced marches, he reached Aberdeen on the 11th, just as the transports from Leith were entering the harbour. They docked the next day. He learned on his arrival that the rebels had scooped up all of the boats on the north side of the Tay, thus blocking the overland route to the capital; he would have to rely upon the transports to bring him there. He loaded his stores onto them immediately, for he was anxious to depart, but contrary winds prevented them from sailing until the 15th.[198]

Meanwhile, Tweeddale was firing off replies to Cope's letters of the 29th, 31st and 3rd. Two of them are especially interesting. The first, dated 7 September, awaited (or found) Cope at Aberdeen. Its contents show that Tweeddale had at last come to understand the pitfalls of what moderns would call 'micro-managing' from afar. (The neologism may be anachronistic when applied to the eighteenth century, but the concept surely is not.) In the Secretary's words, 'you will easily judge it impossible for any Orders to be sent to you from this Place; but as you are on the Spot, you must now be left to act as you shall judge best...'.[199]

The second is even more revealing. It was written on 12 September, and it is not clear when, where or even whether Cope received it. Recognising that the march to the forts had been not just a failure but a disaster, Tweeddale was now trying to disclaim responsibility for its consequences: Charles dominant in the Lowlands; the capital in jeopardy. 'I must observe,' he announced tartly, that

> toward the end of my Said Letter [that is, the one dated 13 August] I added these Words, 'It is impossible at this Distance to give particular Directions; your Judgment and Conduct will enable you to make the best of the Circumstances that may occur.' And I think that all the Orders given were plain and clear; but as...you seem to take Exception to the above quoted Words, I must declare to you my Opinion, that whatever Orders are given to a Commander in Chief, his own Prudence and Judgment must direct him in the Execution of them, according as Circumstances may happen.[200]

If it was indeed Tweeddale's intention to let Cope act at discretion, he expressed himself as infelicitously as Lord Raglan later did at Balaclava when issuing the ambiguous order that sent the Light Brigade charging, the wrong way, into the Russian guns.[201] And there were the same fatal results.

On the 15th, the winds off Aberdeen turned favourable. So eager was Cope to get underway that 'in one Tide he embarked the whole Army, even against the wishes of the Sea People, and got out of the Bay'.[202] He expected to land at Leith, Edinburgh's harbour, the following day. But bad luck continued to dog him. First, the tide ebbed, and he could not proceed further until nightfall. Then the wind changed again to his detriment, slowing his progress. And as he approached Leith, on the afternoon of the 16th, it died out altogether, so that the transports could not enter the Firth. Accordingly, he made for Dunbar, on the eastern edge of the coast, dropped anchor there the next morning, and prepared to set his men ashore.

He was a day too late.

All of Edinburgh also knew that Charles was coming, and its citizens prepared: some to welcome him, others to resist.

Archibald Stewart, Provost of Edinburgh and thus its civil and military leader, resisted, or said he did. His critics, though, were sceptical: they suspected him of being a covert Jacobite and of playing a double game. Certainly his behaviour was equivocal. He ordered repairs to the obsolete and decaying city walls – some of them jerry-built structures erected in haste after the disastrous battle of Flodden more than two centuries earlier – and mounted them with cannon from warships at Leith. But he refused to borrow sailors to man the cannon, on the excuse that sailors lacked the skills to fire them accurately – which may indeed have been the case, except that there was nobody else who knew how to fire them at all. In addition, Stewart raised new military units to defend the city. He author-ised the formation of six volunteer foot companies, of about sixty-five men each, after lawyers advised him that he could legally do so without awaiting royal permission provided that he called them 'volunteer com-panies' rather than a 'regiment'.[203] Then, when permission arrived, he raised a regiment as well. Known as the 'Edinburgh Regiment' (not to be confused with Colonel John Roy Stewart's Edinburgh Regiment on the Jacobite side), its notional strength was 1,000 men, its actual strength 250 to 600.[204] He had, besides these, two long-established local units at his dis-posal – the Trained Bands (on paper, 1,000; in reality probably rather less) and the Town Guard (100)[205] – plus other small bodies that sprang up as the crisis mounted. But he refused at critical moments to order his forces into action – and in truth many of their members were reluctant to go into action themselves, especially when action loomed. Imprisoned after the war on a charge of criminal negligence, he was acquitted following a lengthy trial. In all likelihood he was not disloyal – merely indecisive and overwhelmed. Besides, he was seeking re-election (the voting began, inconveniently, on 10 September, just as the Jacobite threat was becoming imminent), and he wanted to placate as many constituents as possible. He also wanted to keep them safe whichever side won.

John Home, future dramatist and historian, and Alexander Carlyle, future minister of the Kirk, also resisted, and there is no doubting their sincer-ity and enthusiasm. They joined the College Company of the Volunteers, composed, as the name implies, of university students and graduates: Home on the 9th, Carlyle on the 14th after breaking short a holiday to return to the city and enlist. All six companies were created on the 12th, for Stewart had only authorised them on the 7th, and the first handbills calling for volunteers were circulated on the 9th. The companies underwent just two days of training, on the 13th and 14th, using arms from Edinburgh Castle. Then, shortly before ten o'clock on the morning of Sunday the 15th, they assembled in the College Yard and awaited orders to march west out of the city and confront the enemy.[206]

At fifty-five years of age, Patrick Crichton – merchant, family man, devout Presbyterian and ferocious Whig – was too old and too settled to make armed resistance. But he fulminated in his diary against the 'theiving naked ruffians' of the latter-day Highland host (although he admitted grudgingly that the 'hillskippers' had shown surprising 'disiplin', and that their leaders had dealt severely with the few who had not). He fulminated also against Edinburgh's politicians, who in his view either lacked resolution, or – like Stewart – were in active correspondence with the foe.[207]

None of it availed. On 13 September, the army of Charles Edward Stuart, its energies restored by two nights of camping in the open air, stepped out briskly from Dunblane. Proceeding south, it paused at Doune Castle, where it deposited its remaining Royal Scots prisoners – the rank and file, who, unlike the officers, had not been admitted to parole – and then crossed the River Forth at the Fords of Frews, eight miles west of Stirling. Charles had expected to encounter Gardiner's dragoons there, for the regiment was stationed nearby, the passage was easy to defend, and the dragoons had been boasting of what they would do to the Jacobite rabble. But they evidently thought better of it as the rabble drew closer, and retreated east to Linlithgow. After feinting briefly toward Glasgow, Charles turned east himself, in Edinburgh's direction, and halted that night outside Stirling.

On the 14th, the Jacobites resumed their progress toward the capital. Passing by Stirling, they came within range of the Castle's cannon, which the garrison fired at them. Some of the shots fell dangerously near to Charles, but did no damage, and the Jacobites marched ahead without breaking step, shouting defiant cheers. They camped in the evening next to Callendar House, just beyond Falkirk.[208]

Charles's host at Callendar House was William Boyd, Earl of Kilmarnock, a bankrupt who took this opportunity to cast his lot with the Jacobites (for which he ultimately paid with his head). He had spent the afternoon hobnobbing with Gardiner's dragoons – he thought himself a Hanoverian then – and told Charles of their whereabouts. George Murray responded by leading 500 to 1,000 men on a pre-dawn raid to

Linlithgow, hoping to catch them unaware.[209] But their camp was empty, for they had fallen back again, this time to Corstorphine, three miles from Edinburgh. In consequence, Charles was able to enter Linlithgow unopposed later in the morning. It was Sunday, and to show respect for the Sabbath he directed that all but his bodyguard remain outside the town and that religious services not be disturbed. Nevertheless, the local Presbyterian minister decamped – in order, wrote Murray of Broughton, 'to enduce the ignorant vulgar to believe that…he would have been insulted and persecuted' if he had preached.[210]

As the Jacobite army neared Linlithgow on that Sunday morning, at least some of the volunteers in the College Yards were proclaiming, with loud huzzas, their eagerness to march out of the city and engage the enemy. It was critical that they do so, for without them General Guest, who commanded the available regular forces in Cope's absence, would not deploy the dragoons. His thinking accorded with the military teachings of the period, which held that cavalry ought only to fight when there was adequate infantry support. Volunteer sentiment was by no means unanimous – there were many who preferred to make their stand behind the dubious shelter of the walls – but a messenger was nevertheless sent to inform Guest that the necessary support would be forthcoming. Reassured, Guest directed his other dragoon regiment, Hamilton's, which was stationed at Leith, to join Gardiner's at Corstorphine.

At about the same time, Edinburgh's fire alarm bell sounded. It was the signal for the volunteers to proceed to the Lawnmarket, reassemble there, and then continue on to Corstorphine via the Grassmarket and the West Port. Provost Stewart, sharing for the moment in the burgeoning martial mood, ordered most of the Town Guard, and as much of the new-formed Edinburgh Regiment as could be mustered, to go to Corstorphine also. As they congregated in the Lawnmarket, where their officers tried desperately to separate those who were willing to venture further from those who were not, the volunteers' spirits were lifted by the appearance of Hamilton's dragoons, who clanged their swords together and cheered while riding past on their way to rendezvous with Gardiner's. The young men of the six companies returned the cheers, and some (but by no means all) of them prepared to follow.[211]

The alarm bell put an immediate end to church services inside the city. At Patrick Crichton's church in Glencorse, eight miles south – too far for the bell's sound to carry – a messenger came to warn of the rebels' approach. The minister, heedless, droned on. Crichton, though, had no more patience for sermons: he left at once, and, with his two children, climbed a hill he called 'Leepshill', in the Pentlands. Looking west, he could see in the distance the two dragoon regiments, mounting guard together at Corstorphine. But the volunteer companies had not arrived.[212]

Nor would they. As the churches emptied, parishioners, to their horror, recognised friends and relatives amongst the volunteers and importuned these loved ones not to throw away their lives. To their pleas were added those of clergy, who harangued the amateur warriors to the same effect. The entreaties struck home, and more volunteers dragged their feet. Asked for further instructions in light of the changing circumstances, Stewart dithered, although he had been all for the enterprise earlier. At last the volunteers were marched back to the College Yards and dismissed, with some retained to do guard duty. Only the Town Guard and a small component of the Edinburgh Regiment – about 180 men in all – sallied forth to meet the dragoons, and they were not enough to provide the necessary foot support. (Guest had wanted 300.) The dragoons, accordingly, left a small advance party of thirty men and an officer to keep watch at Corstorphine, and then retired to the vicinity of the capital, bringing the infantry with them.[213]

Edinburgh's doom was sealed the next day. Early in the morning, Brigadier General Thomas Fowke, freshly arrived from London, took command of both dragoon regiments, and reviewed them for the first time at their camp outside the West Port. He did not like what he saw. 'I found many of the Horses Backs not fit to receive the Riders, many of the Men's and some of the Officers Legs so swell'd, that they could not wear Boots; and those who really were to be depended upon, in a manner overcome for want of Sleep.'[214] Nevertheless he marched them at Guest's direction to the eastern end of Colt Bridge, two miles west of the city. Their advance guard remained at Corstorphine, a mile further off. Upon reaching Colt Bridge, Fowke was dismayed to see that the ground was 'full of Defiles, inclosed by Stone-Walls, and quite unfit for Dragoons to act upon'.[215] With no other option at this point, he stationed the regiments there anyway. Before noon the entire Town Guard and about 120 men from the Edinburgh Regiment joined them. This was still shy of the needed 300, though, and in making the men available Stewart had stipulated that they be back in the city by nightfall for watch duty.[216]

At about 3p.m., Patrick Crichton stopped by and chatted with Colonel Gardiner. The Colonel, he wrote, 'was in bad habit of body' – he was in bad habit of mind too, as we shall discover shortly – and his men seemed 'fatigued'. Hamilton's troops 'looked better, but alace they were Irishmen!' In all, they did not impress Crichton as men who 'wowld stand to it'.[217] Events would soon prove him right.

The Jacobites, meanwhile, had camped Sunday night some three miles east of Linlithgow and a dozen miles from Edinburgh. Now they were marching six abreast[218] in a steady approach to the capital. Before setting out, Charles had the Duke of Perth distribute arms to Highlanders who were without them: muskets for the lucky ones, Lochaber axes '& other instruments of War' for the rest.[219] En route, he fired off a letter to Provost Stewart, summoning him to surrender or suffer dire consequences.[220] At two o'clock he ended the day's march at Corstorphine, close by the advance party of dragoons, and took up quarters at Gray's Mill, just south-east of the village, in the home of tacksman David Wright.[221] Then, an hour or two later, he sent an advance party of his own to report on the dragoons' dispositions. Patrick Crichton heard a scout tell Gardiner that this advance party was coming. Bidding a hasty farewell to the Colonel, he sought safety at the far side of a field and watched developments.[222]

Like so much else about the '45, what happened next was in the eye of the beholder. As Fowke and his officers explained it afterward, Fowke had already concluded that under the circumstances – the debilitated condition of the dragoons; the inhospitable terrain; the impending departure of the foot – it made no sense to resist, especially now that night was approaching. When the Jacobites came into view, therefore, he sent the Town Guard home, recalled the advance guard, which fell back 'slowly and without Confusion', and led both regiments in a measured, unhurried withdrawal. Since Provost Stewart, citing lack of provisions, would not let them stay inside the city, they proceeded around its northern edge, 'in order' and at a 'very slow' pace. Continuing east in the same unhurried manner, and stopping at least twice on the way, they prepared to settle in for the night at Prestonpans. The site was chosen to accommodate Colonel Gardiner; still feeling ill, he had wanted to sleep at his own house, which was nearby.[223]

Others tell a different tale. The Jacobite advance party – in Crichton's recollection, some 400 strong; in Home's rather less, but well mounted[224] – fired its pistols at the Hanoverian one. The latter wheeled and scurried to the other side of the Colt Bridge, 'carrying its fears into the main body'.[225]

The main body then wheeled in turn and together the dragoons rode past Edinburgh, rather more precipitately than Fowke and his subordinates remembered, skirting the north side of the city over elevated ground 'in full view' of the populace and 'not draw[ing] brydle till they came to Musselburgh'.[226] The Town Guard was left to shift for itself.

If the 'Canter of Coltbridge' (as it is popularly known) truly began as a tactical retreat, which is what Fowke would have us believe, it did not long remain one. After the dragoons had halted at Prestonpans, one of their number fell into a disused coal pit. The loud rattling of his 'sidearms and accoutrements', as Carlyle describes it, put the wind up the others. Terror-stricken, they took flight, scattering their weapons and equipment along the road. Most did not stop until they reached Haddington, twenty miles from their starting point at Colt Bridge, and some sped all the way to North Berwick or Dunbar on the coast. Carlyle led a salvage party that collected as many of the abandoned weapons as possible and forwarded them to their owners.[227]

With the dragoons went the last hope of saving Edinburgh. The alarm bell sounded again, this time to summon the inhabitants to a meeting, which began at the Goldsmith's Hall and then, when the crowd became too large for the premises, was moved to the New Church. All was confusion. Stewart had sent for advice to the crown officials – Justice Clerk Lord Milton, Lord Advocate Robert Craigie, and Solicitor General Robert Dundas – but those worthies had left town. While the meeting was in progress, Charles's surrender demand arrived – the one that he had sent from the road, or perhaps from Corstorphine, earlier in the day. At first Stewart refused to read it, for he saw upon opening it that Charles had signed it as Prince Regent, and he was afraid he would be perceived as ratifying that usurped title. But the crowd insisted, so at last he gave in. Its contents, when disseminated, strengthened the hand of the pro-surrender faction – as did a cry from an unidentified passing horseman that the Highlanders were 16,000 strong. The volunteers, who at the tolling of the bell had assembled again in the Lawnmarket, sent messengers to Stewart asking for orders, but the Provost had none to give them; they, in consequence, after consulting with their officers, marched to the Castle and returned their weapons. At this point, the citizens recognised that the game was up, and the meeting produced a consensus: that a deputation be sent to Charles in quest of surrender terms. The deputation left for Gray's Mill at about 8p.m.[228]

Charles had little time for repose at Factor Wright's house. One item of business was to receive the newly-arrived Lord Elcho, who would later command a troop of Lifeguards (raised after Prestonpans) and write memoirs that were highly unflattering to the Prince. Elcho's sentiments are understandable. Upon hearing Charles complain that evening that he was destitute – his war chest having evaporated to fifty guineas, according to Elcho; to a mere guinea, according to Charles himself[229] – Elcho then and there lent him 1,500 guineas, which Charles never repaid.

Then Charles dealt with the deputies from Edinburgh. Through Murray of Broughton, he gave them short shrift. He had Murray tell them, orally and in writing, that he would not negotiate with his subjects; the most he would do was give them two or three hours to consult with their constituents. Thereafter they could choose: capitulate or face attack. The deputies returned to the city at ten with Murray's letter.[230]

Meanwhile, the situation there had altered, for Cope's transports had been sighted beating across the Firth to Dunbar. Now there was a real prospect that Edinburgh might be relieved – as well as the prospect of treason trials if its officials surrendered prematurely. The city fathers sent messengers to recall the deputies before they reached the Prince, but were too late. There was talk of trying once again to mount a defence, but that too came to naught: the volunteers had already dispersed, and Guest insisted upon sending the dragoons to Cope no matter what the citizens did. Only one resort remained: to dispatch another deputation to Charles, seeking more time, in hopes that Cope might come to the rescue before the new deadline. If the Jacobites defeated him, Edinburgh could surrender then.

Charles, though, got wind of what was afoot, and took measures of his own. Soon after the first deputation left him, he sent Lochiel, O'Sullivan and Keppoch at the head of 800 to 900 picked men,[231] with Murray of Broughton for a guide, to capture the city by stealth. When the second set of deputies arrived at 2 a.m. on the 17th, he abruptly turned them away. As their coach bore them homeward, the raiders positioned themselves outside the Netherbow Gate and sought a means of entry. At last fortune favoured them. At 5 a.m. a coach lumbered up to the gate. It was the one with the returning deputies. When the gate opened to admit it, the Highlanders swarmed in after it and took over the city bloodlessly while the inhabitants slept. Only the Castle remained in government hands.[232]

Charles received the news soon afterwards at Gray's Mill. At about the same time, a messenger told it to Cope aboard his transport off Dunbar.[233]

4

PRESTONPANS 1745

The sow was unlucky. She had walked across a line of Camerons as they advanced three abreast up Falside Hill, a mile and a half south of Prestonpans village, on the afternoon of 20 September. Deeming her a bad omen, about twenty of the Highlanders plunged their dirks into her, and she perished at once in screaming, writhing agony. It was a portent of what the following day would bring to the government side.[1]

Charles had entered Edinburgh with the main body of the army at about 10a.m. on the 17th, five hours after O'Sullivan and the others captured the place, O'Sullivan having meanwhile met with the magistrates and in a 'high' tone admonished them to cooperate.[2] (This appears to have been his usual way of dealing with civil authority: George Murray reports that he behaved similarly to the magistrates of Perth before Charles restrained him.)[3] Circling south-east to avoid the lowering guns of the Castle, which fired a few desultory and ineffective rounds as it passed, the procession turned left when it was safe to do so and marched north into King's Park, adjacent to Holyrood Palace. A portion of the park wall had been broken down to allow access to the grounds. Charles was resplendent in Highland attire, a St Andrew's star flashing on his chest. His Highlanders made a less impressive appearance, at least in the eyes of a disgruntled Patrick Crichton, who – in town to observe the spectacle – recalled them afterward as a 'loosie crew', 'catching the vermin from ther lurking places abowt ther plaids and throwing them away'.[4] He acknowledged, though, that they kept good order, and others confirm that they behaved admirably throughout their stay, refusing liquor and paying for requisitioned goods.[5] By Crichton's own admission his was one of the few unwelcoming faces in a vast, cheering crowd, most of whom – especially the women – were so enthusiastic that Charles, who had dismounted to descend a steep hill, was forced to mount again in order to escape their tumultuous attentions.[6]

Dismounted once more, he approached the palace, the first Stuart and first member of royalty to set eyes upon it since the future James II and VII had lived there as viceroy of Scotland more than sixty years ago. A hastily cleaned set of apartments awaited him. Before he reached the palace entrance, James Hepburn of Keith – republican, Jacobite and ardent Scottish nationalist (the latter expression reconciles the seeming oxymoron of the first two) – separated himself from the crowd, stepped in front of Charles, and, with raised sword, preceded him into the building.[7]

After that melodramatic gesture, the sequel was almost anti-climactic. It occurred at midday, on the heels of Hepburn's performance. Amid pageantry and pibrochs ('pibrowchs', Crichton called them),[8] the Highlanders formed a large circle, five or six rows deep, around the market cross as thousands of spectators looked on from the outside. Within the circle, the reluctant city heralds read out the Commission of Regency and the Manifesto: the same ones that Tullibardine had declaimed at Glenfinnan, and that had been echoed in many locations since.[9] According to Home, who like Crichton was a hostile eyewitness, 'the populace…huzzaed; and a number of ladies in the windows strained their voices with acclamation, and their arms with waving white handkerchiefs in honour of the day'.[10]

Then, to business. Charles directed O'Sullivan to conduct a diligent 'cherche' (search) for the Town's arms – those, that is, that the Volunteers had not delivered for safekeeping to the Castle. The 'cherche' (or 'charch', as O'Sullivan alternatively spelled it) turned up 1,200 stand of muskets, only half of which were serviceable. These were distributed to men who lacked muskets of their own. O'Sullivan thought them a godsend, but Murray of Broughton differed; he believed that the army had ample muskets already.[11] Other reports do not bear him out, however, and the inescapable conclusion is that even after the 'cherches' muskets remained in short supply.

The next morning – Wednesday, 18 September – Charles posted guards throughout the city, replacing the Town Guard,[12] and issued a proclamation ordering the townspeople and the inhabitants of the adjacent countryside to surrender all privately-held weapons. His purpose in seeking these, Murray of Broughton tells us, was not to add them to his own armoury but to prevent their being used against him.[13] At about the same time, he sent Elcho to Provost Stewart's house to demand, from that unhappy magistrate and his colleagues, 1,000 tents, 2,000 targets, 6,000 pairs of shoes and 6,000 canteens. Stewart set artisans to work producing them.[14]

Later in the day, drummers beat up for volunteers, and gained, by rough calculation, 160 recruits. They were assigned to the Duke of Perth's infantry regiment, joining some forty MacGregors who had enlisted in it earlier.[15] Confusingly, this regiment did not fight under Perth's direct command at Prestonpans, where he led the right wing and the regiment was brigaded with the left.

The army camped in the King's Park on the 17th and 18th. On the evening of the 19th, news arrived that Cope had disembarked his troops at Dunbar and was advancing upon Haddington, sixteen miles east of the capital. Charles was delighted: he had feared that Cope would retire to Berwick and await reinforcements, thereby avoiding battle again, just as at the Corrieyairack.[16] Now it was clear that Cope's eagerness for combat matched his own. The Prince moved his camp to Duddingston, which was south-east of the Park – thus, closer to the enemy – and summoned a council of war.

The Duddingston village house where the council took place still exists; its modern address is No. 8, The Causeway.[17] (A commemorative plaque appears above the door.) There were three issues to discuss.

The first was whether to await Cope at Edinburgh or march east and offer him battle. This, in present-day vernacular, was a no-brainer: the unanimous consensus was to seek him out, preferably near Musselburgh, two miles from the city, or, if he was not there, wherever else he might make a stand.[18]

The second question, a contentious one, was which unit would occupy the right of the battle line, traditionally the place of honour in Scottish armies. The MacDonalds asserted an ancient entitlement to the position, but so, inconveniently, did Lochiel's Camerons and George Murray's Athollmen. At Perth, Charles or Murray had brokered an agreement whereby the disputants would draw lots when battle loomed, but, the MacDonalds now chafing, Murray proposed another solution: he would waive his own clansmen's claim – being poorly armed, they were in any case better suited for the reserve – and the Camerons and MacDonalds would alternate days. This meant that if a battle were fought on one day, the MacDonalds would be on the right, but, if it were fought on the next, the post would go to the Camerons. It also meant that the two clans would take turns in the van of the march, because, as explained in a previous chapter, it was the Jacobites' practice to march in long lines three abreast, and then, when confronting the enemy, execute a quarter turn to form a line of battle. Given the direction of their approach, the quarter turn in this instance would be to the left, so the van would constitute the army's right wing. The officers acceded to this arrangement, except for Sir John MacDonald, who blustered against it furiously and accused Murray of trying to sow dissension in the army.[19]

Charles next asked the chiefs whether their men, untested in battle, would fight. Keppoch, speaking for the rest, opined that they would. Upon hearing this, Charles expressed the desire to lead them in person, but the chiefs demurred: if he were killed, they said, the cause would die with him, and they would go home if he persisted. The Prince gave in – reluctantly, because, despite the carpings of his detractors, he did not lack courage – and settled for leading the reserve.[20]

The Jacobite army left Duddingston in the morning: Murray of Broughton says at nine o'clock, Elcho at six. (The former is more likely.)[21] Before departing, Charles famously drew his sword – he did not lack a flair for the dramatic either – and announced to the entire body, 'Gentlemen, I have flung away the Scabbard'. Cope, he vowed, 'shall not escape us as he did in the Highlands'.[22] O'Sullivan also records the speech, albeit in slightly different language.[23] It had somehow been determined that the Camerons would fight on the right if a battle took place that day, and therefore they marched in front, under George Murray's command, preceded only by Strathallan's handful of cavalry, who rode ahead as scouts.[24] So eagerly did the foot advance, however – O'Sullivan recalled that they 'had more need to be curbed then [sic] pressed' – that there was scant distance between them and the horse.[25]

The troops passed over the ancient and beautiful bridge that spans the Esk at Musselburgh – some call the bridge Roman; others date it to the sixteenth century – and approached Pinkie House, country seat of the absentee Lord Tweeddale. This they spared, as they habitually spared Hanoverian property. (There is a charming tale of how, at Kirkliston, the MacDonalds of Glencoe zealously protected the home of the Earl of Stair, whose grandfather had directed a notorious massacre of their ancestors, and who himself commanded the government forces in England.)[26] Here Strathallan's scouts reported that Cope's army had been sighted near Tranent, barely four miles away. This was confirmed soon afterwards by Colonel John Roy Stewart. He, with another officer, had also ventured forth on a scouting mission, and the two of them now returned, bringing as prisoners a pair of government scouts – former Edinburgh Volunteers – whom they had overheard in imprudent discourse at a local tavern.[27] According to the reports, Cope was heading in the direction of Falside Hill, slightly south of the Jacobites' line of march and just west of the mining town of Tranent.

The news alarmed George Murray, who believed that he knew the ground well (although he turned out not to know it as well as he imagined), and who also knew the temperament of his men. He was anxious to deny Cope the high ground, both for tactical reasons and for reasons of morale; in his own words, it was essential to the confidence of Highlanders that they 'got above the enemy'. There was no time to be lost. Accordingly, he gathered up the Camerons, and without awaiting orders – indeed, without so much as notifying Charles or anyone else in the rear – 'I struck off to the right hand through the fields, without holding any road… In less than half an hour, by marching quick, I got to the eminence'.[28] The time was 2p.m., more or less. Satisfied that he had pre-empted Cope, Murray slowed down so that the rest of the force could catch up. He and his men then looked left toward the north. What they saw must have surprised them.

About half a mile away and 100 to 150 feet below them, on level ground, the army of General Sir John Cope was lining up to face them.

Murray had misread Cope's intentions. The Hanoverian general had no interest in Falside Hill.

He had reached Dunbar on 17th September, in the morning, and learned of Edinburgh's surrender. The dragoons met him on the shore shortly before noon, their flight having ended at Dunbar, perhaps because their horses wouldn't swim.[29] It took him the better part of two days to disembark his men and artillery. He'd wanted to set out at once to reconquer the capital, but seeing the state of the dragoons thought better of it: they were, he wrote charitably to Tweeddale the next day, 'extremely fatigued with the forced marches they had made to arrive here', and thus in no condition to accompany him immediately.[30] Their own Colonel Gardiner was less forgiving: he confided to Alexander Carlyle – come to Dunbar to offer his services to the government – that they had panicked, and that 'not above ten' could be counted on even now.[31] Fatigued or panicky, they needed time to recover, so Cope decided to rest them another night and depart for Edinburgh the following day.

There was some question as to whether he should depart for Edinburgh at all just yet. Based on the reports that were coming in to him – the ones, that is, that he chose to listen to – he thought himself badly outnumbered. He also knew (for Tweeddale had told him at Aberdeen)[32] that he would soon get reinforcements. A Dutch battalion, which the Netherlands government had rushed to Britain in obedience to a thirty-year-old treaty, was expected momentarily. So imminent was its anticipated arrival that when the wind diverted Cope's flotilla to Dunbar, he sent messengers to sea in quest of the Dutch commander, warning him that all of the northern harbours were in rebel hands and that the Dutchman should land south of the Forth. (In fact, the battalion, likewise blown off course, was already ashore at Burlington, and preparing to march across the border.) Seven more Dutch battalions had reached the Thames, and ten British ones, recalled from Flanders, were heading there.[33] One option, then, was for Cope to remain at Dunbar, or withdraw further south, until the reinforcements joined him. Again he summoned a council, where some of his officers, including Gardiner, advocated this option vigorously. But Cope overruled them. Delay, he feared, would benefit the rebels: they too would increase their numbers, and would tighten their hold on the Lowlands and the capital. He was eager to execute a plan, which he had arranged in concert with Guest, whereby the latter would use the Castle's two garrison companies, from Lascelles's regiment, to 'beat down a Portion of the Town-Wall, should the rebels keep within it, in order to admit his Army'. And he was confident that his troops, untested though most of them were, possessed the training and discipline to beat a larger force of mere 'Militia'.[34] Gardiner accepted the decision – he had no choice – but he grumbled about it to young Carlyle.[35]

A word about this Colonel Gardiner. After the battle, Hanoverian Britain was in dire need of heroes, and Cope for obvious reasons didn't suit. So Gardiner was cast in the role. He was in some respects qualified for it. He perished at Prestonpans, and though his hagiographers[36] have exaggerated his exploits there, at least he did not run like the rest. His martyrdom was the more poignant in that he received his death wounds next to his home, which stood (and still stands) at the south-western edge of the battlefield – received them, indeed, within sight of his wife and daughters – and then, carried insensible from the field, lay for a time in his own garden[37] before being moved to the manse of the Tranent parish kirk, where he gave up the ghost.[38]

And he was deeply devout, which some think a further requisite for heroism. Small wonder that his biographer Dodderidge endows him with the shining qualities of Foxe's martyrs or of Charles I as depicted in the *Eikon Basilike*.

But he no more deserved this apotheosis than Charles did. In fact, he was a dangerous old lunatic (even his friend Carlyle acknowledged him a 'fanatic').[39] A roué in his youth, he had turned to God upon beholding a vision of Christ or the Devil – or, as some have it, reading an inspirational religious text given him by his mother – when awaiting a meeting with one of his mistresses.[40] He inflicted creatively sadistic punishments on his troops, not for pleasure, as Henry Hawley was wont to do, but (as he told them while they suffered) for the good of their souls.[41] During the days before the battle he lugubriously predicted his approaching death to Fowke, to Fowke's brigade major Captain Singleton, and heaven knows how many others.[42] In this he revealed, if not the gift of grace, at least that of prophecy – and a level of depression (perhaps other pathologies besides) that rendered him quite unfit to lead a regiment. One wonders whether his troopers' poor performance, both before and during the battle, resulted at least in part from lack of confidence in their chief.

The dragoons were not the only dubious helpmates to join Cope at Dunbar. Also presenting themselves were those remnants of the Edinburgh Volunteers who were still spoiling for a fight: eighty to ninety of them, Carlyle and Home among them.[43] Failing to meet with him in town, they resolved to accompany him on his march in hopes he would find employment for them. He eventually would – but not the military employment they had expected and coveted.

Cope began his march on the capital on the morning of Thursday, 19 September. He must have started late, for Carlyle and his fellow volunteers, finding no quarters in or near Dunbar, had spent the night at Linton, five miles to the west, and the army did not catch up with them till midday.[44] They then fell in with it. Its westward progress has been described as Hogarth-like,[45] the men advancing in a long, straggling line that extended over several miles, the country folk following and mingling with them freely.[46] Carlyle thought this unwise: he worried that local Jacobites would have too much opportunity to gather information and to demoralise the troops by regaling them with exaggerated tales of the rebels' numbers and savagery.[47] If the locals tried, they seem not to have succeeded, because Cope remembered the foot as advancing with 'Alacrity and Spirits',[48] and according to Colonel Whitefoord 'even the Dragoons breathed nothing but Revenge'.[49]

In the afternoon, the army reached Haddington, eleven miles from Dunbar. Cope had hoped to press on further. Learning, however, that no water was available west of the town, he settled in for the night.[50]

There was some excitement later in the day: a false alarm, precipitated by a passing wedding party – the groom, as chance would have it, being younger brother to Lord Elcho – which a few of Cope's officers somehow mistook for the Jacobite vanguard. The drums beat, and 'the Line turned out, and was immediately formed'.[51] Carlyle thought the officers over-anxious, but Cope, making the best of a bad job, 'thank'd them for their Alertness; and they returned him an Huzza'.[52]

That evening Carlyle and his comrades at last communicated with Cope through their commanding officer George Drummond, arch political rival of Archibald Stewart and a once and future Provost himself. Quickly taking their measure, as he had taken that of the dragoons, Cope declined their military services, and invited them to scout for him instead. This they agreed, reluctantly, to do. Drummond chose sixteen of them for the task, including Carlyle. They rode out at intervals, in pairs, for the rest of the night, seeking signs of enemy movements. It was two of these young men who fell into John Roy Stewart's hands while they were breakfasting on white wine and oysters at a local inn. After a harrowing morning in captivity, they were released at the behest of a fellow student in the Jacobite camp. The others met with no adventures, and gained no information either.[53]

Cope left Haddington at around nine o'clock on the morning of the 20th. He planned to advance as far as Musselburgh, which lay within striking distance of the capital and could thus serve as a launching point for an assault if the Jacobites, as anticipated, stayed within the walls. It also provided suitable ground for action if they ventured out to fight.

For the first few miles Cope kept to the post road, which, if he had pursued it, would have brought him through Tranent and then over the high ground of Falside Hill. That is what George Murray had expected him to do. But when he reached the adjacent villages of Elvingston and Trabroun, three or so miles into the march, he veered off the road at an oblique right angle and proceeded north-west for about another three miles until he came to St Germains. From there he turned slightly to his left and resumed his former westerly direction across level terrain nearer to the coast. This seems counter-intuitive, for it meant abandoning the high ground and lengthening the route. Certainly Carlyle initially found it so. But even this brash young man later changed his mind and admitted that Cope, or whoever was directing him (Carlyle, remember, doubted whether the general had 'any will of his own'), had known what he was doing.[54] The high ground was broken and uneven – full of 'Defiles and Inclosures'[55] – and hence unsuitable for cavalry and artillery. The smooth, flat country that Cope was now entering allowed him to move the dragoons and cannon forward more rapidly and deploy them more effectively in event of action.[56]

In assuming that the route change had not been Cope's own idea, Carlyle may have stumbled closer to the truth than he realised. Accompanying the army were a number of the judges and other civic leaders who had fled the capital just before its collapse. Most were local notables who were closely familiar with the territory, and it would have been natural for Cope to consult them. Major Caulfield implied as much when he testified, at the Inquiry, that 'On *Friday* Morning, those who knew that Country, and those were People of high Rank and Station, mention'd two Ways, one above *Tranent*, the other between that Village and the Sea', and had recommended the latter.[57] Cope was wise to follow their advice.

The immediate objective remained Musselburgh. Cope and his officers still calculated that the Jacobites would cower within Edinburgh, the conventional wisdom being that Highlanders were afraid to wage open battle against regulars, especially regulars who possessed both artillery and cavalry, which Highlanders were reputed to fear almost as much as they did cannon.[58] From Musselburgh, Cope could storm the capital once Guest's two garrison companies had sallied forth from the Castle and breached the walls. To that end, he sent a scouting party forward from St Germains to seek out a suitable campsite in the Musselburgh vicinity, preferably west of the town. This was no ordinary scouting party, for it consisted of Cope's highest-ranking subordinates. There was the Earl of Loudon, Cope's adjutant-general and colonel of the freshly raised New Highland Regiment. There was Major Caulfield, the quartermaster-general. There were Lieutenant-Colonel Whitefoord and the Earl of Home (not to be confused with John Home). These were volunteers, normally assigned to other regiments – Whitefoord to the Marines,[59] Home to the foot guards[60] – who had happened to be in the area as Cope was passing through and had offered him their services. Whitefoord had joined him at Stirling, and thus had been with him from the beginning; Home had joined only the other day at Dunbar. Accompanying them was Hew Dalrymple, Lord Drummore, a former Sessions Judge, recently named a Justiciary Lord, whose estates lay nearby. He was one of the dignitaries who had betaken themselves from Edinburgh when the Jacobites were at the gates. He had attached himself to the army, and was displaying an unbecoming taste for adventure. He would soon get his fill.[61]

Approaching Musselburgh, these five saw, through their glasses, more than they had bargained for: not just prospective campsites, but Strathallan's cavalry, closely followed by the rest of the Jacobite army. The conventional wisdom was wrong: the rebels had renounced the shelter of the walls and were obviously seeking battle. First Loudon, then the other officers, galloped back to tell Cope, with the adventuresome Drummore staying on for a time to observe the enemy further.[62] It was now about noon.[63]

When Cope heard the news, his vanguard had reached a low-lying level field, about a mile square. It rested between Tranent, which occupied an eminence a half-mile south, and – following the map from east to west – the coastal villages of Port Seton, Cockenzie and Prestonpans on its northern periphery. The village of Seton lay a short distance to the east. In Carlyle's words, 'this field was entirely clear of the crop, the last sheaves having been carried in the night before; and neither cottage, tree or bush were in its whole extent, except one solitary thorn bush', which stood near its centre.[64] Thus, it afforded maximum play to the Hanoverian cavalry and artillery: two branches in which they enjoyed overwhelming superiority, and of which the rebels were reportedly afraid.

It also had other features to recommend it. It was completely protected on three sides, 'as in a fortification', a frustrated James Johnstone would observe when he saw it soon afterwards.[65] A half-mile north was the Firth, which, controlled by the Royal Navy, offered security and a limitless source of supply. To the west, Bankton House, home of Colonel Gardiner, and, above it, its near neighbour Preston House, each surrounded by ten-foot high park walls, with a pair of narrow defiles running east–west through the properties: one just north of Preston House, the other separating the two estates. It would take a hardy force to pass that way under fire. To the south, extending as far as Tranent and the base of Falside Hill, a veritable obstacle course of natural and man-made booby traps.

To begin with, the ground nearer the field – known as Tranent Meadows – was marshy, so that no attacking army could negotiate it safely. The marshes, to be sure, were drained by ditches, but these presented impediments of their own. The most formidable of them – eight feet wide by four feet deep – ran almost the entire length of the field on its southern extremity, establishing an impenetrable boundary between it and the marshes. For good measure, the area beyond the marshes was punctuated with 'bottle mines' for the gathering of coal. The mines were built according to a design that is unknown today. Each had a small opening at the top, which then ballooned into a larger cavity just below the surface: hence the nickname. The opening alone could trip up an unwary soldier, and, if the roof above the cavity had collapsed, which seems to have occurred with dismaying frequency, the broken ground would make rapid movement even more difficult and dangerous.[66]

Only two tracks gave access over the marshes. One was a wooden railway – its cars were horse drawn – that was used to transport coal from the mines to Cockenzie. Barely a mile long, it originated slightly south of a steep gully, called the Heugh, that bordered the western edge of Tranent kirk. After dropping into the gully and emerging at its far end, it plunged northward down Falside Hill, crossed the marshes and the ditch, and bisected the field. The other track was a cart road, also originating in Tranent and culminating at Cockenzie. It began further east and ended further west, so that the two tracks intersected with one another, midway through the field, to form an almost perfect saltire. As Tomasson and Buist rightly conclude, neither track posed a threat; each was 'narrow and easy to defend'.[67]

Secure on its northern, western and southern flanks, the position was vulnerable from just one direction: the east. And the Jacobites, of course, were coming from the west.

Cope knew a good thing when he saw it. He elected to stop where he was, adopt a defensive posture, and let the enemy come to him. Anticipating that the rebels would continue to advance in the same direction – that is, due east – he stationed his forces in a north-south line near the western edge of the field. The line thus faced west, with a slight south-westerly tilt, its left flank pointing towards the ditch, 'a pretty good distance from it',[68] and its right towards the Forth. Directly ahead were the walls and two defiles of the Bankton and Preston estates. To get at him that way, his foe would have to race in narrow columns through the defiles: a thankless, indeed a suicidal, task. To make it more so,

Cope had his men drive breaches through the walls in several places, thereby creating a freer field of fire.[69]

But the rebels, we know, did not continue to advance in the same direction and run the gauntlet of the defiles. Instead, they scrambled up Falside Hill, the Camerons in the van. Upon sighting them, Cope wheeled his line a quarter-turn to the left, facing it south. He then marched it forward 100 paces to the near side of the ditch. There it stopped, with the ditch in front and the Meadows and the hill beyond. This was the movement that the Jacobites had witnessed earlier. The two armies could now see one another plainly. Each hurled a defiant cheer at the other.[70]

How did the two sides measure up against one another, in numbers and weapons, on this eve of battle?

NUMBERS

The question about numbers is difficult to answer – indeed is impossible to answer with exactitude – for either army. In the Jacobites' case, it is because the numbers were in constant flux due to desertions and new arrivals; in the Hanoverians', because Cope's records were captured at Prestonpans and vanished afterward. Though the reasons are different, the result is the same: we are reduced to informed guesses. The guesses to date have fluctuated widely.

The Jacobites themselves were uncertain of their strength. Their figures range from 1,800 (Johnstone)[71] through to 3,000, or 3,036 if one includes the cavalry (Elcho).[72] Their foes similarly disagree about them. John Home, who had counted them carefully in Edinburgh, estimated them initially at under 2,000, but later revised the figure to 2,400 to allow for latecomers.[73] There were, in fact, quite a few of those: John Murray, Lord Nairne, cousin to George Murray and Tullibardine, came on the 18th with 250 more Athollmen in tow; MacLachlan of MacLachlan reported with 150 of his clansmen the same day; and approximately 100 Grants from Glen Moriston and Glen Urquhart, defying their equivocating chief, showed up on the 19th or on the early morning of the 20th.[74] Richard Jack, a mathematician who had helped to repair Edinburgh's fortifications during the frantic few days before the city fell, likewise attempted an exact count, but somehow reached inconsistent conclusions: 2,740 at Edinburgh, and from 1,600 to 1,800 on the battlefield.[75]

Jack appears to have been an eccentric – a better word might be crack-pot – but on this subject he was closer to the mark than most, at least if we take the average of his two totals.

There is no consensus among modern historians either, though the gaps are narrower. Compare the following: 2,550 ('*Muster Roll*');[76] 2,500 (Susan Kybett);[77] 2,400 (Tomasson and Buist, who rely on Home);[78] between 2,300 and 2,400 (Reid).[79] Others suggest lower figures, as we shall see momentarily.

At the upper end, Sir Walter Scott outdoes even Elcho with 4,000.[80] But the wildest overestimate comes from Sir John Cope: 5,500.[81] Perhaps Cope should have known better, because Home and Jack had reported their findings to him before the battle,[82] but he thought he had more reliable sources.[83] He was wrong about that. The error did not affect his decisions, for he believed his regulars would beat the Jacobite 'banditti' regardless of numbers. He was wrong about that too.

Even the Jacobite cavalry was of indeterminate size. As a working hypothesis I have accepted Elcho's figure of thirty-six,[84] but other sources are less precise. Murray of Broughton recalls only that it was 'not above fifty'.[85] That is O'Sullivan's count also.[86] Tomasson and Buist estimate it at 'between thirty and forty'.[87] Whatever the unit's actual numbers, it was too small to participate in the fighting; its functions were to scout and, in Elcho's words, 'to take prisoners in case of a Victory'.[88]

The guesses, informed or otherwise, about Hanoverian strength have fluctuated widely as well. Jarvis reviews and critiques many of them in his essay 'Cope's Forces, August 1745'.[89] The most outlandishly high one, 4,000, is James Johnstone's.[90] Johnstone's anonymous editor errs toward the opposite extreme: he postulates 2,100,[91] which is surely too low, as is Tomasson and Buist's and Fitzroy Maclean's 2,200.[92] Lowest of all is Cope's own estimate (in which his officers concurred) of slightly over 2,000: 1,400 foot, 600 horse, plus 'a small Number' of Highlanders.[93] One wonders whether, by exaggerating the numerical imbalance in both directions, he was trying to rationalise the disaster. In between, we have Elcho's 3,000[94] and Murray of Broughton's 2,700 – the latter based on intelligence reports.[95] These are more realistic, but still too large.

Striving heroically for accuracy, Reid offers up a figure of 2,034 rank and file for the horse and foot combined. If we add sixteen per cent for the officers – Jarvis's rule of thumb[96] – this produces a total of 2,360 on the government side. Reid's is a more convincing effort than the others, but his conclusion is still conjectural. Another convincing effort appears in the *Scots Magazine* article that reported the battle. As quoted by Jarvis and Reid, its author identified 2,191 rank and file.[97] If we apply the sixteen per cent rule, this would have given Cope about 2,540 officers and men overall. Each of these calculations has its supporters.[98] We may come closest to the truth if we do as I facetiously proposed doing with mathematician Jack's calculations about the Jacobites: split the difference. That would leave us, and Cope, with 2,450 effectives, including the two dragoon regiments. Those mustered, together, perhaps 650 officers and men[99] – well below their notional strength of 435 each, but still at least thirteen times larger than the Jacobite cavalry – although 'effectives' is in their case a courtesy title. On the other hand, the Jacobites enjoyed somewhere in the vicinity of a 3 to 2 infantry advantage.

Some historians refuse to commit themselves on the size of either army, except in the broadest generalities. Hook and Ross go no further than to say that each fielded between 2,000 and 2,500 troops.[100] Moray McLaren also hedges, but reduces the ranges to between 2,200 and 2,500.[101] One cannot blame them for their caution.

In summation: The two armies were more or less equally matched; each contained slightly fewer than 2,500 men; each overestimated the strength of the other. It would be incautious to hazard more.

WEAPONS

When it comes to weapons, though, the various accounts are remarkably congruent. The Hanoverians' personal arms were as described in the chapter on 'Armies', minus the swords, which Cope had left at Stirling and the men would probably not have carried in any event. As for the Jacobites, the accounts – from both friendly and hostile observers – are not only congruent but downright picturesque. Let the sources speak for themselves:

Patrick Crichton (Whig):

> I observed these armes, they were guns of different syses, and some of innormowows lengh, some with butts tured up lick a heren, some tyed with puck threed to the stock, some withowt locks and some matchlocks, some had swords over their showlder instead of guns, one or two had pitchforks, and some buts of sythes upon poles with a cleek, some old Lochaber axes.[102]

John Home (Whig, and government volunteer):

[I saw] that about 1400 or 1500 of them were armed with firelocks and broad-swords; that their firelocks were not similar nor uniform, but of all sorts and sizes, muskets, fusees, and fowling-pieces; that some of the rest had firelocks without swords, and some of them swords without firelocks; that many of their swords were not Highland broad-swords, but French; that a company or two (about 100 men) had each of them in his hand the shaft of a pitch-fork, with the blade of a scythe fastened to it, somewhat like the weapon called the Lochaber Axe...[103]

Lord Elcho (Jacobite):

The Princes Army, when it pass'd the Forth, Consisted of 2000 foot – the half completely armed, the others with pitch forks, Scythes, a sword or a pistol, or some only a Staf or a Stick...[104]

James Johnstone (Jacobite):

His [Charles's] army was composed of about eighteen hundred men, badly armed, a part of them having only bludgeons in their hands. They had found very few arms at Edinburgh, as the inhabitants, before the capitulation, had deposited them in the castle...[105]

[O]ur second line...was composed of those who were badly armed; many of them, as we have already observed, having only staves or bludgeons in their hands. Captain MacGregor, of the Duke of Perth's regiment, for want of other arms, procured scythes, which he sharpened and fixed to poles of from seven to eight feet long. With these he armed his company, and they proved very destructive weapons.[106]

Sir Walter Scott (nineteenth-century novelist, with a foot in each camp: his politics Hanoverian, his sentiment Jacobite):

Here was a pole-axe, there a sword without a scabbard; here a gun without a lock, there a scythe set straight upon a pole; and some had only their dirks, and bludgeons or stakes pulled out of hedges.[107]

There is an important *caveat*: Crichton, Home and Elcho made their observations *before* O'Sullivan conducted his 'cherches'. In fact Home, reporting to Cope on 18 September, cautioned him that the firearms deficit would soon be rectified by the distribution of the Town's fire-locks.[108] Scott and the first passage from Johnstone, however, purport to describe the Highlanders as they appeared when they were leaving Edinburgh via the Musselburgh road, while the second Johnstone quote refers to the moments before the battle. To be sure, Scott may have taken some literary licence and Johnstone was notoriously prone to exagger-ate (as he did in estimating the government numbers), but it is doubtful that they invented their descriptions out of whole cloth. If they are even partly correct, the 'cherches' – as Johnstone implies above – were not nearly so productive as O'Sullivan would have us suppose.

What of artillery? For the Hanoverians the answer is clear: they had six one-and-one-half-pound cannon – two borrowed from the castle at Inverness to supplement the four that Cope already carried – plus four coehorns and two 'royals', which were also mortars, but of a heavier type.[109] What they lacked were trained gunners to man them. Responding to Cope's repeated requests, the London authorities had dispatched some to Edinburgh in early September (they arrived on the 4th),[110] but Guest kept them there on the plea that he needed them to defend the Castle.[111] On the night of the 20th – hours before the battle – Cope sent a Lieutenant Craig into Edinburgh to beg for them, and Guest grudgingly released four, plus a bombardier. Accompanied by a guide, and disguised as tradesmen to escape detection, they made for Cope's camp, but, 'unluckily missing their Way', never reached it.[112] Bereft of these, Cope and Master Gunner Eaglesfield Griffith had to rely upon four invalids, including the old Scots army gunner, and either six or nine sailors, the latter borrowed from warships stationed at Dunbar.[113] All were to disappoint him bitterly. The mortars were worthless in any case, because most of their fuses had rotted – 'damnified', as Griffith expressed it – from overlong storage.[114]

For the Jacobites, the truth once more is murky. Of *Du Teillay*'s twenty guns, twelve had been buried near Glenfinnan, leaving eight. Those eight, however, vanish from view soon afterward; we see no further mention of them. Given the Highlanders' distaste for drudgery, the like-lihood is that they never crossed the Corrieyairack. Of course Charles could have helped himself to the Edinburgh city cannon, but these, it will be recalled, were naval guns, hauled up from the Leith warships.

As such, their heavy carriages made them unsuitable for field service.[115] Murray of Broughton states definitively that Charles 'was without cannon' in the Lowlands.[116] Others, though, allude to a single field piece, which Home describes as a 'small iron gun, without a carriage, lying upon a cart, drawn by a little Highland horse'.[117] Its only employment, says Walter Scott, was to fire the signal of march when the army left Edinburgh. Scott also tells us that Charles, thinking it useless, wanted to leave it behind, but the chiefs objected that their men attached symbolic, even superstitious, importance to it.[118] Whether Charles prevailed on this point, or the gun found its way to Prestonpans as a totem, it played no part in the battle. Essentially, then, if not literally, Murray of Broughton was right: the Jacobites had no artillery.

When the Jacobite leaders looked down on Cope's position from Birsley Brae on Falside Hill, just west of Tranent, the view was disheartening. This seems, in fact, to have been one of the few points on which they ever agreed. Their assessments included the following: 'very good' (O'Sullivan);[119] 'advantageous' (Sir John MacDonald);[120] 'impossible to attack' (Murray of Broughton);[121] 'impossible for men to pass' (George Murray.)[122] And this from James Johnstone (in addition to his earlier-quoted encomium):

> [T]he position… was chosen with a great deal of skill. The more we examined it, the more we were convinced of the impossibility of attacking it; and we were all thrown into consternation, and quite at a loss what course to take.[123]

Before long Lord George confirmed that the Hanoverian encampment was unassailable and that his earlier understanding of the terrain had been imperfect:

> I sent Colonel Ker into the meadows to observe well the grounds. He rode in at a gate (gait?) and went to the meadow next the enemy; several of their men got alongst the ditches and shot at him. He did his business very coolly, and then returned and told me it was impossible for men to pass those ditches in a line.[124]

The high ground, then, did not hold the key to victory as he had sup-posed. True, Cope could not attack him there, but neither could he attack Cope.

The rest of the afternoon was taken up with manoeuvring and coun-ter-manoeuvring. It was also marked by repeated miscommunications, or non-communications, between O'Sullivan and George Murray, and (if O'Sullivan is to be believed) an unseemly tantrum on Murray's part.

The first of the communication lapses occurred at about the time that Ker was carrying out his scouting assignment. O'Sullivan does not mention it – perhaps out of embarrassment – but others do. Without first informing Lord George or anyone else, the Irishman sent fifty Camerons[125] to occupy Tranent churchyard, slightly to the right and for-ward of the Jacobites' main position at Birsley Brae: 'for what reason,' wrote Murray in exasperation, 'I could not understand'.[126] In truth the reason was plain enough: to establish defensible outposts along an antici-pated line of attack was completely according to the book.[127] The problem was that Lord George had by now determined that there would be no attack, from either side, over this particular ground. The exercise might nevertheless have been harmless, had not one of the civilians accompa-nying the government army, Customs Collector Walter Grossett, chosen that moment to conduct a scouting mission of his own. The Camerons unwisely revealed their presence by firing at him, whereupon he scurried back to tell Cope about his near-death experience. In response Cope brought two of the cannon to the edge of the ditch (the coehorns would have served the purpose better, but he did not trust their 'damnified' fuses),[128] and fired at the Camerons in turn, wounding several.[129]

At this point the seething Murray – on Lochiel's urging, and without consulting O'Sullivan – withdrew the Camerons from the churchyard and sent them with Lochiel through Tranent to the far, that is, the eastern, side of the town. By the time O'Sullivan found him and expostulated with him for having committed the solecism of exposing his flank to the enemy (an inconsequential fault, since the enemy had neither the inten-tion nor the means of exploiting it), the re-alignment was irrevocably underway. Its purpose was twofold: to get the Camerons out of danger, and to lay the groundwork for assaulting Cope's position on its unpro-tected eastern periphery: the only direction from which Lord George thought it vulnerable. It was during this eastward movement that the Camerons encountered, and butchered, the unfortunate sow.[130]

Meanwhile, Lord George had returned to Birsley Brae and ordered the rest of the army to follow the Camerons. Most of it obeyed.[131]

Most, but not all, for not all of it was there; 250 or more members of Murray's own Atholl Brigade were missing.[132] There had been another communication lapse. It had occurred to Charles, O'Sullivan or both that Cope might use the approaching darkness – it was only around 4p.m., but Britain's Julian Calendar lagged eleven days behind the sun – to bypass the Jacobites altogether and waltz into Edinburgh unopposed.[133] Their concern was by no means implausible, since when Lord George 'struck off to the right' to claim Falside Hill, he left the roads to the capital unguarded. O'Sullivan, therefore, probably at Charles's direction, sent the Atholls back down the hill with instructions to post themselves west of Cope's camp and watch those roads. Neither he nor Charles had notified Lord George.

This communication lapse led to Murray's tantrum – at least according to O'Sullivan, who is the only one to report it. As he tells the tale, Lord George in a 'high tone' (an expression of which O'Sullivan seems fond) asked the Prince where his Brigade had gone, and, when Charles told him, 'threw his gun on the Ground in a great passion, & Swore God, he'd never draw his sword for the cause, if the Bregade was not brought back'. Charles meekly complied. Then, Lochiel intervening to smooth the waters, Lord George relented and let the Athollmen stay where they were.[134] (This seems odd, because by Lord George's account Lochiel at this very moment was leading his Camerons to the far side of Tranent.)[135] But someone must have reconsidered a second time, because at nightfall the Athollmen were on the hill once more, overlooking Bankton House – by whose order nobody knows. The Jacobite sources are sketchy about when this occurred, and the most nearly exact estimates come from the government side: Carlyle ('twilight') and Cope himself ('it was now beginning to grow dark').[136] Later, it is said, Charles had yet another change of heart and wanted to return the Brigade to its original posting west of Cope's camp, but he desisted to keep peace with Lord George.[137]

Again the truth is murky. Murray of Broughton, Elcho, and Lord George, the supposed villain of the piece, all mention the posting but not the tantrum.[138] Perhaps it was Lord George's turn to be embarrassed. Or perhaps the tantrum never happened. (If it had, it is hard to imagine that Murray of Broughton would have passed up the opportunity to cast mud at his namesake.) O'Sullivan is at least right to grumble that the next day's victory would probably have been even more overwhelming if the Athollmen had stayed where they were, because they could have boxed in the defeated Hanoverians and prevented any from escaping.[139]

If nothing else, the incident with the Athollmen provided Alexander Carlyle with the most exciting moments of his brief military career. It also induced Cope to take up new positions for the third and fourth times that day.

Through his acquaintance with Colonel Gardiner, Carlyle had been charged with a potentially important trust: to climb the tower of Prestonpans kirk – his father's church – and monitor the Jacobites' activities. From his vantage point he noticed, first the Atholl Brigade's initial westward movement, and soon afterward a further one toward Dolphingstone. He thereupon rode full tilt to announce his findings to one of Cope's aides.

Cope, however, had already seen and responded to the first movement. Suspecting and probably hoping that Charles meant to attack him from the west (though he was troubled by the Camerons' near-simultaneous eastward movement, which Lord George did not bother to conceal),[140] he resumed something approximating his original position. Now he was facing west by south-west, slightly forward of where he had stood upon first reaching the field. Then, when the Brigade withdrew (Carlyle dutifully reported this also, but again Cope had noticed it on his own), the general concluded that the Jacobites had abandoned this plan of attack. His cause-and-effect analysis was faulty, for no such attack had ever been contemplated, but his conclusion was correct: there was no threat from the west. Accordingly, he turned his men about and marched them to their left until they once more faced south, fronting the ditch, somewhat east of their previous south-facing position, with their artillery strung out across the railway on the eastern end of the line. In that posture they spent the night – all, that is, except the volunteers. These lacked warm enough clothing to sleep in the open, so Cope dispersed them to local billets with instructions to report in the morning. The two armies lay close enough to one another for Sir John MacDonald to overhear 'talking and swearing' in the government camp.[141]

For his part, Carlyle trudged wearily home for supper, darkness having made it pointless to return to the tower. He stopped on the way to receive a final morose blessing from Colonel Gardiner. Finding that he was too exhausted to eat, and that his bedroom had been taken over by fellow Volunteers to whom his parents had offered shelter, he continued on to a neighbour's house and slept there. He did not know it, but his soldiering days were over.[142]

The rebel rank and file still wanted to fight even as darkness fell, and some proposed filling the ditch with fascines to support a frontal attack.[143] But their leaders demurred. Except for a 'pretty brisk' exchange of shots outside Bankton House between the Atholl Brigade and dragoon pickets toward 8p.m., there would be no hostilities on the 20th.[144] For one thing, the hour was too advanced for a full-blown action.[145] For another, Lord George – who appears to have been as much in charge of overall operations as anyone on the Jacobite side – was no more interested in attacking from the south than from the west. His thoughts were focused on the east.

At the inquiry, testifying in his own as well as Cope's defence, Colonel Lascelles described vividly how, 'About nine of the Clock that Night, all the Dogs in the Village of *Tranent* began to bark with the utmost Fury, which, it was believed, was occasioned by the Motions of the Rebels'.[146] It was indeed. To be exact, it was the main body of the Jacobite force, crossing Tranent to link up with the Camerons as Lord George had directed. Though this movement had begun earlier, in daylight, it had apparently been interrupted when he and O'Sullivan exchanged their pleasantries.[147] The 'Motions' continued until about half past ten.[148]

While they were in progress, or perhaps immediately afterward, the Jacobite leaders met in council, where Lord George was trying to persuade the others to fall in with his strategy of encircling the marsh and attacking from the east. It was not a difficult sell. Here, as in their assessment of Cope's position during the afternoon, this bagful of cats reached a rare consensus: to adopt Lord George's plan.[149]

There was a problem, though: circumventing the marsh meant swinging far to the east and then advancing across flat, open ground. By that time the sun would have risen, so Cope would see the advance from a distance and have ample opportunity to prepare. One of Charles's junior officers, Robert Anderson of Whitburgh, came forward to cut this Gordian knot. His father owned the Meadows, and he himself had often hunted upon it. He knew a shortcut that would bring the rebels through it less than a mile east of their present position. He had sat at the edge of the council, too diffident to intervene, as it discussed Lord George's plan. But when the meeting was over, and the others had gone to sleep, he sought out his friend James Hepburn of Keith, of Holyrood fame, and put forward his idea.

Hepburn recognised its merit at once. He did not think that he him-self should relay the proposal to Lord George, for he was Lord George's social equal, and his Lordship had a prickly way of resenting advice from peers.[150] But Anderson, Murray's junior, was no threat. Hepburn therefore advised the young man to awaken the general and deliver the suggestion in person. Anderson did, and Lord George enthusiastically accepted it. He roused the other commanders, including the Prince, who was sleeping on 'a sheaf of peas' nearby. At midnight the council reassembled, and all agreed to follow Anderson's route, using Anderson as a guide.[151] O'Sullivan, away on other business, did not attend either meeting, which may account for the extraordinary harmony.[152]

Toward 3a.m. on the 21st, government patrols detected another east-ward shift in the Jacobite ranks. This time it was the Atholl brigade, come at last from the west side of Tranent to stand at the rear of the line, whence, less well armed than the others, it would remain in reserve.[153]

Also that night came diarist Captain John Maclean, back from his recruitment mission on Mull, to rejoin his Prince. He tells us nothing about the battle, because, he says, its details were already 'well known to severalls', except to mention that afterwards he helped in 'taking Care of the Wounded and gathering the Spoils', and the following day he had charge of some of the prisoners.[154] He tells us nothing about Culloden either, because he was killed there.

One more manoeuvre was necessary before the rebel army was ready to follow Anderson across the marsh. The MacDonalds had to pass the Camerons in order to take up their agreed-upon place at the front of the line: the place that assured them the coveted position on the right in the forthcoming battle. This was accomplished, 'without the least noise or confusion',[155] shortly before 4a.m.[156] The entire force, minus Strathallan's cavalry, began its eastward march immediately afterwards.[157] The cavalry remained behind, either because it was feared that the horses would make too much noise,[158] or because someone had forgotten to issue the necessary order.[159] In any case, this tiny unit would have been useless. By all accounts the men were cheerful, and eager to settle their reckoning with Cope. He had escaped them at the Corrieyairack. He had escaped them at Slochd Mor. He would not escape them now.

Like the Jacobite leaders, Cope and his staff had little sleep. Many of his men had as little as he.

The nineteenth-century historian Robert Chambers first circulated the tale that Cope spent the night of the 20th in comfortable quarters at Cockenzie and in consequence overslept.[160] Others have taken it up, and of course the Skirving song implies the same (which is perhaps where Chambers acquired the notion). But it is untrue. Cope slept that night on the field – if he slept at all. About a fifth of his men – 200 dragoons and 300 foot[161] – were deployed as 'outguards', or sentries, and they reported to him at half hour intervals,[162] bringing 'good Intelligence the whole Night, of every Motion the Enemy made'.[163] He busied himself with other matters as well: he ordered three fires lit in front of the camp, so that the outguards might see better;[164] sent Lieutenant Craig on his futile mission to General Guest;[165] and at one point lobbed a mortar shell into the Jacobite lines. Its 'damnified' fuse failed to burst, however, and he chose not to fire more, lest they too prove ineffective, and the Highlanders in consequence lose their legendary fear of artillery.[166] Amidst this activity, the remainder of the army lay 'in good Spirits on their Arms':[167] the only troops, on either side, who would fight rested.

The government patrols were thorough, ranging over the entire ground and beyond, to the base of Falside Hill on the far side of the marsh, 'near to the rebels',[168] and to the east. But they did not cover the track along which Anderson of Whitburgh was surreptitiously leading their foes. Cope's local civilian experts were ignorant of it.[169]

From three o'clock on – perhaps even earlier – the patrols, 'very alert',[170] had noted ominous eastward movements on the Jacobite side: first when the Atholl Brigade rejoined the main body and later when the entire rebel force began its march. Then, in the neighbourhood of 4a.m., the dragoon outguards reported a development that was more ominous still: in the darkness they had stumbled upon a large party, which could only have been the enemy, advancing north toward Seton. They had hurled a challenge, and when the challenge went unanswered, they galloped back to camp with the news.[171]

Forewarned by the previous reports, Cope was ready and reacted immediately. He ordered a cannon fired, which at one and the same time called in the outguards and roused their sleeping comrades.[172] He then wheeled his men, by platoons, to their left and marched them north at a right angle to the ditch. After they had proceeded only a short distance he halted them and had them execute a quarter-turn to their right.

They now faced east, their right wing – comprised, as we shall see, of the artillery – straddling the railway next to the ditch, their left extending north toward Cockenzie close to where the flat ground began to slope down to the Forth. If one envisions the saltire formed by the intersection of the railway and the cart path, the right rested at the edge of the saltire's south-western arm and the left just north-west of the crossing.[173] According to one observer, the manoeuvre took between fifteen and sixteen minutes.[174] When it was complete, the front line extended about 670 paces from end to end,[175] and each unit occupied exactly the same place, relative to its neighbours, as it had done in the four previous positions.[176]

One of the issues at the Inquiry was whether that line was fully formed before the rebels attacked it. It was. A pair of civilian witnesses – Lord Drummore, the adventuresome judge, and a spectator named David Bruce – attested to this: 'standing stock still', declared the one; 'regularly drawn-up', recalled the other.[177] If they were telling the truth, and there is no reason to doubt it, Cope was not taken by surprise, though Anderson's shortcut had left him less preparation time than he had expected.

The alignment of his troops was essentially in accordance with an Order of Battle which Lord Loudon, as adjutant general, had distributed to the officers before the army left Haddington:[178] an arrangement that Thomasson and Buist aptly likened to 'the final line-up of a Christmas pantomime'.[179] It had survived, more or less intact, the complex manoeuvrings of the preceding day. There were, however, some interesting modifications.

As initially conceived, the front line consisted of two squadrons of Hamilton's dragoons, and Colonel Thomas Murray's Regiment of Foot, on the left; eight companies of Lascelles's and two companies of Guise's (the latter containing the only combat veterans in the entire force, and not many of them either)[180] at the centre; and five companies of Lee's and two squadrons of Gardiner's dragoons on the right. Lascelles's and Guise's companies were brigaded together as a single battalion under the command of Major John Severn. Neither Colonel Lascelles nor Colonel Gardiner was with his own regiment: Lascelles was stationed on the right, as brigadier of that wing, and Gardiner was to serve in the same capacity on the left.[181]

The cannon were to be dispersed along the entire length of the front: two between Hamilton's and Murray's, two between Murray's and Lascelles's, and two between Lee's and Gardiner's. Dispersal of this sort was the usual practice of the period. Only the mortars were to be concentrated on the right, between the cannon and the dragoons. The dragoons were lined up two ranks deep. That was not the usual practice of the period – the norm was three – but there was good reason for the deviation. Cope, knowing that the rebels had almost no cavalry with which to oppose them, wanted to spread them over the widest possible front, so they could ride down the maximum number of enemy foot.

Even under the original plan, the second line, or reserve, was small: the third squadrons of the two dragoon regiments (each mustering barely a hundred officers and men); the old and new Highland regiments (the former drained by desertions, the latter not yet complete and perhaps even without uniforms);[182] and the eighty to ninety Edinburgh Volunteers. It would shrink further by the morning of the battle.

Twenty-four hours later most of the plan's components remained in place, including the left-to-right arrangement of the front line. A few did not.

Firstly, instead of being dispersed, the cannon as well as the mortars were kept together. During the night, when the army faced south, the cannon had stood across the railway at the far left of the line. Now, as a result of that wheeling, eastward movement, they were on the right, immediately to the left of the mortars. All of the pieces were six feet apart. Protecting them, on their right, was an artillery guard of 100 soldiers, detached from the various foot units and stationed between the mortars and the ditch. The reason for the concentration was that Cope – entirely dependent upon the six or nine sailors and the four invalids (including the old Scots army gunner) under the direction of Master Gunner Eaglesfield Griffith – did not have enough manpower to service the weapons if they were scattered. He would soon have even less.[183]

Secondly, under Loudon's scheme, soldiers from the regular line units were to guard the baggage, which Cope had transferred to Cockenzie House, in Cockenzie, for safekeeping, and the Highlanders – new and old alike – were to fight in reserve. But on the afternoon of the 20th he assigned the Highlanders to guard the baggage and ordered the regulars to return to their companies.[184] Evidently he had sized up the former and found them wanting. As for the volunteers, also slated for the reserve,

Cope, remember, had sent them away the previous night with orders to report in the morning. Because the battle started and ended early, however, most of them (like Carlyle) slept through it.[185] This meant that the reserve now consisted only of the two reduced dragoon squadrons.

Thirdly, the plan had been for Gardiner to serve as brigadier of the entire left wing. Today, though, he was on the right, with his own regiment. What is more, he did not even command that regiment, but only one of its squadrons. Probably Cope had sized him up too.[186] If so, Cope never let on; at no point during the inquiry did he criticise the deceased officer. (We have seen that Gardiner, for his part, was less forbearing.) But before and during the battle he made certain that he himself, not Gardiner, performed the brigadier's duties at the left of the government line.[187]

Fourthly, there was no time for the 300 foot outguards, once recalled, to rejoin their companies. Instead, they were hastily assembled into a separate unit and squeezed into the right of the line, between Lee's and the cannon. In consequence there was no room, on the right, to accommodate the two dragoon squadrons standing abreast; the ditch was in the way. So Gardiner's squadron was moved to the rear and the right of the other, just behind the artillery guard.[188] Lieutenant-Colonel Shugborough Whitney commanded the forward squadron. At first the outguards were positioned so far to the right that there was no room, in the front, for either squadron. But Colonel Lascelles moved them closer to Lee's, and Whitney's squadron took over their former space.[189]

It was now about 5a.m.[190] Peering into the half light of the pre-dawn, Cope's men could see what looked like bushes a few hundred yards away, along terrain that had been featureless the night before. But they were not bushes. They were the vanguard of the Jacobite army, coming out of the mist.[191]

They had made their way through the darkness three abreast,[192] as was their wont. They were separated, front to back, into three columns, each arranged in fighting order, so that a simple quarter-turn to the left would transform them instantly into a line of battle. In the first column, commanded by the Duke of Perth, were the MacDonald regiments, marching to claim their station on the right: at their head, Clanranald's (200 men), then Glengarry's, including a company of Grant's (400, or 500 with the Grants), and finally Keppoch's (250). In the second column,

Perth's own regiment (200), the Appin Stewarts (200) and Lochiel's Camerons (600). They would stand on the left under the watchful eye of George Murray. In the rearmost column, comprising the reserve, the Atholl Brigade (250) and the Machlachlans (100) under Lord Nairne and the Prince in person. A number of lesser clans, such as the MacGregors and Glencoe MacDonalds, were scattered amongst the others.[193]

Silently they proceeded east for about half a mile, then turned north onto Anderson's narrow path. Another mile brought them to Riggonhead Farm. There they swung obliquely to their left, so that they were now heading in a north-westerly direction. Five hundred yards beyond they encountered their only obstacle: a four-foot ditch with a wooden bridge over it.[194] The men used the bridge, but Charles in his exuberance tried to leap the ditch, and stumbled to his knees on the far side. Johnstone, who helped him to his feet, thought him disconcerted by the seeming bad omen. The Highlanders, for all their reputed superstition, took no apparent notice of it.[195]

Perth's column passed successfully through the marsh and, turning north again, entered the field, crossing it 500 to 600 yards east of where the railway and cart path intersected. It was the second column – Lord George's – which, emerging from the marsh, encountered the patrolling dragoons.[196] Ignoring their challenge, and the signal gun that followed, that column too marched onto the field, the reserve at its rear.

In the half dark (George Murray recalled that 'day was just beginning to dawn', and Cope that there was 'very little light'),[197] the two front line columns could not clearly see either one another or the enemy. The poor visibility had three consequences.

First, Perth's column kept marching north after Murray's, unbeknownst to it, had halted, wheeled and formed in back of it. This opened up a gap, several hundred yards wide, between the two divisions. The error may actually have worked, psychologically, to the Jacobites' advantage, because when it was light enough for the government forces to see at all, they still could not see distinctly across the distance that separated the armies. Hence they mistook the reserve – which was standing fifty to eighty yards behind the gap[198] – for the enemy centre and assumed that there was yet another reserve beyond it: a misperception that made them think their opponents more numerous than was the case.[199] Cope himself, for instance, asserted at the inquiry that the rebels were drawn up 'in a Line entire, without any Interval',[200] which could explain why he persisted in guessing that there were 5,500 of them.

Second, when Perth finally did come to a halt, he was further east than Murray's division – thus, further away from the government line – and, more significantly, well to the north of it, which means that he was outflanking it on its left by about 100 yards.[201] In addition to gaining him a tactical advantage, this too may have given the government troops, and their commander, exaggerated notions of Jacobite strength.[202] Lord George likewise strayed too far north, though not as much so as Perth. When he pulled up and turned to form his front, there were about 100 paces of open ground between the left – that is, the southern – extremity of his line and the ditch, which put him at risk of being flanked in turn by the government right.[203]

Third, because of the space that had opened up between the two rebel divisions, they were now unable to communicate with one another and therefore could not coordinate their movements. So Murray acted in character: independently. He charged.

Cope at this moment was on the left of the government line, leading up Hamilton's dragoons – a task that under Loudon's plan would have fallen to Gardiner as brigadier.[204] He was dismayed to find that they had not yet drawn their swords, and he ordered them to do so.[205] Observing that the Jacobite right was outflanking him, he resolved to employ cannon 'to annoy' it,[206] and accordingly bade his aide Major Mossman bring over two of the one-and-a-half-pounders from his own right. Mossman delivered the message to Colonel Whitefoord, who with Griffith was directing the artillery. But Whitefoord could not oblige: the civilian drivers who worked the artillery train had run away minutes earlier and taken the horses with them.[207] Mossman returned dejectedly to tell Cope, only to find that the general had meanwhile moved to the right himself.[208] The cannon remained there also.

The sailors and the invalids who served the cannon were the next to run – first the former, then the latter – leaving Whitefoord and Griffith to manage the pieces unaided. The fleeing invalids, moreover, carried off the powder flasks, which meant that the gun that had fired the alarm was now useless; there was no means of reloading it.[209]

The reason Cope had shifted to the right was that he had seen Murray's division in motion and realised that the initial onslaught would be in that direction. He rode there across the entire front of his line, shouting encouragement to his men along the way.[210] Despite the mishap with the cannon, he still anticipated success.[211]

His foe was not long in disabusing him. On Lord George's instructions, the Camerons and their allies veered obliquely to their left as they charged, in order to close the gap between themselves and the ditch and thereby prevent the dragoons from taking them in flank.[212] They surged ahead with the speed that was their hallmark: 'as fast as they Could', as Elcho described it;[213] 'with a Swiftness not to be conceived', in Whitefoord's more famous and more poetic phrase.[214] Their feet rustled audibly against the stubble of the recently harvested corn,[215] and they uttered 'hideous' cries (Elcho),[216] or, in Home's words, spoke and muttered to themselves 'in a manner that expressed and heightened their fierceness and rage'.[217] Walter Scott mentions bagpipes, as do some nineteenth-century historians who follow his lead, but that is a literary invention; the rustling, and the cries or mutterings, were the only noises they made.[218] When they launched their attack it was not yet light, so their 'dark cloaths' (O'Sullivan) helped to conceal them as they cut through the mist.[219] Before they were halfway to the government lines, however, 'the sun rose, dispelled the mist, and showed the armies to one another'.[220]

At that first full sight of the enemy, many of the Jacobite officers shared Cope's expectation that they would be soundly beaten,[221] and small wonder. The government forces were drawn up smartly, except for some momentary confusion amongst the artillery guard, which Fowke put to rights even as the rebels were advancing;[222] once he accomplished this, the redcoats 'made a most gallant appearance'.[223] The rebels did not. Each of their three divisions had originally stood three ranks deep as a result of the left-wheeling movement of their marching column when it formed a line of battle. But they lost all semblance of order once the action began. As Murray's division raced across the field, its broad front dissolved into a column, which soon separated itself into two columns, one immediately behind the other, and then into 'clumps and clusters'.[224] In the forefront were the fastest and bravest[225] – or perhaps those who were simply the most anxious to pass the dreaded cannon. From the government perspective their appearance was even more chaotic. Cope saw before him 'several Bodies; whereof that upon the Left, we judged to be at least 20 in front, and 30 in Depth'.[226] Loudon, noting 'a great Confusion among them', thought them 'form'd into five square Bodies or Columns, that on the Left the largest, and about twenty deep', although he admitted that he had observed only three of those columns himself. He speculated that the hindermost were waiting to discover how the foremost fared before deciding whether to press on.[227] Comparing the state of the two armies, the Jacobites had reason for pessimism.

The rising sun was at their backs as they ran forward, but its rays glinted sharply off the polished weapons and accoutrements of the Hanoverians,[228] and its effects must have been blinding to both sides. When they approached the artillery, Whitefoord, seconded by Griffith, contrived to fire a single round from each of the pieces that were still loaded: the mortars, and five of the six cannon.[229] A private fell dead, an officer was wounded,[230] and the rebel line as a whole 'made a great Shake'.[231] Seeing this, the Hanoverians cheered. But the Jacobites cheered back – and kept running forward.[232]

Now came a critical point in the battle. The Jacobites had not yet reached the cannon, nor had they completely closed the gap between their extreme left and the ditch.[233] It was still possible for the government army to take them in flank and protect the guns. Loudon, or perhaps Whitefoord – Cope and Lascelles thought it was Loudon, but Whitefoord claimed the distinction for himself[234] – ordered Colonel Whitney to ride forward with his dragoon squadron and do both. The dragoons trotted ahead obediently until they came within pistol shot of the rebels, whereupon the latter fired their muskets, killing a few dragoons and wounding Whitney in the sword-arm. The dragoons turned and fled: the rear ranks first, the rest 'in Tens and Twenties'.[235] Their flight had a collateral consequence. Major Mossman at the time was trying to find Cope and tell him that he had been unable to deliver the two cannon, but the fleeing horses blocked his way, and Cope remained for the moment in happy ignorance that his wishes had been flouted.[236]

Ominously, Lascelles, as brigadier on the right wing, had tried to wheel the foot to the right and help the charging dragoons. He was forced to desist, however, when he found some of them 'crouching and creeping gently backwards, with their Arms recovered, which was occasioned by a continued irregular Fire over their Heads'. He was able to restore them to order, but it was too late to do Whitney's any good, and the episode did not bode well for their future behaviour.[237]

The panic among the dragoons spread to the artillery guard, which had been unsteady to begin with. At Fowke's command it gave one fire – 'a very irregular one' – and fled also.[238]

Next it was Gardiner's turn. The Jacobites, already in disarray, had opened their ranks even further to pass through the cannon and the remnants of the artillery guard. Seeing the rebels thus 'broken',[239] someone ordered Gardiner to attack them. It is not clear who issued the order; the Board questioned both Cope and Fowke on this point, and neither could say.[240] His squadron's fate was the same as Whitney's: the troopers took a few hesitant paces toward the enemy, received some musket fire – the Jacobites in the lead having closed up again to deliver it – and made off, flinging away their standards and leaving their colonel, severely wounded, almost alone upon the field.[241] Their panic may have resulted in part from being stampeded by the fleeing artillery guard,[242] but they had been skittish even before they went into action. Fowke had spotted them reining back their horses as they awaited the command to engage, and had rebuked them for their timidity.[243]

The first attacking column now separated into three bodies.[244] ('Bodies' is perhaps an inexact expression, inasmuch as it implies more coherence than seems to have been the case; Elcho, for instance, writes that the respective groups were 'some places 10 deep, others one or two'.)[245] One pursued the fleeing government troops. Another stayed to secure the cannon. About 150 in the rear halted briefly beside the guns and waited for their slower comrades from the second wave to reach the scene. Then, their muskets flung away, they drew their swords, and with the same 'incredible impetuosity' that had marked their charge, fell upon the foot.[246]

The government position was still salvageable. But here Lascelles may have committed a fatal error. According to his own version of events, he again directed the foot to wheel to its right, this time to repel the attacking Highlanders. And again he failed, because the foot, shaky on the prior occasion, collapsed altogether and bolted like the artillery guard and the dragoons.[247]

The nineteenth-century military historian Robert Cadell, a British general himself, has a different view of the affair. He bases it on what he regards as a suspicious time lag in Lascelles's account, and on notes that Lieutenant-Colonel Peter Halkett, who commanded Lee's five companies, inscribed in a copy of the inquiry board's report. As Cadell tells the tale, Lascelles made a common parade ground mistake: he shouted 'left' when he meant 'right'. In consequence, the foot wheeled in the wrong direction and stood for the moment with their backs to the enemy.

By the time he corrected himself the men had lost every trace of composure and there was no containing them.[248]

Halkett mentioned nothing of the sort in a letter he sent the Board on Lascelles's behalf (being out of town, he was unable to testify in person), nor did any of the other witnesses. But they may have been covering for their superior. More recent historians have not mentioned it either, perhaps because they placed no stock in the story. But none of them was a general and Cadell was. It is one of those mysteries about the '45 that no modern inquiry can resolve.

There is no doubt, though, that the foot companies bolted. They did so, moreover, in the most spectacular fashion. They fired once: a regular fire, say Elcho and Cope,[249] but the consensus is that it was not.[250] Then they melted away from right to centre, the rear ranks before the front ones: first the outguards, next Lee's, and finally Lascelles's own regiment with its complement of Guise's – 'as it were by Platoons', in the picturesque expression of two officers who looked on helplessly.[251]

Cope was not content to look on helplessly. He rode frantically to and fro across the crumbling line, crying out to his men, 'For Shame, Gentlemen, don't let us be beat by Such a Set of Banditti', and 'Behave like Britons, give them another Fire, and you'll make them run'.[252] After they had departed the field, he tried to re-form them into a body 'for their own Safety', and to persuade them to re-load, 'in Hopes that they would then be brought to make a Stand'. But it was all to 'no Purpose'; the terrified foot were past listening.[253] By then the rebels, fleeter, because they were more lightly armed, were mixed among them and were wreaking savage execution with swords and scythes.[254]

Fowke at the moment was west of the area, trying unsuccessfully to rally the dragoons. Hearing firing in his rear, 'I gallop'd back, in Hopes it was our own Foot had continued to engage the Rebels'. But when he reached the ground where the foot had stood, 'I heard a Voice call out to me' – it was Captain Wedderburn, who like Whitefoord and the Earl of Home was an unattached volunteer – 'saying, These were the Rebels'.[255] Finding the way to his own side blocked, he faced his horse left and rode north to the sanctuary of the shore. He was luckier than many.[256]

As the Jacobite left was bearing down upon the government right, it occurred to Lord George that he should let his opposite number know what he was doing. So he dispatched an aide to Perth, on the right, informing him that the left was underway and suggesting that Perth get started too. At about that time, the same idea occurred to Perth, so he sent his own messenger – Anderson of Whitburgh, who, having led the approach through the marsh, would naturally have remained with the van – to tell Lord George that Clan Donald was ready.[257] Such were the notions of unified command in the Jacobite army. The two messengers, meeting midway, had little to do but exchange compliments, because events were generating their own momentum.

The right commenced its advance after the left was already in motion, but it soon made up the lost time. It had first to overcome a false start that provided the Hanoverians with their only tactical success of the day. Some of Perth's men tried to sneak up on their opponents under cover of an embankment on the northern edge of the field, where the ground began to slope down to the sea. Noticing this, a Hanoverian officer ordered one of Hamilton's dragoon squadrons to ride north and take up a position opposite them. Checked, they re-joined their main body, and the squadron returned to its proper place in the line. Then the MacDonald regiments attacked in earnest.[258]

The best description of what happened next comes from the vivid pen of Lord Drummore. Arriving from quarters in Cockenzie at about 5.15a.m., he stationed himself about 150 yards north of the field 'to see the Fate of a Battle in which I was most sensibly interested'.[259] From this vantage point he had an unobstructed view of the government left. His subsequent letter to the inquiry board (in which he vigorously defends General Cope) describes the MacDonalds as having moved forward quickly, in two parallel 'Columns, Clews or Clumps', but in surprisingly good order; 'tho' I could see thro' from Front to Rear, yet, to my Astonishment, every Front Man cover'd his Followers, there was no Man to be seen in the Open'. He noticed no shooting, by either side, but Officer of the Day Major Talbot, on the left of the government line, believed that the rebels discharged a few desultory rounds from a distance.[260] Inclining obliquely to their left, much as Lord George's division had done, they raced forward to close with Hamilton's, whom they still considerably outflanked.

Hamilton's did not await them. Spooked, it would seem, by the carnage that was occurring to their right, its two forward squadrons wheeled and fled when the nearest attackers were still sixty yards off:[261] 'not in a Body, but quite broke in two's or so', recalled Drummore;[262] 'like rabbets',

wrote Charles to his father two weeks later (his spelling was as idio-
syncratic as O'Sullivan's); [263] 'like a flock of sheep which after having
run away, gathers together and then begins to run again when seized
by a fresh fear', according to Sir John MacDonald, who was looking
down on the spectacle gleefully with the rest of the Jacobite cavalry. [264]
Captain Clark, commanding the reserve dragoon squadron, counselled
his troopers to open up and let their fleeing comrades through; his plan
was to ride down the MacDonalds when they pursued. But his troopers had different ideas. They 'immediately quitted their officers' and
decamped with the others, and the reserve squadron on the right – the
last of Gardiner's three units – did the same. [265] Cope testified that all four
squadrons, reserve and forward ones alike, 'went off…so much at the
same Instant, that it's difficult to say, which run first'. [266] And Drummore,
who did not lack humour, commented that he could not tell which of
them 'had the Honour' to reach safety soonest, 'but I think it was a very
near Match'. [267]

With the dragoons gone, Cope's only remaining unit, Colonel Thomas
Murray's 57th Foot, about 580 strong, was now, in Drummore's words,
'standing naked' before the enemy. [268] It did not stand long. It emitted
what the judge called one 'infamous' fire – 'Puff, Puff, no Platoon that
I heard' – and headed off in the wake of the dragoons. [269] Drummore
acknowledges that he departed also: 'I hope with more Discretion and
Deliberation than the dragoons did'. [270]

The fighting was effectively over. Nobody knows how long it lasted,
for there were no stopwatches in those days and the participants would
not have had leisure to consult them anyway, but estimates range from
three to just under fifteen minutes. [271] It ended so quickly that Prince
Charles and his reserve were never engaged: though they charged a mere
fifty paces behind the first line, by the time they reached the field the
only enemies they encountered were dead or wounded. [272] The cavalry
was not engaged either. When he saw the government army fleeing, Sir
John MacDonald urged Strathallan to pursue it, but Strathallan protested
that the horses – still, apparently, on the hillside – could not cover the
distance quickly enough. [273] MacDonald, Elcho and a few others rode
ahead anyway in quest of prisoners and collected a few straggling dragoons. [274] So complete was the rout that, on the losing side, 'none of the
soldiers attempted to load their pieces again, and not one bayonet was
stained with blood'. [275]

The morning had been an unmitigated disaster for the King's forces. And it was about to get worse.

'I have always remarked,' wrote Lord George's aide James Johnstone, 'that much fewer men [are] lost in the field of battle than in the subsequent flight.'[276] Johnstone is often unreliable, but in this instance he was, so to speak, dead right.

The dragoons escaped more lightly than the infantry, because they were faster. After quitting the field, some of Hamilton's people headed for the shore,[277] but the majority from both regiments congregated on the near side of the Preston House walls. There they paused, with their horses' rumps to the enemy, while Cope and their other officers strove in vain to turn them around. (Fowke, for instance, was heard to cry out, 'Now Lads, take your revenge', before giving it up as a bad job and riding back to try his luck with the foot.)[278] Then, as bands of rebels came up in back of them and pot-shotted them, they plunged down the north and south defiles that led past Preston House to tiny Preston village,[279] or else sought safety through the breaches that Cope had driven into the walls for a very different purpose the previous day.[280] Finding their horses too bulky to negotiate those breaches, many of them dismounted and left the animals to shift for themselves.[281]

The foot also tried to slip through the defiles and breaches, but were not as lucky, because the dragoons, or their abandoned mounts, blocked their way. In desperation a few tried to climb the walls, only to discover that these were too high.[282] And now came the proof of Johnstone's proposition, in the ghastly form alluded to at the beginning of this book: as the fugitives milled about, with their backs to the battlefield, the ground that they occupied became 'a spectacle of horror...with heads, legs, and arms, and mutilated bodies' (Johnstone);[283] 'wth one stroke, armes, & legs were cout of [cut off], & heads split to the Shoulders, never such wounds were seen' (O'Sullivan).[284] There is grim irony in the fact, for the poor devils had fled precisely in order to avoid these vividly imagined effects of the Highlanders' broadswords, scythes and axes. Their fears proved self-fulfilling.

The horses suffered too. The victors could simply have captured them, but, deeming them better fighters than their riders, chose to slaughter them instead.[285] Lord George, or whoever conducted the training on the Jacobite side, had instructed the men to slash at the beasts' noses during combat, in order to provoke a stampede. There was no opportunity to do this, however, because the dragoons had turned tail once the action started and the rebels saw little of the horses' fronts. So the wounds were inflicted from the rear, and they were pitiful. Cleanly severed legs were the order of the day.[286]

Carlyle, asleep in his neighbour's house, awoke to the sound of the cannon. Dressing quickly, he raced to his parents' home, a short distance away, where he could see almost to the battlefield. By that time, though, the fighting was already over and

> the whole prospect was filled with runaways, and Highlanders pursuing them. Many had their coats turned as prisoners, but were still trying to reach the town in hopes of escaping. The pursuing Highlanders, when they could not overtake, fired at them, and I saw two fall in the glebe… The crowd of wounded and dying now approached with all their followers, but their groans and agonies were nothing compared with the howlings, and cries, and lamentations of the women…

He then set out to do what he could for the victims.[287]

To their credit, the Jacobite officers, from Prince Charles and Lord George on down, also tried to mitigate these horrors as much as possible. Even the Whig John Home admits that Charles provided 'for the relief of the wounded of both armies' and preserved 'every appearance of moderation and humanity'.[288] The Jacobites say the same. 'As Soon as the pursuit began,' recalled Elcho, 'all the Principal Officers Mounted on horseback in order to Save and proteck Gen. Cope's officers as much as they could'.[289] Charles personally ordered that the enemy wounded, officers and men alike, receive the same care as his own;[290] indeed, Murray of Broughton maintains that he had them treated ahead of his own.[291] Of the officers, the most serious cases were brought inside Bankton House, Colonel Gardiner's residence, where, guarded by Captain John Maclean, they were given prompt medical attention; wounded enemy privates were accommodated in its parks and gardens. The less severely wounded officers walked under parole to other nearby homes.[292] Lord George's behaviour appears to have been especially commendable. He distributed provisions to the prisoners – the rank and file, as well as the officers; he lent his own horses to officer prisoners who were unable to walk;

and, when some of the captured officers expressed fear that the Highlanders would plunder them at night, he slept on the floor of their room to protect them. But despite these palliative efforts the 'butcher's bill' on the government side was high.

It should not astonish anyone who has read this far that there is wide-ranging disagreement as to how high. Johnstone speculates that there were 1,300 Hanoverian dead and 1,500 prisoners.[293] This is preposterous, because it adds up to more men than Cope had under his command, but we have seen that Johnstone exaggerated that too. Home weighs in at the low end with 200 dead, including five officers.[294] In between are Elcho (500 privates and seven officers killed, 900 wounded, and 1,400 prisoners – which also does not add up, especially if one remembers that some escaped),[295] O'Sullivan (700 to 800 killed),[296] and Murray of Broughton (300 privates and seven or eight officers killed, 400 to 500 wounded, and most of the rest taken prisoner).[297] Lord George does not speculate as to the number of killed and wounded, but puts the prisoner count at between 1,600 and 1,700.[298] Modern historians – those who venture opinions at all – also differ. Thomasson and Buist adopt Murray of Broughton's figures,[299] while Reid, citing a contemporary newspaper report, opts for a more modest 150 dead.[300] Unsurprisingly, neither expresses any great confidence in these conclusions.

The dead government officers included Captain Brymer of Lee's regiment, who had fought against the Jacobites at Sheriffmuir – the only member of Cope's army to have done so – and had warned his comrades not to underestimate them.[301] To his cost he was right. And of course they included Colonel Gardiner. In his case it is difficult to ascertain exactly what happened, because fact trails into legend. What is certain is that he remained on the field after most of his troopers had deserted him, took at least two bullet wounds in the body, was cut about the head with both a sword and a scythe, and received his death wound from a Lochaber axe, also administered to the head. The latter occurred close by the lone thorn tree, where Lee's and the outguards were – or should have been. (The original tree withered and was cut down early in the last century, but a successor, of unknown provenance, stands near the site.)[302] He was then carried, first to his own garden, and later to the Tranent kirk manse, where he died.[303]

Colonel Peregrine Lascelles, in contrast, had a near-miraculous deliverance, or so he said. When he tried to wheel his platoons the second time, he slipped and fell. Upon rising, he was surrounded by a Jacobite officer and sixteen privates, who declared him their prisoner and confiscated his sword. Seconds later, however, they bolted in pursuit of the fleeing foot and he was at liberty once more. Taking advantage of the gap between the Jacobite left and right wings, he walked through it unchallenged to Seton. His men having left the scene, there were no witnesses to confirm his story.[304]

The Jacobite casualty figures are also debatable, although the range is for obvious reasons narrower. Johnstone estimates forty killed and as many wounded; Elcho fifty-four killed (including four officers) and eighty wounded; and Murray of Broughton and Home thirty-four killed (including three or four officers) and seventy to eighty wounded.[305] The deaths were all from gunshot wounds, often through infection.[306] Vietnam has taught us the limitations of a body count, but even allowing for these the one-sidedness of the rebel victory is apparent.

There were still pockets of resistance, which the rebels set out to eradicate. George Murray reports, for instance, that fragments of the broken foot companies had tried to re-form behind him once the first assault column had passed through them, but the second wave quickly dispersed them. And after the field itself was cleared, he came upon Lieutenant-Colonel Halkett and about twenty of his officers and soldiers, who fired at him and his men from inside the Bankton enclosures. Lord George could have destroyed them – he had a hundred men at his back – but he made his own side hold its fire and convinced Halkett and the others to surrender. He later wrote, 'nothing gave me more pleasure that day, than having it so immediately in my power to save those men....'.[307]

His generosity soon paid dividends, for there was another piece of unfinished business on hand: Cope's baggage, which the Highland companies were guarding behind the walls of Cockenzie House. Lord George sent Lochiel's Camerons over to claim it. Cope might have been wiser to trust the Highlanders on the battlefield, because despite his misgivings about them they were initially inclined to defend the place. But Halkett knew that this would be futile, and Lord George had him go there, on parole, to dissuade them. When he explained the situation to them, they surrendered. The booty included, not only Cope's papers, but also his military chest, which provided two to three thousand pounds for Charles's depleted coffers. Halkett, like his captor George Murray, seems to have been an exceptionally decent man; he and Captain Sweetenham were among the few Hanoverian officers who honoured their parole throughout the war.[308]

The Duke of Perth had his own unfinished business with one of those Highlanders. This was company commander Sir Patrick Murray of Auchertyre – the very one who had tried through duplicity to arrest him at dinner in his home. Seeking Auchertyre out after his surrender, Perth murmured to him with exquisite courtesy: 'Sir Petie, I am to dine with you today'. Auchertyre's answer is not recorded.[309]

Of the 1,400 government foot (taking Cope's low-end figure), only about 170 escaped: 'by extraordinary swiftness or early flight', writes John Home. Having in Cope's words 'dispersed and shifted for themselves all over the Country', 105 of them reached Edinburgh and reported for duty at the Castle on Monday the 23rd; the rest eventually arrived at Berwick.[310] Again, the dragoons were luckier.

When Cope saw them pouring through the two defiles, he pursued them down the south one, hoping to head them off before they passed Preston Village. Upon arriving at its terminus, he found that the Earl of Home, Loudon, and other officers had anticipated him. Home was standing in the road, pistol pointed in the air, and, with his colleagues, was herding about 450 dragoons into an enclosed field immediately south-west of the village. Once there, the dragoons were separated into a squadron and two smaller bodies. At this exact moment, a large group of rebels appeared at the end of the defile, but seeing the dragoons arranged in orderly fashion showed no interest in attacking them; on the contrary, they 'stood in awe' of them. (Both Cope and Loudon used this same curious expression.) Observing their hesitation, the Hanoverian officers tried to persuade the dragoons to take the offensive, but without success: they would not move 'one Foot', declared Cope and Loudon disgustedly. (Again, both employed the same language to convey their chagrin.) The officers, deeming the walled-in field unsafe, then tried to move the dragoons further west. Initially they rode behind the troopers, as was customary during retreats, but those in the lead began to gallop off, so they dashed to the front in order to contain them. Once this was done, the dragoons 'were form'd three different Times towards the Enemy, to make the retreat as decent as possible'. A hurried conference now took place, at which the officers agreed that it was imprudent to go to Edinburgh, because they had not enough men to defend the city; instead, they would retire to Berwick and join forces with the Dutch. Accordingly, the tiny troop turned south, crossed Birsley Brae by a road that is known to this day as 'Johnnie Cope's Road', and headed in gloom toward the border.[311]

Battles often spawn legends, and Prestonpans has produced its share. None of them is true.

We have already addressed the one that has Cope sleeping comfortably at Cockenzie the night before the battle. He did not. The others are also specious.

That the Jacobite army paused to pray before charging.[312] It did not. It was incapable of such coordinated action, and the two front wings could not have seen one another clearly enough in the dark to have executed it.

That Cope (in the words of the song) 'sent [Charles] a challenge from Dunbar'. (Patrick Crichton believed this as well.)[313] He did not. Eighteenth-century armies did not indulge in such quixotic gestures. Besides, this one would have played into Charles's hand, by implicitly recognising him as a legitimate belligerent. Cope would not have done that.

That Cope promised his men eight hours of plunder if they recaptured Edinburgh.[314] He did not, any more than George Murray issued the spurious 'no quarter' order that Cumberland used to justify government atrocities after Culloden.[315] There is no evidence to support the story, and it is completely out of character. Colonel Whitefoord testified at the inquiry that during the march to the forts and back, Cope 'kept such exact Discipline in his Army, that no Outrage was committed by the Soldiers, nor was there one Complaint from his going North till his Return'.[316] No serious historian has ever suggested otherwise.

That Cope or Lascelles, anticipating defeat, secreted a white cockade – the Jacobite symbol – about his person and donned it to facilitate his escape. (Johnstone says it was Cope, Murray of Broughton Lascelles.)[317] Cope certainly did not, for he did not anticipate defeat, nor did he escape by sneaking undetected through enemy lines. It is theoretically possible for Lascelles to have done it, but it is also unlikely. If the rumour had substance, it would have reached other ears besides Secretary Murray's, and the members of the inquiry board would have taxed him about it. They did not.

Finally, the Skirving song has it that Cope brought with him the first news of his own defeat, and that Lord Mark Ker, who was in charge of the Berwick garrison, chaffed him for being the only general in history ever to have done so. James Johnstone repeated the tale,[318] and some modern writers have accepted it.[319] Well, no.

What happened, rather, was this. Cope halted briefly at Lauder on his way to Berwick, 'to refresh the Men'.[320] While there, he took the opportunity to dash off a disconsolate letter to Tweeddale. After reporting the stark details of the battle, he concluded poignantly:

> I have been unfortunate, which will certainly give a Handle to my Enemies to cast blame upon me. I cannot reproach myself. The Manner in which the Enemy came on, which was quicker than can be described (of which the Men have long been warned) possibly was the Cause of our Men taking a most destructive Pannick... The fatigue and Concern I have had, renders me incapable of being more particular.[321]

The party quartered that night at Coldstream and crossed the border into Berwick the next day. Ker knew about Prestonpans before Cope arrived; he found out, in fact, the previous morning, within hours after it ended. The two men did meet. They were not fond of each other – Ker, remember, had coveted Cope's command – but their discourse was unremarkable.[322]

After arranging medical treatment for those who needed it, Charles presided over a celebratory meal on the battlefield, with a minister in attendance to give a blessing. The meal took place at a table set up near the cannon – but not, declares Murray of Broughton, within sight of the dead and wounded as Charles's detractors claimed (though how he could have avoided them, in that location, is difficult to imagine).[323] He spent the night at Pinkie House, Tweeddale's mansion just outside Edinburgh. The following morning, as his pipers played 'When the King Enjoys His Own Again', he re-crossed the ancient Esk bridge at the head of 800 foot and entered the capital in triumph.[324]

5

AFTERMATH

The three adjacent villages of Prestonpans, Preston and Tranent, each with an eye on tourism, vied for the honour of naming the battle, but Prestonpans soon supplanted the others.[1] Jacobites, though, called it Gladsmuir, the name of another nearby village, because of an ancient prophecy that the Scots would win an important victory there.[2] Important it was, at least in the short term.

In Edinburgh, where he held opulent court, Charles – now master of most of Scotland – issued a proclamation forbidding public rejoicing, inasmuch as the blood that was shed on both sides was that of his father's subjects. He briefly besieged the Castle, but abandoned the attempt when its garrison bombarded the town and the citizens begged him to desist. He also issued proclamations designed to reassure the public on both sides of the border about his future policies; however, with his eye on his remaining two crowns, especially the English one, he equivocated on his former pledge to dissolve the union, to the dismay of many of the chiefs. Indeed, so bent was he on claiming his English inheritance that he toyed with the idea of pursuing Cope immediately. He gave that up, though, and decided to stay where he was for the time being in order to rebuild his strength: a wise decision, since many of his victorious soldiers had gone home with their battlefield booty.[3]

The invasion of England finally began at the end of October. The majority of the chiefs – above all George Murray – participated only on the basis of Charles's promises that English Jacobites and the French would support them. But the support was not forthcoming, except for a few hundred Englishmen from the Manchester area who were mobilised into the ill-fated Manchester Regiment; Charles could not, this time, make things so by wishing. After capturing the border town and castle of Carlisle, the expedition, about 5,500 strong,[4] advanced unopposed as far as Derby, 130 miles from London.

There the chiefs called in the promises. When Charles came up empty-handed, they forced him to turn around and retreat to Scotland. Against advice, he left the Manchester Regiment in Carlisle, to defend the castle, after he and the rest of his army had re-crossed the border: a symbolic gesture that betokened his determination to return. A shocking percentage of the Manchesters, their officers and non-commissioned officers in particular, paid for that gesture with their lives, and there would be no return.

The chiefs had good reasons, political as well as military, for their reluctance to proceed further. For one, their agendas (as we moderns say) were different than their Prince's: theirs cantered upon Scotland, whereas he, with more grandiose dreams, coveted all three kingdoms. But even if their goal had been the same as his, attacking London was risky. The rebels could probably have captured the city, but it might have become a death trap, just as the Prestonpans battlefield, for all of its initial allure, became one for Cope. Three armies were converging upon them – Marshal Wade's, based in Newcastle; the newly-arrived regiments from Flanders under the command of the Duke of Cumberland; and the assorted collection from Finchley and vicinity whom Hogarth immortalised in his famous painting of the Guards – and a colourful double agent, Dudley Bradstreet, had duped them into thinking that there was a fourth.[5] In addition, the London mob was unpredictable, comprised as it was of Irish labourers, who were potential allies, and vigorous and violent anti-Papists who might have massacred them and the Irish alike.

In the end, though, they should have kept going, as Charles had desperately wanted them to do: not because they necessarily would have won, but because at least they had a chance. Prior to Derby, they had morale, mystique and momentum in their favour. Once they reversed direction, they lost all three, and had no chance whatever: their footsteps thereafter pointed inexorably toward Culloden. As a result, Prestonpans had important short-term consequences – the invasion, and its effects upon the English psyche (as well as upon Britain's military position in Europe), were no small things – but not long-term ones. The rebellion ended in a Hanoverian triumph, exactly as if Cope had prevailed – which of course implicates the question, at the beginning of the book, of whether human action can ever have important long-term consequences.

The military board convened exactly three weeks before the first anniversary of the battle. It met on five consecutive days – Monday 1 September to Friday 5 – from 10a.m. until 3p.m., and then held a special session on the 24th to hear mathematician Richard Jack, who claimed to have assisted with the artillery at Edinburgh and Prestonpans as a volunteer. All sessions were open to the public, and were well attended. There were at least 150 spectators at each one.[6]

More than forty witnesses testified. Most were Cope's former officers, but some were civilians: Duncan Forbes, Lord Drummore, and Jack, among others. All except Jack strongly supported the three men whose conduct was under scrutiny, and Jack's testimony was so implausible (for instance, he described Cope's artillery as having stood on rising ground, when there was no such ground anywhere on the totally flat battlefield)[7] that the board was clearly right to disregard it; indeed, some of his more bizarre assertions suggested megalomania or outright dementia. The majority of the witnesses gave evidence in person, but some (for instance, Loudon), being away on the King's business, submitted letters instead. Others who did appear – Cope for one; Whitefoord for another – supplemented their oral testimony with written statements, which, like the letters, were read aloud. The witnesses who were present were closely questioned.

The board's report is not dated, but must have been issued by early January of the following year, because it was certified for publication on the 5th of that month.[8] All three men were completely exonerated.

Addressing itself first to Cope, the board reviewed and ratified every one of his actions: his march to Dalwhinnie; his approaches to the chiefs; his by-passing of the Corrieyairack; his continuing on to Inverness; and his preparations for, and conduct of, the battle. It then concluded, unanimously:

> That he did his Duty as an Officer, both before, at, and after the Action: and that his Personal Behaviour was without Reproach.

> And that the Misfortune, on the Day of Action, was owing to the shameful Behaviour of the Private Men; and not to any Misconduct or Misbehaviour of Sir *John Cope*…[9]

The board next went on to clear Fowke and Lascelles of wrongdoing as well. Here too, the findings were unanimous.

A constant frustration, in writing this book, has been that little is certain about the battle of Prestonpans except that it happened and the Jacobites won. As in any courtroom trial, the trick is to construct an approximation of the truth out of conflicting testimony by witnesses with widely varying motives and perspectives (except that the lawyer has an advantage over the historian in that he or she has the opportunity to cross-examine). Some of my conclusions, accordingly, are tentative, as the reader will discern from many of the endnotes. One is not. I count it among the few additional certainties that, as to Cope at least, the board was right.

Of Thomas Fowke and Peregrine Lascelles, I am less confident; the board may have sanitised the former's management of the Canter of Coltbridge and the latter's escape from the battlefield. Assuredly dragoon squadron leader Whitney (killed at Falkirk) would not have let Lascelles off so lightly: he sent that officer a stinging letter, after the battle, questioning whether Lascelles could have peregrinated as far as he did, by the time he did, if he had tarried to do his duty under fire.[10] And even in Cope's case there are alarm bells. His unflagging support from his officers is impressive, but they may have had their own stake in the outcome; had he been found culpable, the net might have extended next to them. (That, however, does not explain his warm endorsements from civilians, the egregious Jack excepted.) The same phrases appear, with suspicious frequency, in the remarks of different witnesses, suggesting collusion. ('Stood in awe', as used by both Cope and Loudon, is one example – and since Loudon was testifying by letter, from afar, it is not as though he had been sitting in the board room when Cope delivered the phrase, and decided on his own to repeat it. Besides, there are other examples.) Moreover, Cope enjoyed the favour of the King, as the luckless Admiral Byng did not – indeed, he was welcome at court throughout the war[11] – and this may have weighed somewhat with the board. But the fact is that there was no fair basis on which to fault him.

The anonymous publisher of the board's report, whom we now know to have been Benjamin Robins, agreed. He declared in his preface that, after attending the hearings and studying the evidence, he regretted his earlier harsh assessment of the general and was releasing the report 'to make him the best Reparation in my Power'.[12]

Others among Cope's contemporaries, on both sides of the battle lines, vigorously dissented. They included, curiously, some of

the very folk – Murray of Broughton, James Johnstone – who com-
mended his choice of ground. Their principal criticisms distil into the
following. He should not have marched north; rather, he should have
remained below the Forth, defending its fords, and thereby confining
Charles to the Highlands, where the rebels would soon have melted
away for lack of supplies and money.[13] Having undertaken the march,
he should have stayed at Dalwhinnie once he deemed the Corrieyairack
impassable, instead of inspiriting his enemies by appearing to flee before
them to Inverness.[14] He should have brought his men's swords with him
– not left them at Stirling.[15] He should have done what Charles feared
he might do: slip through the Jacobite lines and recapture Edinburgh
when Lord George left the roads to the capital unguarded.[16] He should
have chosen a different battlefield, one that would not have boxed him
in with ditches and enclosures – say, the real Gladsmuir – where the
dragoons could manoeuvre freely. (This, from Murray of Broughton,
who had described the Prestonpans battlefield as 'impossible to
attack'.)[17] Having chosen Prestonpans, he should have attacked, instead
of adopting a defensive posture, which, again, inspirited his enemies.[18]
He should have waited at Berwick for the Flanders battalions and the
Dutch.[19]

Most of these carpings are risible. Staying at Dalwhinnie made no
sense: as Cope and his council rightly concluded, the Jacobites could
have by-passed him and swept into the Lowlands, and it would have been
his troops, not theirs, who melted away for lack of supplies. The swords
would have made no difference. The only ones that might have been
effective were the broadswords of the Highland companies, and those
companies were not on the battlefield; they were guarding the baggage
at Cockenzie. The decorative hangers of the regular infantry would have
been useless, if, indeed, that infantry could even have been persuaded to
carry them, which British foot were often unwilling to do. The Edinburgh
option made no sense either: not unless Cope destroyed Charles's army
first. Otherwise he would have found himself inside the city, surrounded
by a foe that was gaining recruits almost daily, and he would have been
boxed in well and truly. To paraphrase scripture, it little profits a man to
gain his country's capital if in doing so he loses his country. Suggesting
a different battlefield, in the same general locality, falls ill from the pen
of one – Murray of Broughton – who, besides lacking military experience, had praised, just six pages earlier, the field that Cope had chosen.[20]

As for attacking the Jacobites from below in their camp on Falside Hill, anyone visiting the site even today would recognise the proposal as suicidal, and it would have been more so then when the intervening ground was mottled with ditches, marshes, and collapsed bottle mines.

The only two criticisms that merit serious consideration, therefore, are the first and the last: that he should have remained below the Forth, and that he should have awaited reinforcements at Berwick.

The most vigorous proponent of the former was James Johnstone. We have already seen that Johnstone vastly overestimated Cope's manpower. As Johnstone's own editor points out in a footnote, Cope had neither enough troops nor enough artillery to protect the Forth's numerous crossings,[21] and would have had to disperse his meagre forces dangerously even to try. The critique also overlooks the fact that Cope's principal reason for marching north was to seek recruits from the putative loyal clans. This was an eminently sensible objective, especially since his most trusted civilian advisors had assured him of success.

Besides, he had no choice. As he reminded the Board, he had his positive orders.[22]

It is true that Cope himself had wanted to 'alter my design', and stay put, when he received mistaken information that the French had landed in force to the north of him. It is also true that he bitterly regretted not having done just that upon discovering that the expression 'loyal clans' was an oxymoron. What he had in mind, though, was different from what Johnstone was suggesting. His strategy – had Tweeddale left him free to pursue it – would not have been to defend the Forth crossings and bottle up his foes in the Highlands (an impossible task), but rather to keep his army concentrated, let the Jacobites pass into the Lowlands, and do battle with them there.[23]

Which leads into the second criticism: why would Cope seek battle, at Prestonpans or anywhere else, especially after he had come to believe – erroneously, but still he believed it – that the Jacobites outnumbered him by something like two to one? Why not await reinforcements?

This was Murray of Broughton's plaint, and one might note at the outset that it is at odds with one of that gentleman's other arguments: namely, that Cope should not have inspirited his enemies by shirking a possible confrontation at Dalwhinnie. But it is flawed even on its own merits. Charles too might have augmented his forces if Cope had let him prance about in the meantime unmolested. And Cope was reasonable in thinking that he would win regardless of any perceived numerical disparity. He had cavalry, and he had artillery. The Jacobites had neither, and by all accounts feared both.[24]

What is more, he *would* have won, if Whitney's squadron had done its duty and flanked the rebel left as its colonel had ordered.[25] The defeat, therefore, was not the product of flawed strategy, flawed tactics or flawed intelligence. It was the product of flawed soldiering. And for that, Cope was not responsible. He had to play with the hand he was given. Nor could he have anticipated that his men would fail him, inasmuch as their morale was high until the moment of action.

What happened to shake that morale? In Cope's view and others', it was 'The Manner in which the Enemy came on, which was quicker than can be described...'.[26] Though the men had 'long been warned' to expect this, no warning could prepare them for the reality: so different from the measured pace of the European warfare for which they were trained.

Cope's explanation is accurate as far as it goes. What he did not say, because eighteenth-century minds were not acculturated to think in such terms, was that the fears engendered by the unfamiliar 'celerity'[27] of the charge fed into deeper fears: those arising from the cultural and ethnic biases of Englishmen and Lowlanders against the dreaded Highland Other. Such feelings, of course, are not unique to Great Britain. And that is why Johnstone's anonymous editor is right when he observes that irregulars 'will almost always defeat an equal or even a greater number of regular troops'[28] – especially, he might have added, when the regulars are inexperienced and impressionable. Culloden was the exception that proved the rule, and the King's soldiers there were veterans.

A decade later Edward Braddock, another British general who has been unjustly traduced in history texts and popular myths, suffered an even more crushing defeat at the hands of irregulars near present-day Pittsburgh, in North America. Like Cope, and even more than Cope, he had conducted a march worthy of a Hannibal – until, a half dozen miles from its conclusion, he was set upon by French-led American Indians, who to Britons closely resembled Highlanders in their weapons, tactics and savagery. His own troops were – *déjà vu* all over again – mostly raw levies, and they panicked, crumbled and were butchered.[29] Braddock, less fortunate than Cope, was among the victims. So was the brave and decent Peter Halkett – Sir Peter and a full colonel now – who perished with his son. One wonders what memories flashed through his mind at the end.

We have concluded our story. It remains to trace the fate of the principal actors.

Of the Moidart Seven, O'Sullivan and Sir John MacDonald faded into obscurity, to the point where their dates of death are unknown. MacDonald, as a French national, surrendered and was repatriated after Culloden, then disappears from view.[30] While the rebellion lasted (and indeed for years to come), O'Sullivan quarrelled famously with George Murray about the choice of ground at Culloden and divers other matters. When it ended, he fled with Charles to the Western Isles, made his way separately to France, rejoined the Prince in Paris, and from there went to Rome, where he wrote his *Narrative* at James Francis' request. Returning to France, he re-joined the French army, married, and fathered a son, who lived till 1824. He fell out for a time with Charles, but the falling-out seems to have been one-sided: a mark of Charles's growing paranoia. The last mention of him in any record is in late 1760, after which he too disappears from view.[31]

Strickland was at Carlisle when the city fell to Cumberland. His sudden death there, from a stroke or heart attack, spared him a worse fate.[32]

Tullibardine, like MacDonald, surrendered following Culloden. Not being a French subject (despite having spent half his life in that country), he was consigned to the Tower, and died a prisoner in July 1746 – less than three months after the battle. His death, too, may have been a deliverance.[33]

Thomas Sheridan was another who did not long survive the rebellion, but at least he lived his last months in freedom. Escaping to Rome, he died in November 1746.[34]

Parson George Kelly arrived in France before the others: Charles sent him across the Channel in late September to report the Prestonpans victory. He did not return. Upon Charles's own arrival, Kelly became his secretary, and was blamed by fellow Jacobites for encouraging his burgeoning alcoholic excesses. Eventually they fell out (do we see the beginning of a pattern here?). Estranged from his former master, Kelly died, in Paris, in 1762.[35]

Banker Aeneas MacDonald was the longest lived of the Seven, dying in Paris during the French Revolution, perhaps as one of its victims. He was in Barra on 16 April 1746, the day of Culloden, collecting money owed to the Prince: a mission that led to yet another falling out, because Charles wrongly suspected him of pocketing it. He too surrendered afterward, but was eventually released in exchange for what appears to have been some very half-hearted cooperation with government interrogators. He then went back to France, where from the 1750s onward he avoided politics and devoted himself entirely to business.[36]

As for the remaining Jacobite leaders:

James Drummond, Duke of Perth, did not live to fall out with Charles Edward. He died in May 1746, on board a ship that was carrying him to France.[37]

Donald Cameron of Lochiel reached France safely, but not for long: he died there in 1748. Charles, true to his bond, procured for him the colonelcy of a French regiment, to compensate him for his lost estates – the much-encumbered Sobieska jewels being unavailable.[38]

Captured and imprisoned after Culloden, John Murray of Broughton saved his neck and gained a British pension by testifying against the slippery Lord Lovat – mostly about the discussions at Invergarry between Charles and Fraser of Gortuleg, which Murray had witnessed. For that betrayal, embittered former comrades called him ever afterward 'Mr Evidence Murray', though Lovat would probably have gone to the block without Murray's testimony, and the Secretary withheld revelations that might have incriminated others. Charles, uncharacteristically, forgave him – the two men had an apparently cordial meeting in 1763 – but he was among the few: Walter Scott recalled that his father flung out of a window a teacup from which Murray had drunk. Deserted by his wife, Murray died in 1777 – perhaps in a madhouse.[39]

Lord George Murray had predicted in his valedictory letter to his Whig brother that his allegiance to the Cause would ruin him, and he was right. He led the last, futile Highland charge at Culloden. A day later, with typical frankness, he sent a reproachful missive to Charles, criticising him and O'Sullivan for mismanaging the war. He then retired to Holland, a permanent exile. Charles, who had always believed him a traitor, refused to have anything to do with him, spurned his efforts at reconciliation, and on one occasion tried to have him arrested. He died, still in Holland, in 1760. He had his flaws, but he was a good man, and deserved better of his Prince.

This is not the place to trace the four-decades-long decline of Charles Edward Stuart, culminating in his sordid death in 1788. That sad tale of increasing isolation and emotional disintegration has been well told by many others, though nowhere as well as in Frank McLynn's aptly-entitled *Charles Edward Stuart: A Tragedy In Many Acts*, Oxford, 1991.

He had an overweening ego – that much is obvious – but in fairness one must recognise that there was no clear line, in his mind, between ego, hereditary right, and his religious duty to enforce that right: a duty of which even a sceptic such as he must have been sensible. To his eternal credit, he was never cruel to his enemies. But he was cruel to his friends, and even crueller to himself.

John Hay, Marquess of Tweeddale, resigned his Secretaryship in January 1746 amid allegations of incompetence, and the office lapsed until the next century. His political career was not quite over, however, for he was named Lord-Justice-General in 1761, the year before he died.[40] He is best known for his comment on the performance of the dragoons: 'The dragoons have no excuse but that they are from Ireland'.[41]

Duncan Forbes was in no small sense a casualty of the '45. He spent considerable sums, from his own pocket, raising and equipping troops and trying to keep wavering chiefs in the fold, and the government never repaid him. He also fell out of favour, after the war, for urging clemency on Cumberland – a message that the 'Martial Boy' (as his adulators called him) did not want to hear. His depression over these displays of ingratitude may have contributed to his death in 1747. The self-medication that he likely prescribed for the depression – recall the opening pages of the 'Run-Up' chapter – would have contributed also. He remained a staunch friend to Cope, testifying for him at the inquiry (where he blamed himself for misgauging clan loyalties),[42] and writing him to express support when the rest of Hanoverian Britain was demanding the general's head.[43]

Relieved of his command after Prestonpans, and reviled by much of the country, Sir John Cope nevertheless found solace even before the Board exonerated him. He had bet ten thousand pounds that his successor would be beaten too, and at Falkirk he won his wager.[44] It is said that his was among the only cheerful faces in the room when the news of that battle reached St James.[45] It must have been especially gratifying that the losing general was Henry Hawley, who had railed against him over the Prestonpans debacle. In addition, the Duke of Cumberland, upon superseding Hawley, solicited Cope's advice.[46] Evidently his misfortune had not depleted his credit with people who mattered.

Nor did it blight his career. He never again commanded in the field, but that was because of a worsening gout condition and not because he was in official disfavour. In 1749 we find him serving, with Hawley, on a board that was reviewing the organisation and drill of the cavalry.[47] In 1751, he was posted to the general staff in Ireland, and appears to have kept the position until his death nine years later.[48]

Though his career continued to flourish, his personal life was marred by tragedy: his only legitimate child, a diplomat, hanged himself in 1756. However, he also fathered an illegitimate son and daughter, both by the same mother, and he sent them to good schools. The son, who was older by a year, was born in May 1747, so the general was evidently finding solace of another sort while his professional conduct was still under scrutiny.[49]

In a narrative that is already replete with uncertainties, it is fitting to end by noting that the date of Cope's death is in doubt. He died on either 28 July or 1 August 1760,[50] at 26 St James's Place, a handsome house that he built during the '45 (German aircraft destroyed it during World War II),[51] and was buried in St James's church, Piccadilly on the 5th.[52] His second wife, Elizabeth, whom he had married in 1736, was the executor of his will, the principal beneficiaries of which were the two illegitimate children. It is an interesting aside that when the widow died in turn, fourteen years later, the illegitimate daughter, also named Elizabeth, was living with her in apparent amity.[53]

Urbanisation and industrialisation have altered the East Lothian landscape. But the Prestonpans battlefield remains relatively pristine, although the ditches, marshes and mines are gone. One modern intrusion may even be for the better: a nearby artificial hill, overlooking the field from the south. Originally built as a ski slope, it was converted into an observation post and monument when the skiing venture failed.[54] The view is excellent, and an exhibit at the top depicts and explains the battle.

Imagination does the rest. You can climb the Pentlands with Patrick Crichton's ghost and watch the dragoons assemble at Corstorphine. You can stand in the Prestonpans kirk tower with Alexander Carlyle and observe the mysterious westward movements of the Atholl Brigade. And if you ascend to the pinnacle of Arthur's Seat and look east, you can see, in the mind's eye, the doomed red-coated army, a dressy, finical little man at its head, marching with alacrity and spirits to Haddington from Dunbar.

NOTES

INTRODUCTION

1   *Encyclopaedia Britannica* (11th Edition),
    vol. 10, New York, 1911, pp.609, 611.

2   George Thomson, *The First
    Churchill: The Life of John, 1st Duke of
    Marlborough*, London, 1979, pp.142, 155.

3   Frank McLynn, *The Jacobites*
    ('McLynn, *Jacobites*'), London, 1985,
    p.106 (rebellion came 'within an ace'
    of success); W.A. Speck, *The Butcher:
    The Duke of Cumberland and the
    Suppression of the '45* (paperback ed.),
    Caernarfon, 1995, p.203 (it 'had not
    seriously threatened' the regime).

4   Benjamin Robins (ed.), *The Report
    of the Proceedings and Opinion of the
    Board of General Officers, On Their
    Examination into the Conduct, Behaviour
    and Proceedings of Lieutenant-General Sir
    John Cope, Knight of the Bath, Colonel
    Peregrine Lascelles, and Brigadier-General
    Thomas Fowke* ('Cope'), London,
    1749, p.1 (preliminary statement by
    board). Henceforward, when the
    reference is to Cope's testimony, only
    the page number will be cited; when
    the reference is to the testimony of
    another witness, or to the Appendix,
    the witness's name, or the Appendix
    number, will be cited in parentheses
    after the page number. References to
    the board's statements, or the editor's
    preface, will be also be identified in
    parentheses after the page number, as
    above.

5   Cope, p.vi (editor's preface); General
    Sir Robert Cadell, *Sir John Cope
    and the Rebellion of 1745* ('Cadell'),
    Edinburgh and London, p.274.

6   John Home, *The History of the
    Rebellion in the Year 1745* ('Home'),
    London, 1802, p.55.

7   Alexander Carlyle, *Autobiography of
    Alexander Carlyle of Inveresk* ('Carlyle'),
    London and Edinburgh, 1910, p.146.

8   Fitzroy Maclean, *Bonnie Prince Charlie*
    ('Maclean'), New York, 1989, p.54.

9   Cope, p.iii (editor's preface) (emphasis
    in original).

10 Michael Hook and Walter Ross, *The
    'Forty-Five: The Last Jacobite Rebellion*
    ('Hook and Ross'), Edinburgh, 1995,
    p.55. I have reproduced only selected
    stanzas. Robert Burns later wrote
    equally unflattering lyrics to the same
    melody. Some versions mix the two
    sets of lyrics.

11 T.P.H., 'Cope, Sir John', *Dictionary of
    National Biography* ('*DNB*'), Oxford,
    1900, p.1092.

12 Stephen Brumwell, 'Cope, Sir John',
    Oxford Dictionary of National Biography
    ('*ODNB*'), Oxford, 2004, p.314.

13 Peter de Polnay, *Death of a Legend: The
    True Story of Bonnie Prince Charlie* ('de
    Polnay'), London, 1952, p.25.

14 Katherine Tomasson and Francis
    Buist, *Battles of the '45* ('Tomasson and
    Buist'), New York, 1962, p.79.

15 Evelyn Lord, *The Stuarts' Secret Army:
    English Jacobites 1689–1752*, Harlow,

2004, p.192.

16 Rupert Jarvis, 'Cope's March North, 1745' ('Cope's March'), in Rupert Jarvis, *Collected Papers on the Jacobite Risings*, vol. I ('Jarvis'), Manchester, 1971, p.20.

17 Bruce Lenman, 'Introduction: The Jacobite Army and its Achievement', in Alastair Livingstone, Christian Aikman and Betty Hart (eds), *No Quarter Given: The Muster Roll of Prince Charles Edward Stuart's Army, 1745–46* (3rd Edition) ('*Muster Roll*'), Glasgow, 2001, p.xxii (Stuart restoration would have wrought significant changes in British domestic and foreign policy); McLynn, *Jacobites*, pp.120–121 ('unlikely that a mere change in dynasty…would greatly alter underlying trends and policies'); Daniel Szechi, *The Jacobites: Britain and Europe 1688–1788* ('Szechi'), Manchester, 1994, p.136 ('So what?').

I THE RUN–UP

1 Cope, p.105 (App. I).

2 Andrew Lang, *Prince Charles Edward Stuart* ('Lang'), London, 1903, p.107.

3 Moray McLaren, *Bonnie Prince Charlie* ('McLaren'), New York, 1972, p.50.

4 Bruce Lenman, *The Jacobite Risings in Britain 1689–1746* ('Lenman, *Risings*'), Aberdeen, 1995 (paperback), p.210.

5 Howard Nenner, *The Right to be King*, Chapel Hill, 1995, p.31; Paul Monod, *Jacobitism and the English People, 1688–1788* ('Monod'), Cambridge, 1989, p.18.

6 Anon., *The Trials of King Charles I and Some of the Regicides* (7th Edition), London, 1861, p.47.

7 Monod, pp.18–20.

8 The terms 'Presbyterian' and 'Episcopal' are juxtaposed only for simplicity's sake. 'There were never two large and distinct churches in seventeenth-century Scotland; rather, there were two groups of men struggling for control of the Church of Scotland.' Lenman, *Risings*, p.56.

9 Gerald Warner, *The Scottish Tory Party: A History* ('Warner'), London, 1988, p.9.

10 Christopher Duffy, *The '45* ('Duffy'), London, 2003, pp.554–569.

11 George S. Pryde (ed.), *The Treaty of Union of Scotland and England 1707*, London, 1950, reprinted Westport, Conn., 1979, p.44.

12 Bruce Lenman and John Gibson, *The Jacobite Threat – England, Scotland, Ireland, France: a Source Book* ('Lenman and Gibson'), Edinburgh, 1990, pp.107–108.

13 David Daiches, *Bonnie Prince Charlie* ('Daiches'), London, 1973, p.62 (over 8,000); Warner, p.32 (9,000); Szechi, p.78 (10,000).

14 Bruce Lenman, *The Jacobite Cause* (2nd Edition) ('Lenman, *Cause*'), Edinburgh, 1992, p.83. But see Duffy, p.146 (original six companies had 60 men apiece). Since three of the original companies were commanded by captains and three by lower-ranking captain-lieutenants, it seems more probable that the former were larger. H.D. MacWilliam, *The Black Watch Mutiny Records* ('Mutiny Records'), London, 1910, p.xxxi.

15 Duffy, p.146; John Prebble, *Mutiny: Highland Regiments in Revolt 1743–1804*, Harmondsworth, 1975, p.26 (tartans), p.27 (blackmail).

16 *Mutiny Records*, p.xxiii.

17 Anon., *A Short History of the Highland Regiment* ('Short History'), originally published 1743, reprint edition Cornwallville, 1963, p.21 (Lovat's captaincy); W.C. MacKenzie, *Lovat of the Forty-Five*, Edinburgh and London 1934, pp.37–38 (his religion).

18 Frank McLynn, *France and the Jacobites* ('McLynn, *France*'), Edinburgh, 1981, pp.13, 42–47.

19 Frank McLynn, *Charles Edward Stuart:*

A Tragedy In Many Acts ('McLynn, *CES*'), Oxford, 1991, pp.66–82; Daiches, pp.88–104; Lenman and Gibson, pp.182–190.

20 Lenman, *Risings*, p.236.

21 McLynn, *France*, p.13; Lenman and Gibson, p.185.

22 McLynn, *France*, pp.19–20.

23 Duffy, p.43. But see McLynn, *France*, p.24 (10,000).

24 Evan Charteris (ed.), *A Short Account of the Affairs of Scotland in the Years 1744, 1745, 1746* by David, Lord Elcho ('*Affairs*'), Edinburgh, 1973, p.234; Robert Bell (ed.), *Memorials of John Murray of Broughton* ('*Memorials*'), Edinburgh, 1898, p.428 (App. II-9).

25 Monod, pp.45–69, 161–232.

26 Id., pp.111–118 (smugglers), 225 (cities and towns), 228 (London Irish), 271 (gentry).

27 Duffy, pp.53, 60–61.

28 McLynn, *France*, pp.85–88, 116–163.

29 Murray Pittock, *The Myth of the Jacobite Clans* ('Pittock'), Edinburgh, 1995, pp.57–58.

30 McLynn, *Jacobites*, p.67 (Scottish population); M. Dorothy George, *London Life In the Eighteenth Century* (2nd ed.), Chicago, 1984, p.319 (English).

31 Pittock, p.60; Duffy, p.50.

32 Szechi, p.77.

33 Pittock, p.84.

34 Szechi, p.18.

35 The two communions did not formally unite until 1867. Pittock, p.105.

36 Monod, p.142.

37 Lenman, *Risings*, p.130 ('most'); Duffy, p.76 ('Only a minority').

38 Lenman, *Risings*, p.130.

39 Duffy, p.77; Szechi, p.20.

40 Lenman, *Cause*, pp.76, 88.

41 Pittock, pp.97–99.

42 Lenman, *Risings*, p.223.

43 Lenman, *Risings*, pp.129–132, *Cause*, pp.86–87; Monod, pp.139–140.

44 Duffy, p.71.

45 Id., p.77.

46 Id., p.552.

47 Alexander MacBean, 'Memorial Concerning the Highlands', in Walter Blaikie (ed.), *Origins of the 'Forty-Five*, Edinburgh, 1975, pp.89–90.

48 Pittock, p.84 ('confessional issue' probably 'paramount').

49 Eveline Cruickshanks, *Political Untouchables: The Tories and the 'Forty-Five* ('Cruickshanks'), New York, 1979, p.9.

50 Id., p.4; McLynn, *Jacobites*, p.81.

51 Cruickshanks, p.6.

52 Bruce Lenman, 'The Place of Prince Charles and the '45 in the Jacobite Tradition', in Robert Woosnam-Savage (ed.), *1745: Charles Edward Stuart and the Jacobites* ('Woosnam-Savage'), Edinburgh, 1995, p.11; Linda Colley, *In Defiance of Oligarchy: The Tory Party 1714–60* ('Colley'), Cambridge, 1982, pp.41–44.

53 Monod, pp.16, 23; Colley, pp.28–49.

54 Duffy, p.43; Cruickshanks, p.70; McLynn, *Jacobites*, p.63.

55 Supra n.9.

56 Warner, p.18.

57 Id., p.11.

58 Id., p.24 (emphasis added).

59 Stuart Reid, *1745: A Military History of the Last Jacobite Rising* ('Reid, *1745*'), New York, 1966, p.6.

60 Duffy, p.91.

61 Reid, *1745*, p.5; McLynn, *CES*, p.176.

62 Duffy, pp.552–553, 565–566.

63 Id., pp.553–554 (MacKenzies, Grants); McLynn, *CES*, p.176 (MacLeods, MacKintoshes).

64 Duffy, p.565; Bruce Lenman, *The Jacobite Clans of the Great Glen 1650–1784* ('Lenman, *Clans*'), Aberdeen, 1995 (paperback), pp.155–156.

65 Lenman, *Risings*, p.256, *Clans*, p.167.

66 McLynn, *Jacobites*, p.73.

67 John Prebble, *The Lion in the North*, Harmondsworth, 1973, pp.33–34, 37–38, 232–233; Lenman, *Risings*, p.139.

68 Lenman, *Risings*, p.139.

69 Id., pp.245–246.

70 Pittock, p.55; Duffy, pp.89–90.

71 Pittock, p.60; Duffy, p.80.

72 Duffy, p.80. But see McLynn, *Jacobites*, p.67 (Highlanders constituted over half Scotland's population ten years after Rising despite Rising-related population losses).

73 McLynn, *Jacobites*, p.70 (debts and titles); Lenman, *Clans*, pp.22–23 (Campbell tacksmen).

74 Lenman, *Risings*, p.248; McLynn, *Jacobites*, p.73.

75 Lenman, *Risings*, p.255; Hook and Ross, pp.14–15.

76 Lenman, *Risings*, p.146.

77 McLynn, *Jacobites*, p.88.

78 Katherine Tomasson, *The Jacobite General* ('Tomasson'), Edinburgh and London, 1958, p.20.

79 Duffy, pp.79–80; McLynn, *CES*, p.162.

80 McLynn, *France*, p.18.

81 Duffy, pp.48–49, 542; Lenman, *Risings*, p.205; McLynn, *Jacobites*, pp.82–83, *CES*, p.181; Pittock, p.82; Szechi, pp.23, 34; Monod, pp.45–69, 95–125, 161–266.

82 Pittock, p.82.

83 Monod, pp.16, 23.

84 McLynn, *Jacobites*, p.147; Monod, p.81.

85 McLynn, *Jacobites*, p.148.

86 Lenman and Gibson, p.212.

87 McLynn, *Jacobites*, p.148.

88 Id., pp.77, 79.

89 McLynn, *France*, p.236.

90 Szechi, pp.150–151 (quoting Stuart Papers); Cruickshanks, pp.47–49.

91 McLynn, *CES*, p.519.

92 Lenman, *Risings*, p.256.

93 Pittock, passim.

94 Szechi, pp.2–6.

95 *Memorials*, p.180; Duffy, p.174 (6,000 in Britain); Rupert Jarvis, 'Cope's Forces, August 1745' ('Cope's Forces'), in Jarvis, p.44.

96 Cope, pp.105–106 (App. I).

97 Id.

98 Szechi, p.103.

99 Cope, pp.106–107 (App. II).

100 Id., pp.107–109 (App. II–IV).

2 THE ARMIES

1 Jarvis, Cope's Forces.

2 J.A. Houlding, *Fit For Service: The Training of the British Army 1715–1795* ('Houlding'), New York, 1981, pp.101–115; I.F. Burton and A.N. Newman, 'Sir John Cope: Promotion In the Eighteenth Century Army' ('Burton and Newman'), in *The English Historical Review*, vol. 78 no. 309, October 1963, pp.655–668.

3 Burton and Newman, p.658. While commander-in-chief in Scotland, Cope once tried to fill a vacancy with his own candidate over the head of the most senior officer who had bid for the position. The officer beseeched Duncan Forbes to intervene on his behalf. The outcome is unknown. Duncan Warrand (ed.), *More Culloden Papers* ('*MCP*'), vol. III, Inverness, 1927, p.211.

4 Burton and Newman, p.661.

5 Duffy, p.132; Houlding, pp.172–195 (regulations and treatises), 271–273 (officer training).

6 Houlding, pp.109–110. But see Stuart Reid, *Like Hungry Wolves: Culloden Moor 16 April 1746* ('Reid, *LHW*'), London, 1994, pp.33–34 (took ten years to become a captain).

7 A.J. Guy, 'King George's Army, 1714–1750' ('Guy'), in Woosnam-Savage, p.43.

8 Houlding, p.50; Peter Harrington, *Culloden 1746: the Highland Clans' Last Charge* ('Harrington'), London, 1991, p.28 (regimental strength). But see Guy, p.43 (1,000). Lucky to muster half: Harrington, p.28; Duffy, p.132; Reid, *LHW*, p.35.

9 Burton and Newman, p.661.

10 Id.

11 Houlding, pp.102, 107–108.

12 Id., p.117 n.32; Harrington p.26; Reid,

LHW, p.29.

13   Reid, *LHW*, p.29.
14   Houlding, p.117; Harrington, p.26.
15   Houlding, p.118; Reid, *LHW*, p.29.
16   Reid, *LHW*, pp.29–30; Duffy, p.132.
17   Houlding, p.118.
18   Id., p.16 n.31.
19   Id., pp.120–125; Harrington, p.26.
20   Houlding, pp.1–45, 55–98 *passim*
      (dispersal and effect on training),
      301–302 (difficulty of finding suitable
      facilities); Duffy, p.146; Reid, *LHW*,
      p.31.
21   Reid, *LHW*, p.36.
22   Id., pp.34–35; Harrington, p.28.
23   Houlding, pp.260–261, 277–279. But
      see Peter Smith, *The Invasion of 1745:
      The Drama in Lancashire and Cheshire*,
      Manchester, 1993, p.26 (infantry in
      1740s marched at 75 paces a minute).
      Use of drum for signalling: Gen.
      Richard Kane, *Campaigns of King
      William and Queen Anne; from 1689,
      to 1712. Also, A New System of Military
      Discipline, For a Battalion of Foot in
      Action...* ('Kane'), 1745, pp.115–120.
24   Houlding, p.139; Reid, *LHW*, p.37;
      Harrington, p.29.
25   Reid, *LHW*, p.38.
26   Houlding, p.151.
27   Percy Sumner (ed.), 'General
      Hawley's "Chaos"' ('Chaos'), in
      *The Journal of the Society For Army
      Historical Research*, vol. 26, 1948, pp.91,
      93. 'Chaos' was an essay that Hawley
      wrote either for his own amusement
      or for presentation to the Duke of
      Cumberland. The title was his.
28   Benjamin Cole, *The Soldier's Pocket
      Companion, Or the Manual Exercise of
      our British Foot...* ('Cole'), London,
      1746 (facsimile edition), passim;
      Houlding, pp.261–263; Reid, *LHW*,
      p.31.
29   Cole, pp.65–87.
30   Houlding, p.262.
31   Harrington, p.29; Reid, *LHW*, p.37.
32   Houlding, pp.262–263, 279–280.
33   Id., pp.90, 263.

34   Id., p.281; Reid, *LHW*, p.38; Duffy,
      p.140.
35   Chaos, p.93.
36   Id.
37   Houlding, pp.322–346.
38   Houlding, p.xx; Harrington, pp.26–
      27; Reid, *LHW*, p.35.
39   Houlding, p.44 n.86 and text.
40   Harrington, p.26.
41   Houlding, p.91; Reid, *LHW*, p.35.
42   Houlding, pp.49–50.
43   Guy, pp.43–44.
44   Duffy, p.132; Houlding, p.xxi.
45   Kane, pp.111–115; Houlding, pp.90–
      93.
46   Houlding, pp.90–93; Duffy, pp.140–
      141; Reid, *LHW*, pp.36–37.
47   Duffy, p.140; Reid, *LHW*, p.38.
48   Duffy, p.140; Reid, *LHW*, p.36.
49   Houlding, p.93.
50   Id.
51   Reid, *LHW*, p.38.
52   Duffy, p.140; Reid, *LHW*, p.37. But
      see Harrington, p.29 (four to five
      rounds per minute); Guy, p.47 (one or
      two).
53   Reid, *LHW*, p.37. See Houlding,
      pp.262–263 (better marksmen might
      score hits 20 to 25 per cent of the
      time from 70 to 75 yards).
54   Houlding, p.93; Duffy, p.141.
55   Reid, *LHW*, p.38.
56   Duffy, p.141.
57   Houlding, pp.264–265; Harrington,
      p.31; Reid, *LHW*, p.39.
58   Houlding, pp.126, 264.
59   Harrington, p.31.
60   Reid, *LHW*, p.39. But see
      Harrington, p.32 (barrel was 27 to 36
      inches long).
61   Reid, *LHW*, p.39; Harrington, p.33.
62   Reid, *LHW*, p.39.
63   Harrington, p.32.
64   Reid, *1745*, p.28, *LHW* p.39;
      Houlding, p.94; Duffy, p.142.
65   Reid, *LHW*, p.39.
66   Id.
67   Houlding, p.xii.
68   Id., p.11.

69 Harrington, p.33.

70 Id.

71 Tomasson and Buist, p.31.

72 Duffy, pp.143–144.

73 Jarvis, 'The Lieutenancy and the Militia Laws', in Jarvis, pp.102–103.

74 Id., pp.98–100, 103–107.

75 Id., p.104.

76 Reid, *1745*, p.85; Alexander MacLean, 'Jacobites At Heart: An Account of the Independent Companies' ('MacLean, Jacobites'), in Lesley Scott-Moncrieff (ed.), *The 45: To Gather An Image Whole*, Edinburgh, 1988, p.124.

77 Reid, *1745*, p.85; MacLean, Jacobites, p.125; Duffy, p.147; Harrington, p.34; James Fergusson, *Argyll In the Forty-Five* ('Fergusson'), London, 1951, p.37; Carolly Erickson, *Bonnie Prince Charlie: A Biography* ('Erickson'), New York, 1989, p.150. These writers disagree about the numbers and dates of the commissions.

78 Cope, p.5.

79 Jarvis, Cope's Forces, p.44.

80 Cope, p.5 (unit names and depletions from drafts); Jarvis, Cope's Forces, pp.30–31, 45 n.47; Duffy, pp.131, 145–146; Reid, *1745*, pp.12–14, *LHW*, pp.11–12 (unit origins and assignments); Duffy, p.131 (quoting General Hawley's description of Sempill's as two-third Scottish; the context is that Hawley was so desperate for warm bodies that he would accept them in spite of their provenance).

81 Cope, p.5; Jarvis, Cope's Forces, p.45 n.25.

82 Reid, *1745*, p.13; *LHW*, p.11.

83 Jarvis, Cope's Forces, p.44.

84 Houlding, p.353; Duffy, p.131.

85 Jarvis, Cope's Forces, p.35.

86 Tomasson and Buist, p.29.

87 Houlding, p.46.

88 Duffy, p.142.

89 Reid, *1745*, pp.13–14, *LHW*, p.11.

90 Cope, p.54 (Master-Gunner Griffith).

91 Tomasson and Buist, p.29.

92 Sir John Clerk of Penicuik, *Memoirs* (John Gray, ed.), Edinburgh, 1892, p.180.

93 Houlding, p.104.

94 Burton and Newman, pp.655–656; *MCP*, vol. III, pp.216–217; Cadell, p.28.

95 Burton and Newman, *passim*; *DNB*, p.1091; *ODNB*, pp.314–315.

96 Lenman, *Risings*, p.251.

97 *MCP*, vol. III, pp.211, 215–216.

98 James Johnstone, *Memoirs of the Rebellion of 1745 and 1746* ('Johnstone'), London, 1820, p.11 (ed. note).

99 *MCP*, vol. III, p.218.

100 Cadell, p.28.

101 *DNB*, p.1091.

102 *Johnson's Revised Dictionary As Improved By Todd and Abridged By Chalmers* ('Johnson's Dictionary'), Boston, 1828, p.385; George Crabbe, *English Synonymes* ('Crabbe'), New York, 1831, p.386; *Webster's New International Dictionary of the English Language* (2nd ed. unabridged) ('Webster's 2nd'), Springfield, 1961, p.950.

103 Webster's 2nd, p.950.

104 Except where otherwise noted, the material in this section is based on Duffy, pp.99–123; Reid, *1745*, pp.199–211 (App. 3); *LHW*, pp.40–48; and Allan Carswell, '"The Most Despicable Enemy That Are"', in Woosnam-Savage, pp.29–40.

105 See, e.g., *The Orderly Book of Lord Ogilvy's Regiment in the Army of Prince Charles Edward Stuart 10 October, 1745, to 21 April, 1746*, Special Number, vol. II, *Journal of the Society of Army Historical Research*, Heaton Mersey, 1923.

106 But see Reid, *LHW*, p.44 (quoting General Hawley as saying the line was four deep).

107 Cope, p.49 (Lieutenant-Colonel Whitefoord); Cadell, p.40; A. Francis

Steuart (ed.), *The Woodhouselee MS.* ('*Woodhouselee*'), London and Edinburgh, 1907, p.22.

108. M. Newton, 'The History of the Fiery Cross: Folklore, Literature and Fakelore', in *History Scotland*, vol. 5 no. 3, pp.34–35, May/June 2005.

3 TO EDINBURGH

1   Alistair and Henrietta Tayler (eds), *1745 and After* ('O'Sullivan'), London, 1938, p.13 (Introduction). This book consists principally of the *Narrative* of John William O'Sullivan, but also includes, among its footnotes, unnumbered notes by the editor and numbered notes containing excerpts from the unpublished memoirs of Sir John MacDonald. The Taylers identify them by writing (Ed.) or (M), respectively, at the end of the note, and I shall do the same, after the page cite. Unidentified page cites are from O'Sullivan's *Narrative*.

2   McLynn, *CES*, p.137 ('a military dud'); John Prebble, *Culloden*, New York, 1962, p.93 ('the fool O'Sullivan'). But see Duffy, p.103 ('professional and devoted'); Reid, *1745*, p.19 ('highly competent').

3   E.g., Home, p.36 (60 and 16); *Affairs*, p.238 (60 and 14); 'Journal of Aeneas MacDonald' ('Aeneas MacDonald'), in Robert Forbes (ed.), *The Lyon in Mourning* ('*Lyon*'), vol. I, reprint ed. Edinburgh, 1975, pp.284–285 (64 and 16).

4   McLynn, *CES*, p.118.

5   Id. (4,000); Johnstone, p.2 (ed. note) (3,800).

6   Hook and Ross, p.18.

7   McLynn, *France*, pp.33–34 ('no French minister had any… knowledge'); Lenman, *Risings*, p.242 ('it is clear that the French government knew…').

8   McLynn, *France*, p.33.

9   Supra n.1.

10   McLynn, *CES*, p.109.

11   O'Sullivan, p.3 (Introduction); Duffy, p.65; Home, p.40.

12   Johnstone, p.3.

13   McLynn, *CES*, p.119.

14   *Affairs*, p.237.

15   McLynn, *CES*, p.120; O'Sullivan, p.6 (Introduction); Duffy, p.165; Johnstone, p.3.

16   Johnstone, p.20.

17   Supra n.1.

18   Supra n.3.

19   *Muster Roll*, p.19.

20   Maclean, p.32.

21   'Duncan Cameron's Account' ('Duncan Cameron'), in *Lyon*, vol. I, p.203.

22   Aeneas MacDonald, p.287.

23   Supra n.21.

24   Duncan Cameron, p.204 (old acquaintance); O'Sullivan, p.52 n.2 (M) (passing cattle boat).

25   Aeneas MacDonald, p.289.

26   Cope, p.7.

27   Duncan Cameron, p.205.

28   O'Sullivan, p.55.

29   Id., p.53 (Walsh and O'Sullivan), and n.1 (M) (Walsh); McLynn, p.130 (Walsh and Sheridan).

30   O'Sullivan, p.54 and n.2 (M). But see Aeneas MacDonald, p.289 (meeting occurred off Eriskay).

31   John Gibson, *Lochiel of the '45: The Jacobite Chief and the Prince* ('Gibson, *Lochiel*'), Edinburgh, 1994, p.7.

32   O'Sullivan, p.55 and n.4 (M). Some put the date later, e.g., Aeneas MacDonald, p.292 (3 August); Duffy, p.168 (11 August).

33   McLynn, *CES*, p.131.

34   O'Sullivan, p.54 n.2 (M).

35   'Conversation…with Mr. Hugh MacDonald', in *Lyon*, vol. III, p.50.

36   O'Sullivan, p.54 n. (Ed.).

37   Home, pp.39–40.

38   Gibson, *Lochiel*, pp.1, 21.

39   McLynn, *CES*, p.132.

40   Gibson, *Lochiel*, p.63.

41   McLynn, *CES*, p.576 n.43; Lenman, *Clans*, p.159.

42 Home, p.44.

43 'Conversation With Young Glengarry' ('Glengarry'), in *Lyon*, vol. III, pp.119–121; Gibson, *Lochiel*, p.66.

44 Glengarry, p.121.

45 Gibson, *Lochiel*, p.64. But see Hook and Ross, p.23 (7 August).

46 O'Sullivan, p.58 and n.3 (M) (two barges).

47 Id., p.58.

48 Duffy, p.167.

49 O'Sullivan, p.58.

50 Id., p.57 n.4 (M).

51 Iain Brown and Hugh Cheape (eds), *Witness to Rebellion: John Maclean's Journal of the '45 and the Penicuik Drawings* ('Brown and Cheape'), East Linton, 1996, p.21.

52 McLynn, *CES*, p.135.

53 *Muster Roll*, p.123; Alistair and Henrietta Tayler, *Jacobites of Aberdeenshire and Banffshire in the Forty-Five* ('Aberdeen and Banffshire'), Aberdeen, 1928, p.9.

54 O'Sullivan, p.60 n. (Ed.).

55 Duffy, p.168.

56 E.g., O'Sullivan, p.59.

57 Maclean, p.48.

58 Hook and Ross, p.26; Duffy, p.170.

59 *Aberdeen and Banffshire*, p.17.

60 John Jesse, *Memoirs of the Pretenders and Their Adherents* ('Jesse'), London, 1858, p.131.

61 McLynn, *CES*, p.136 (700); *Memorials*, p.168 (750); Hook and Ross, p.26 (800); O'Sullivan, p.59–60 n.3 (M) (900).

62 Gibson, *Lochiel*, p.74.

63 O'Sullivan, pp.59–60 n.3 (M).

64 Duffy, p.171. See Rosalind Marshall, *Bonnie Prince Charlie* ('Marshall'), Edinburgh, 1988, p.75; Erickson, p.118, Maclean, p.49 (blue border); Jesse, p.134 (Latin motto); Aeneas MacDonald, p.292 (no motto).

65 Hook and Ross, p.12.

66 *Memorials*, pp.168–169.

67 Johnson's Dictionary, p.675; Crabbe, p.301.

68 For some of the many (not always consistent) descriptions of the ceremony, see, e.g., Jesse, p.131; *Memorials*, pp.168–169; Hook and Ross, p.26; Maclean, pp.47–49; Duffy, p.171.

69 *Memorials*, p.168; O'Sullivan, p.60 n.3 (M); McLynn, p.136.

70 Duffy, p.171; Hook and Ross, p.26.

71 Duncan Cameron, p.207 (quoting a Major MacDonnell).

72 Cope, pp.169–170 (App. XLVI), pp.175–176 (App. XLVII).

73 Reid, *1745*, p.14. But see Cope, p.124 (App. XVIII) (Cope issued order).

74 Maclean, p.47.

75 Duffy, p.172; O'Sullivan, p.59. But see Cadell, p.52 (Sweetenham kidnapped from an inn).

76 Duffy, p.173; Cadell, p.47.

77 O'Sullivan, p.61.

78 Cope, p.110 (App. VI).

79 Id., pp.6–7, 110–113 (App. VI–IX).

80 Id., pp.110–111 (App. VII).

81 Fergusson, pp.11–17; Cope, pp.114–116 (App. XI).

82 *MCP*, vol. IV, p.14.

83 Cope, p.116–117 (App. XII).

84 Adrian Goldsworthy, '"Instinctive Genius": The depiction of Caesar the General', in Kathryn Welch and Anton Powell (eds), *Julius Caesar as Artful Reporter: The War Commentaries as Political Instruments*, London, 1998, pp.197–198.

85 Cope, p.124 (App. XVIII).

86 Id., p.119 (App. XIII).

87 Id., p.171 (App. XLVI).

88 Id., pp.8, 21.

89 Id., p.21.

90 Id., p.49 (Whitefoord); Cadell, p.40; *Woodhouselee*, p.22.

91 Cope, p.44; Duffy, p.141; *Woodhouselee*, p.38.

92 Cope, p.118 (App. XIII) (emphasis added).

93 Id., p.122 (App. XV), pp.172–173 (App. XLVII).

94 Id., p.173 (App. XLVII); Jarvis, Cope's March, p.11.

95 Cope, p.120 (App. XIV).

96 Id., pp.122–123 (App. XVI) (emphasis added).

97 Id., p.123 (App. XVII).

98 Id., pp.127–131 (App. XIX–XXII).

99 O'Sullivan, p.60 n.3 (M).

100 Cadell, p.24.

101 Id.

102 Id.; McLynn, p.136.

103 O'Sullivan, p.61; *Memorials*, p.170.

104 McLynn, p.137; Duffy, p.179.

105 O'Sullivan, p.61; *Memorials*, p.168.

106 O' Sullivan, pp.61–62; *Memorials*, p.170; Duffy, pp.179–180.

107 O'Sullivan, p.62.

108 *Memorials*, pp.170–171.

109 McLynn, *CES*, p.577 n.86.

110 *Memorials*, p.170.

111 Id., p.171.

112 O'Sullivan, p.62.

113 Id.

114 Duncan Cameron, p.207.

115 O'Sullivan, p.62.

116 Cope, p.121 (App. XV).

117 Jarvis, Cope's Forces, p.42 (estimated strength 1913); Cope, pp.16–17 (accession of Lascelles's companies at Crieff and Loudon's forty or fifty at Taybridge).

118 Cope, p.21 (cannon); id., p.21; id., p.22 (Master Gunner and Commissary Griffith) (1,500 stand of arms). But see id., pp.16, 17, 22 (Cope, contradicting himself, says 1,000 stand of arms).

119 Cope, p.5.

120 Id., p.23 (Griffith).

121 Id., p.17; id., pp.21–24 (Griffith, Major Talbot, Whitefoord.)

122 Cadell, p.51; Hook and Ross, p.32.

123 Id.

124 Cadell, pp.36, 46, 50; Cope, p.17; id., p.23 (Griffith), 132 (App. XXIV).

125 Cope. pp.15, 132 (App. XXIV).

126 Id., pp.16, 132 (App. XXVI).

127 Id., pp.16–17.

128 Id., p.17.

129 Cadell, pp.21, 47. Glengarry loyalties remained flexible to the end. Another son, Alastair, the eldest, has long been outed as 'Pickle the spy', who betrayed Lochiel's brother Archibald Cameron to the hangman in the aftermath of the 'Elibank Plot' – the last serious attempt at a Jacobite restoration – in 1753. O'Sullivan, p.63 n. (Ed.).

130 Duffy , p.569. But see Cadell, p.47 (identifying 'Menzie' as Glenorchy's kinsman 'Monzie', who had no connection to the Menzies clan).

131 Cope, p.17.

132 Id., p.13.

133 Id., p.45 (Whitefoord).

134 Id., p.17; id., p.18 (Whitefoord, Major Severn, and Captain Leslie).

135 Duffy, p.184 (1,400); Reid, *1745*, p.18 (1,800); *Memorials*, p.175 (1,400 at Glenfinnan, plus later accessions of about 400, minus an unspecified number of desertions); Cope, p.19 (Sweetenham); id., p.20 (1,822 to 1,880, based on intelligence from Duncan Forbes).

136 Cope, p.19.

137 O'Sullivan, pp.62–63. But see *Memorials*, p.172 (Charles received the news even sooner, when he forded the River Lochy immediately after leaving Moy).

138 Hook and Ross, p.34.

139 *Memorials*, pp.173–175. Murray of Broughton's account is not unbiased; excoriated, by former comrades, for having testified against Lovat, he may have been trying to redeem his own reputation at Lovat's expense.

140 McLynn, *CES*, p.137; Duffy, p.181; O'Sullivan, p.68; id., p.63 n.1 (M) (giving inconsistent accounts of when some of these levies arrived).

141 *Memorials*, p.175 (ed. note).

142 Id., p.176.

143 O'Sullivan, p.64 n.2 (M); Duncan Cameron, p.208.

144 *Memorials*, p.176.

145 Cope, p.20; id. (Duncan Forbes).

146 Id., pp.45–46 (Whitefoord).

147 Cadell, pp.55–56.

148 Cope, pp.24–32; id., pp.46–47 (Whitefoord) (description of council proceedings); id., pp.25–26 (council report).

149 Cope's figure does not quite tally with Jarvis's, supra n.117.

150 Cope, p.153 (App. XXXIV).

151 Id., p.65 (Colonel Lascelles).

152 Id., pp.46–47 (Whitefoord).

153 O'Sullivan, p.63; Memorials, p.182. Murray, or his editor, has Charles entering the pass on the 27th, a day before he actually did.

154 E.g., Tomasson and Buist, p.34; Martin Margulies, 'Unlucky or Incompetent? History's Verdict on General Sir John Cope, Part II', in History Scotland, vol. 2 no. 3, p.26, May/June 2002.

155 Cope, p.156 (App. XXXIV); Jarvis, Cope's March, pp.7, 17–20.

156 Lenman, Clans, p.155.

157 Cope, pp.30–31.

158 Jarvis, Cope's March, p.19.

159 Cope, p.31 (Wilson).

160 Memorials, p.177.

161 Jarvis, Cope's March, p.5.

162 Memorials, p.177; O'Sullivan, p.64 n.3 (M).

163 O'Sullivan, p.64 and n.2 (M) (20 miles); Memorials, p.178 (14).

164 The word 'amuse' is Murray's. Memorials, p.178.

165 O'Sullivan, p.65.

166 Memorials, pp.184–185; O'Sullivan, pp.65–66; Cope, pp.152–155 (App. XXXIV).

167 Lenman, Clans, pp.151–156 (Cluny's blackmailing activities); McLynn, p.140 ('soothing, close application', pledge of Sobieska jewels as security); Glengarry, p.121 (jewels as security); Duffy, p.565 (relationship to Lochiel, Lovat).

168 Jarvis, Cope's Forces, p.32.

169 Cope's activities at Inverness: Cope, pp.32–33; id., pp.33–34 (Duncan Forbes), 47 (Whitefoord), 150–154 (App XXXIII, XXXIV).

170 Cope, p.33 (Duncan Forbes).

171 Affairs (Introduction), p.71.

172 Cope, p.154 (App. XXXIV).

173 Id.

174 Id., p.47 (Whitefoord).

175 Cope, p.184 (App. LII).

176 Duncan Cameron, p.208; McLynn, CES, p.140. But see O'Sullivan, p.66; Duffy, p.185 (1 September).

177 Memorials, p.186.

178 Id., pp.188–189; O'Sullivan, p.67.

179 Memorials, p.186.

180 O'Sullivan, p.66.

181 Id.; Muster Roll, p.215.

182 Muster Roll, p.19; McLynn, CES, p.140; Hook and Ross, p.40 (200 Robertsons, but says they joined at Perth). But see Muster Roll, p.229 (only about 100 Robertsons).

183 Memorials, p.187 (but wrong on date).

184 Supra Chapter 2, n.105.

185 O'Sullivan, p.69.

186 Duffy, p.103; Tomasson, p.2.

187 O'Sullivan, p.67.

188 Affairs, p.251; O'Sullivan, pp.67–68, 68 n.1 (M).

189 Tomasson, pp.20–21 (reproducing letter in full).

190 But see Duffy, pp.103–104 ('genuinely formidable'; 'one of the best').

191 Duffy, p.104 (quoting Horace Walpole).

192 Memorials, pp.156–158; Aeneas MacDonald, pp.290–292.

193 George Murray, 'Marches of the Highland Army' ('Marches'), in Robert Chambers (ed.), Jacobite Memoirs of the Rebellion of 1745, London, 1834, pp.30–31.

194 Memorials, p.190.

195 O'Sullivan, p.69.

196 Id., p.67.

197 Id., p.69.

198 Cope, pp.33–34; id., p.48 (Whitefoord).

199 Id., pp.135–136 (App. XXVIII).

200 Id., p.187 (App. LV).

201 C. Woodham Smith, The Charge of the Light Brigade, New York, 1953, p.224.

202 Cope, p.48 (Whitefoord).

203 Home, pp.68–70 (legalities), 73, 78 (numbers); Carlyle, p.121 (numbers).

204 Notional strength: Home, p.63; actual strength, Hook and Ross, p.45 (250), Duffy, p.193 (600).

205 Duffy, p.193; John Gibson, *Edinburgh in the 'Forty-Five* ('Gibson, *Edinburgh*'), Edinburgh, 1995, p.6 (Trained Bands' strength mostly on paper).

206 Home, pp.71–74, 78–81; Carlyle, pp.121–125. Home also became a minister, but is better known in his other capacities.

207 *Woodhouselee*, pp.17, 24; id., p.6 (Crichton's authorship probable but not definitively established).

208 Jacobite army movements: *Memorials*, pp.191–192; O'Sullivan, pp.69–70; Marches, pp.33–35; McLynn, *CES*, p.145; Duffy, pp.188–192.

209 *Memorials*, p.192 (500 men; mistakenly says that Charles led raid); O'Sullivan, p.70 (800); Marches, p.35 (1,000).

210 *Memorials*, p.192.

211 Home, pp.79–83; Carlyle, pp.124–125.

212 *Woodhouselee*, p.14. Neither the name 'Leepshill' nor any of its imaginable variants appears in modern atlases, and I was unable to identify it through inquiries.

213 Home, pp.81–85; Carlyle, pp.126–130; Cope, pp.71 (Brigadier Fowke), 75 (Brigade Major Captain Singleton).

214 Cope, p.70 (Fowke).

215 Id., p.76 (Adjutant Cowse).

216 Id., p.74 (Singleton).

217 *Woodhouselee*, p.19.

218 *Memorials*, p.193.

219 O'Sullivan, p.71.

220 Home, p.86 (letter went out between 10 and 11a.m., when Jacobites were still on the march). But see *Memorials*, p.193; Duffy, p.197 (sent from Corstorphine, after march had ended in early afternoon).

221 Johnstone, p.18 (ed. note).

222 *Woodhouselee*, pp.20–21.

223 Cope, pp.71, 75–76 (Fowke, Singleton, Cowse, Adjutant Ker).

224 *Woodhouselee*, p.20; Home, pp.87–88. Home specifies no number, but implies that the group was small. If it was indeed well mounted, it could not have been 400 strong; the Jacobites at this point had nowhere near that number of cavalry.

225 Home, p.88.

226 Id. ('in full view'); *Woodhouselee*, p.21 ('not draw[ing] bridle').

227 Carlyle, pp.137–138; Home, pp.102–103 n. See Cope, p.77 (Captain Clark, Adjutants Cowse, Ker) (admitting that some dragoons panicked and fled near Prestonpans, though minimising episode and attributing it to false rumours, spread by locals who hoped to avoid having to provide forage, that the rebels were close by).

228 Home, pp.88–93; Carlyle, pp.134–138; Gibson, *Edinburgh*, p.17; Cope, p.76 (Customs Collector Walter Grossett, placing time an hour earlier).

229 *Affairs*, p.255, text and ed. note.

230 *Memorials*, p.194; Home, pp.94–95.

231 Home, p.96 (800); *Affairs*, p.256 (800); O'Sullivan, p.71 (900).

232 Home, pp.95–96; *Memorials*, pp.194–195, O'Sullivan, pp.71–75, *Affairs*, pp.256–257; Gibson, *Edinburgh*, pp.17–18. But see O'Sullivan, pp.71–75 (gate was opened to accommodate an exiting coach, carrying a dragoon officer back to his regiment).

233 O'Sullivan, p.73; *Affairs*, p.257; Duffy, p.197; Cope, p.35.

4 PRESTONPANS 1745

1 Tomasson and Buist, p.55; *Affairs*, p.268.

2 O'Sullivan, p.73.

3 Marches, pp.31–32.

4 *Woodhouselee*, pp.25–26.

5 Id., p.24; *Memorials*, p.197.

6 *Woodhouselee*, p.25; *Affairs*, pp.258–259.

7 Home, pp.100–101.

8 *Woodhouselee*, p.26.

9 Id., pp.25–26; Home, pp.101–102; *Affairs*, p.261; *Memorials*, p.198. But see O'Sullivan, pp.73–74; Duffy, p.198 (apparently following O'Sullivan); Johnstone, p.18 (giving other dates for ceremony).

10 Home, pp.101–102.

11 O'Sullivan, pp.73–74; *Memorials*, p.198.

12 *Affairs*, p.265.

13 *Memorials*, p.198.

14 *Affairs*, pp.261–262.

15 *Memorials*, p.198; *Muster Roll*, pp.65, 174; Duffy, pp.571–573.

16 Tomasson and Buist, p.55; *Affairs*, p.268.

17 Steve Lord, *Walking With Charlie: In the Footsteps of the Forty-Five* ('Lord'), Witney, 2003, p.120.

18 *Affairs*, p.265.

19 Tomasson & Buist, pp.47–48; Tomasson, pp.44–45; O'Sullivan, p.76 n.2 (M). But see *Memorials*, p.202 n. (discussion took place day before battle and it was Lochiel who yielded).

20 Tomasson and Buist, p.48; Jesse, p.173. But see Johnstone, pp.19–20 (impugning Charles's courage, for which his own editor rebukes him, id.). Elcho is supposed to have called Charles a coward after Culloden, but does not mention having done so either in *Affairs* or in his unpublished Journal. *Affairs* (Introduction), pp.92–95.

21 *Memorials*, p.200; *Affairs*, p.266.

22 *Memorials*, p.200.

23 O'Sullivan, p.75.

24 Id.; *Memorials*, p.200; Marches, p.36.

25 O'Sullivan, p.75; Tomasson and Buist, p.49; Duffy, p.13.

26 Duffy, p.107.

27 O'Sullivan, p.76; *Memorials*, p.199; *Affairs*, p.265 n.1.

28 Marches, p.36. See O'Sullivan, pp.76–77; *Affairs*, p.267; *Memorials*, p.200 (confirming Lord George's account, although the latter two mistake Falside Hill for its neighbour Carberry Hill).

29 Cope, p.72 (Fowke).

30 Id., p.191 (App. LVIII).

31 Carlyle, p.141.

32 Cope, p.186 (App. LIV).

33 Id., p.192 (App. LIX); Duffy, pp.174, 212–213.

34 Cope, pp.49, 51 (Whitefoord); Cadell, p.181; *Woodhouselee*, p.37.

35 Carlyle, p.141.

36 E.g., Philip Dodderidge, *Some Remarkable Passages In the Life of the Honourable Col. James Gardiner* (2nd Edition), Leith, 1802, pp.193–203; Walter Scott, *Waverley* ('Scott'), London, 1972, pp.504–505 (Notes); Jesse, pp.183–185.

37 Reid, *1745*, p.36.

38 Peter McNeill, *Tranent and Its Surroundings* ('McNeill, *Tranent*'), Edinburgh and Glasgow, 1883, p.114; Jesse, p.184; Carlyle, p.153. But see O'Sullivan, p.76 n. (Ed.) (died in his garden).

39 Carlyle, p.62.

40 Duffy, p.192; Carlyle, pp.19–20.

41 Cadell, pp.101–103.

42 Cope, p.75 (Singleton).

43 Id., p.102 (George Drummond).

44 Carlyle, p.142.

45 Tomasson and Buist, p.44.

46 Home, pp.105–106.

47 Carlyle, p.143.

48 Cope, p.36.

49 Id., p.51 (Whitefoord).

50 Cope, pp.143–144 (Caulfield), 49 (Whitefoord).

51 Id., p.48 (Whitefoord).

52 Id.; Carlyle, pp.143–144; *Affairs*, pp.264–265 n.6 (ed. note).

53 Carlyle, pp.144–145; *Memorials*, p.199 N.B.

54 Carlyle, p.146.

55 Cope, p.37.

56 Id.; id., pp.143–144 (Whiteford); Carlyle, pp.146–147; Home, p.106 n.; Duffy, p.12.

57 Cope, p.144 (Caulfield).

58 Id., p.64; Home, pp.106–107; *Affairs*, p.266.

59 Jarvis, Cope's Forces, p.39.

60 Home, p.105.

61 Cope, p.37; id., p.48 (Whitefoord), 137 (Loudon), 145 (Drummore).

62 Id.

63 Cope, p.65 (Lascelles).

64 Carlyle, p.147.

65 Johnstone, p.24.

66 · The field is described in virtually all the cited sources. I am indebted to the Rev. Tom Hogg for explaining the bottle mines.

67 Tomasson and Buist, p.51.

68 Cope, p.146 (Drummore).

69 Id.

70 Id., pp.38–39; id., pp.137–138 (Loudon), 145–146 (Drummore) (movements of government army); Manuscript, notes of anonymous Hanoverian officer, Scottish Public Record Office ('Manuscript'), copy provided by Rev. Tom Hogg, p.1 (100 paces); Home, p.109 (cheer).

71 Johnstone, p.22.

72 Affairs, pp.269–270.

73 Home, pp.103, 111 n.

74 McLynn, p.149; Jesse, p.172; Duffy, p.13. But see Affairs, p.262 (1,000 Athollmen – a figure that is way too high).

75 Cope, pp.84, 100 (Volunteer Richard Jack).

76 Muster Roll, pp.229–230 (App. II).

77 Susan Kybett, Bonnie Prince Charlie: A Biography of Charles Edward Stuart ('Kybett'), New York, 1988, p.142.

78 Tomasson and Buist, p.49.

79 Reid, 1745, p.34 (by individual units).

80 Scott, p.325.

81 Cope, pp.43, 100.

82 Home, p.103; Cope, p.84 (Jack).

83 Cope, p.59 (spectator David Bruce) (Cope relied on a Mr Baillie, Steward to Solicitor-General Dundas, who went 'among the Rebels' on eve of battle and estimated them at 5,000).

84 Affairs, p.253.

85 Memorials, p.200.

86 O'Sullivan, p.75.

87 Tomasson and Buist, p.49.

88 Affairs, p.270.

89 Jarvis, Cope's Forces, p.25 et seq.

90 Johnstone, p.22.

91 Id., p.22 (ed. note).

92 Tomasson and Buist, p.58; Maclean, p.81.

93 Cope, p.43; id., p.101 (Mossman, Severn, Talbot, Clark, Ker, Cowse).

94 Affairs, p.264.

95 Memorials, p.200.

96 Jarvis, Cope's Forces, p.31.

97 Id., p.31; Reid, 1745, p.32.

98 E.g., Duffy, p.12; Kybett, p.143 (Scots Magazine).

99 Duffy, p.12; Jarvis, Cope's Forces, p.29; Reid, 1745, p.32.

100 Hook and Ross, p.54.

101 McLaren, p.68.

102 Woodhouselee, p.26.

103 Home, p.104.

104 Affairs, p.253.

105 Johnstone, p.22.

106 Id., p.26.

107 Scott, p.324.

108 Home, p.104.

109 Cope, p.54 (Whitefoord, Griffith); Home, p.118. The Rev. Tom Hogg has informed me, however, that according to local tradition cannonballs weighing from six to nine pounds have been excavated in the locality – indeed, he has seen and handled one of them himself – and there has been no other fighting, anywhere close by, that would account for their presence. Neither he nor I can explain the discrepancy between the sizes of these cannonballs and and the weapons described at Cope's Inquiry.

110 Hook and Ross, p.52 (Lord Milton letter to Cope).

111 Tomasson and Buist, p.41.

112 Cope, p.49 (Whitefoord); id., p.40; id., p.55 (Craig).

113 Id., p.91 (nine); id., p.55 (Whitefoord) (six).

114 Id., p.49 (Whitefoord), 91 (Griffith).

115 Tomasson and Buist, p.47.

116 *Memorials*, p.191.

117 Home, p.104; Elcho, p.257; Scott, pp.324–325, 504 (Notes).

118 Scott, pp.324–325; Jesse, pp.178–179.

119 O'Sullivan, p.77.

120 Id., p.76 n.1 (M).

121 *Memorials*, p.200.

122 Marches, p.37.

123 Johnstone, p.24.

124 Marches, p.37.

125 But see *Affairs*, p.267 (300 Camerons).

126 Marches, pp.37–38; *Memorials*, p.200; *Affairs*, p.267 (attributing the order to Charles); Cope, p.39; id., p.138 (Loudon) (describing movements).

127 O'Sullivan, p.77 n.2 (M).

128 Cope, p.88 (Grossett).

129 Id., p.39; id., p.88 (Grossett). Cope thought he killed several, but Jacobite sources do not mention fatalities.

130 *Affairs*, p.268; Tomasson and Buist, pp.54–55.

131 Marches, pp.37–38; *Affairs*, p.267.

132 Size of Brigade: *Muster Roll*, p.230 (250). But see Home, p.115, Carlyle, p.149 (300–400); *Memorials*, p.207 (500).

133 Carlyle, p.149 ('about four in the afternoon'); Marches, p.38 ('evening'); Cope, p.39 ('about an hour before sunset').

134 O'Sullivan, p.78.

135 Marches, p.38.

136 Carlyle, p.149; Cope, p.39.

137 O'Sullivan, p.79; *Memorials*, p.201.

138 *Memorials*, p.201; *Affairs*, p.267; Marches, p.38.

139 O'Sullivan, p.79.

140 Cope, p.138 (Loudon).

141 Cope's manoeuvres: Cope, p.39, id., p.138 (Loudon), Duffy, p.15–16; Carlyle's activities: Carlyle, p.149–150; Volunteers: Cope, p.102 (Drummond), Cadell, pp.210–211, Tomasson and Buist, p.57; overhearing 'talking and swearing': O'Sullivan, p.80 n.1 (M).

142 Carlyle, pp.149–150.

143 *Affairs*, p.267; *Memorials*, p.201.

144 Cope, p.65 (Lascelles). But see *Affairs*, p.269 and O'Sullivan, p.80 n.1 (M) (10p.m.). Elcho also says that some dragoons were 'kiled', but government sources mention no casualties.

145 *Memorials*, p.201.

146 Cope, p.66 (Lascelles).

147 The sources are hopelessly inconsistent as to when this movement took place. Compare, e.g., Duffy, p.16 and Tomasson and Buist, p.59 with Reid, p.30 and Johnstone, p.25. I have reconciled them in the way that seems to me most probable: that the movement began, was interrupted, and then resumed.

148 Id.

149 Marches, pp.38–39.

150 Cadell, p.210.

151 *Affairs*, p.269; *Memorials*, p.202; Johnstone, p.25; Home, p.115. But see Marches, p.39 (not mentioning Anderson).

152 Tomasson and Buist, p.60.

153 Cope, p.40; Home, p.115. But see Marches, p.38 (2a.m.).

154 Brown and Cheape, p.22.

155 Marches, p.39.

156 Id.; O'Sullivan, p.80; *Memorials*, p.202.

157 Marches, p.39; Home, p.115.

158 Marches, p.39.

159 *Memorials*, p.202.

160 Cadell, pp.214–215.

161 Cope, pp.39–40.

162 Manuscript, p.2; Tomasson and Buist, p.59.

163 Cope, p.40; id., p.139 (Loudon).

164 Id., p.49 (Whitefoord).

165 Id., p.40; id., p.55 (Craig).

166 Id., p.49 (Whitefoord).

167 Id., p.144 (Caulfield).

168 Id., p.39; id., p.139 (Loudon).

169 Cadell, pp.217–219.

170 Cope, p.66 (Lascelles).

171 Id., p.40; Tomasson and Buist, p 61.

172 *Affairs*, p.270; Johnstone, p.26.

173 Cope, p.40; id., p.139 (Loudon); Cadell, p.221; Duffy, p.17 (map);

Tomasson and Buist, p.68 (map). The maps differ in minor details.

174 Cope, p.89 (Jack). Though unreliable in other particulars, Jack is uncontradicted on this one.

175 Tomasson and Buist, p.62; Duffy, p.18.

176 Home, p.117.

177 Cope, pp.59 (Bruce), 148 (Drummore).

178 Id., p.38.

179 Tomasson and Buist, p.45.

180 Houlding, p.353; Duffy, p.131.

181 Cope, pp.38, 44.

182 Reid, *1745*, p.33.

183 Cope, p.40; id., pp.54 (Griffith), 90–91 (Whitefoord, Griffith).

184 Id., p.40.

185 Id., p.102 (Drummond).

186 Cadell, p.223; Tomasson and Buist, p.64.

187 Cadell, p.223.

188 Cope, p.40.

189 Id., p.68 (Captain Collier).

190 Id., p.147 (Drummore).

191 Johnstone, p.26; Duffy, p.18.

192 Home, p.116.

193 Duffy, pp.18 (diagram), 578 (App. III) (Orders of Battle); Reid, p.31 (diagram); *Affairs* (diagram between pp.272–273); Home (diagram between pp.108–09); *Muster Roll*, p.229 (App. II) (numbers).

194 Home, p.116.

195 Johnstone, p.26.

196 *Affairs*, p.270.

197 Marches, p.39; Cope, p.41.

198 Tomasson and Buist, p.62 (fifty); *Memorials*, p.203 (eighty).

199 Tomasson and Buist, p.62.

200 Cope, p.97.

201 Id., p.58 (Cowse).

202 Id.

203 Marches, pp.39–40.

204 Cope, p.41.

205 Duffy, p.18.

206 Cope, p.41.

207 Id., p.41; id., pp.49 (Whitefoord), 60 (Mossman).

208 Id., p.60 (Mossman).

209 Id., pp.54–55 (Griffith, Whitefoord).

210 Id., p.41.

211 Id., p.51 (Whitefoord).

212 Marches, p.40; Cope, p.41; id., p.57 (Talbot).

213 *Affairs*, p.27.

214 Cope, p.49 (Whiteford).

215 Home, p.118.

216 *Affairs*, p.271.

217 Home, p.118.

218 Scott, p.339; Jesse, p.182; Lord Mahon, *History of England From the Peace of Utrecht to the Peace of Versailles 1713–1783*, vol. III, Leipzig, 1853, p.251. But see Cadell, p.244.

219 O'Sullivan, p.80.

220 Home, p.118.

221 Id.

222 Cope, p.72 (Fowke).

223 Id.

224 Id. ('clumps and clusters'); *Affairs*, p.271; Marches, p.40 (two columns).

225 Home, p.118.

226 Cope, p.41.

227 Id., p.140 (Loudon).

228 Home, p.118.

229 Cope, p.54 (Whitefoord, Griffith).

230 Home, p.119.

231 Cope, p.140 (Loudon).

232 Id., p.41; id., p.140 (Loudon); *Memorials*, p.203.

233 Marches, p.40; Cope, p.41.

234 Cope, p.41; id., pp.49 (Whitefoord), 66 (Lascelles).

235 *Affairs*, pp.271–272; *Memorials*, p.203; Cope, p.41; id., p.140 (Loudon). The quote is Loudon's.

236 Cope, p.60 (Mossman).

237 Id., p.66 (Lascelles); 68 (Captain Blake).

238 Id., p.41; id., p.57 (Adjutant Ker), 73 (Fowke). The quote is Ker's.

239 Id., p.41; id., p.140 (Loudon).

240 Id., pp.43–44; id., pp.73–74 (Fowke).

241 Id., p.41; Elcho, p.271 ('closed up again'); Cadell, pp.236–237; Scott, pp.505–506 (Notes) (Gardiner); O'Sullivan, p.82 ('flinging away their standards').

242 Cope, p.57 (Adjutant Ker).

243 Id., p.79 (Brigade Major Captain Singleton).

244 Cope, pp.66–67 (Lascelles).

245 Affairs, p.272.

246 Memorials, p.203 ('incredible impetuosity'); Cope, pp.66, 69 (Lascelles); Affairs, pp.271–272.

247 Cope, pp.66–67, 69 (Lascelles).

248 Cadell, pp.241–242.

249 Affairs, p.272; Cope, p.42.

250 Cope, pp.50 (Lascelles), 56 (Earl of Home), 140 (Loudon).

251 Id., p.57 (Major Talbot, Major Severn) ('...by platoons...'); id., p.140 (Loudon) (rear to front).

252 Id., pp.60–61 (Captain Forbes, Captain Pointz, Lieutenant Greenwell).

253 Id., p.42.

254 Id., p.140 (Loudon) (mixed among them); Johnstone, p.27 (scythes).

255 Id., pp.73 (Fowke), 80–81 (Singleton) (emphasis in original).

256 Id., p.73 (Fowke).

257 Home, p.117.

258 Cope, p.139 (Loudon).

259 Id., p.147 (Drummore).

260 Id.; id., p.57 (Talbot).

261 Memorials, p.203; Cope, p.41; id., pp.57 (Talbot), 147 (Drummore). But see Cope, p.58 (Cowse) (MacDonalds reached dragoons and attacked them in flank; witness persisted even after Board noted inconsistency with other testimony).

262 Id., p.147 (Drummore).

263 Lang, p.167.

264 O'Sullivan, p.82 n.1 (M).

265 Cope, p.58 (Clark).

266 Id., p.41.

267 Id., p.148 (Drummore).

268 Id., p.147.

269 Id., p.148.

270 Id., pp.147–148.

271 Id., p.56 (Earl of Home); Affairs, p.276.

272 Johnstone, p.27.

273 O'Sullivan, pp.80–81 n.1 (M).

274 Id., p.82 n.1 (M); Affairs, p.276.

275 Home, p.120.

276 Johnstone, p.30.

277 Memorials, p.203.

278 Cope, p.80 (Singleton).

279 Id., p.78 (Captain Chrystie).

280 Affairs, p.272.

281 O'Sullivan, p.82.

282 Id., pp.80–81; Affairs, p.272; Johnstone, p.28.

283 Johnstone, p.28.

284 O'Sullivan, p.81.

285 Affairs, pp.273–274.

286 Johnstone, pp.26–27.

287 Carlyle, pp.151, 154–155.

288 Home, p.122.

289 Affairs, p.272.

290 Marches, pp.41–42.

291 Memorials, p.205.

292 Marches, pp.42–43; Browne and Cheape, p.22.

293 Johnstone, p.28.

294 Home, p.120.

295 Affairs, pp.274–276.

296 O'Sullivan, pp.83–84.

297 Memorials, p.205.

298 Marches, p.41.

299 Tomasson and Buist, p.77.

300 Reid, 1745, p.38.

301 Home, pp.121–122.

302 H. Hannah, The Thorn Tree, Prestonpans, http://www.prestoungrange.org/prestonpans/html/battle_1745/thorntree_4.html (accessed 1 July 2006).

303 Duffy, pp.20–21; Reid, 1745, pp.35–36; Tomasson and Buist, pp.73–74.

304 Cope, p.69 (Lascelles).

305 Johnstone, p.28; Affairs, p.274; Memorials, pp.204–205; Home, p.121.

306 Memorials, p.205.

307 Marches, p.40.

308 Id., p.41; O'Sullivan, pp.82–83; Affairs, p.273. But see Memorials, p.203 (emissary was Capt. Basil Cochrane of Lee's).

309 Aeneas MacDonald, p.292.

310 Home, p.120; Cope, p.42. But see Hook and Ross, p.56 (200 foot

311 Cope, pp.42–43; id., pp.55–56 (Earl of Home), 140–141 (Loudon) ('as decent…').

312 McLynn, *CES*, p.153; Jesse, p.182; McNeill, *Tranent*, p.112.

313 *Woodhouselee*, p.32.

314 McNeill, *Tranent*, p.111.

315 Lenman and Gibson, pp.225–226; *Affairs*, pp.461–462 (App. G).

316 Cope, p.51 (Whitefoord).

317 Johnstone, p.28; *Memorials*, p.204.

318 Johnstone, p.28.

319 Marshall, p.99.

320 Cope, p.43.

321 Id., pp.193–194 (App. LXI).

322 Id., p.43 (arrival at Berwick); Tomasson and Buist, pp.42, 78 (relations and meeting with Ker).

323 O'Sullivan, pp.83–84 n.1 (M); *Memorials*, p.205.

324 Home, p.122; *Affairs*, p.277; *Memorials*, p.209. But see Gibson, *Edinburgh*, p.32 (arrived in evening).

5 AFTERMATH

1 Hook and Ross, p.56; Marshall, p.97; Peter McNeill, *Prestonpans and Vicinity*, Tranent, 1902, pp.217–218.

2 Hook and Ross, p.56.

3 McLynn, *CES*, pp.156–165; Gibson, *Edinburgh*, pp.32–54; Duffy, pp.200–207.

4 Frank McLynn, *The Jacobite Army in England*, Edinburgh, 1983, pp.24–25; Duffy, p.104.

5 D. Bradstreet, *The Life and Uncommon Adventures of Captain Dudley Bradstreet* (G.S. Taylor, ed.), London, pp.125–127.

6 Cope, pp.vii–viii (Preface), 1–2 (Report).

7 Id., p.89; id. (Jack).

8 Cope, p.194 (certification by Gould). The year is mistakenly given as 1746 rather than 1747.

9 Id., pp.102–103.

10 Tomasson and Buist, p.78; Duffy, p.23.

11 Cadell, p.272.

12 Cope, p.xv (editor's preface).

13 *Memorials*, pp.181–82; Johnstone, pp.12–17; Home, pp.62–63.

14 *Memorials*, pp.182–183.

15 *Woodhouselee*, p.38; Duffy, p.141 (reporting complaints of soldiers).

16 *Memorials*, pp.208–209.

17 Id., pp.206–207.

18 *Affairs*, p.267.

19 *Memorials*, pp.205–206.

20 Id., p.200.

21 Johnstone, pp.14–15 (ed. notes).

22 Cope, pp.13, 63.

23 Id., p.173 (App. XLVII).

24 In the end the Dutch were unavailable anyway: though one agreement bound them to fight for Britain, another prohibited them from doing so against France, which soon afterward activated the prohibition by sending a French regiment – the Royal Ecossais – to Charles's aid. Lenman and Gibson, p.207.

25 Cope, p.51 (Whitefoord).

26 Id., p.194 (App. LXI); id., pp.140 (Loudon), 148 (Drummore).

27 Id., p.148 (Drummore).

28 Johnstone, pp.17–18 (ed. note).

29 Paul Kopperman, *Braddock At the Monongahela*, Pittsburgh, 1977, pp.14–15: the best, I believe, of many excellent studies of Braddock's campaign.

30 O'Sullivan, p.6.

31 Id., pp.24–34, 236, 252–253, 264.

32 Id., p.3; *Affairs*, p.237 n.4.

33 O'Sullivan, pp.1–2; *Affairs*, p.236 n.2.

34 O'Sullivan, p.5; *Affairs*, p.236 n.3.

35 O'Sullivan, pp.5–6; *Affairs*, p.237 n.3; Gibson, *Lochiel*, p.158.

36 O'Sullivan, pp.2–3; *Affairs*, pp.237–38 n.5.

37 *Affairs*, p.234 n.2.

38 Gibson, *Lochiel*, pp.155–168.

39 *Memorials*, pp.xxix–xxxi; *Affairs*, p.233 n.3.

40 Hook and Ross, p.28.

41 *Affairs*, p.272 n.1.

42 Cope, p.14 (Duncan Forbes).

43 Cadell, p.273.

44 Geoff Bailey, *Falkirk or Paradise!
    The Battle of Falkirk Muir* ('Bailey'),
    Edinburgh, 1996, p.187; *DNB*, p.315.

45 Maclean, p.166; Cadell, p.272.

46 Bailey, p.187.

47 Houlding, p.197 and n.83.

48 *ODNB*, p.315.

49 *MCP*, vol. III, p.219.

50 Compare *MCP*, vol. III, p.219 (1
    August); *ODNB*, p.315 (28 July).

51 http://www.british-history.ac.uk/
    report.asp?compid=40626, p.14.

52 *MCP*, vol. III, p.219; Cadell, p.282.

53 *MCP*, vol. III, p.219.

54 Lord, pp.120–121.

SELECT BIBLIOGRAPHY

Aikman, Christian, Hart, Betty, and Livingstone, Alastair, *No Quarter Given: The Muster Roll of Prince Charles Edward Stuart's Army, 1745–46* (3rd Edition), Glasgow, 2001.

Bell, Robert (ed.), *Memorials of John Murray of Broughton*, Edinburgh, 1898.

Cadell, Gen. Robert, *Sir John Cope and the Rebellion of 1745*, Edinburgh and London, 1898.

Carlyle, Alexander, *Autobiography of Alexander Carlyle of Inveresk*, London and Edinburgh, 1910.

Charteris, Evan (ed.), *A Short Account of the Affairs of Scotland in the Years 1744, 1745, 1746*, by David, Lord Elcho, Edinburgh, 1973.

Duffy, Christopher, *The '45*, London, 2003.

Forbes, Robert (ed.), *The Lyon In Mourning*, Edinburgh, 1975.

Gibson, John, *Edinburgh In the '45: Bonnie Prince Charlie at Holyrood*, Edinburgh, 1995.

Gibson, John, *Lochiel of the '45: The Jacobite Chief and the Prince*, Edinburgh, 1994.

Harrington, Peter, *Culloden 1746: The Highland Clans' Last Charge*, London, 1991.

Home, John, *The History of the Rebellion in the Year 1745*, London, 1802.

Hook, Michael, and Ross, Walter, *The 'Forty-Five: The Last Jacobite Rebellion*, Edinburgh, 1995.

Houlding, J.A., *Fit For Service: The Training of the British Army 1715–1795*, Oxford, 1981.

Jarvis, Rupert, *Collected Papers On the Jacobite Risings*, Manchester, 1971.

Johnstone, James, *Memoirs of the Rebellion In 1745 and 1746*, London, 1820.

Lenman, Bruce, *The Jacobite Cause* (2nd Edition), Edinburgh, 1992.

Lenman, Bruce, *The Jacobite Clans of the Great Glen 1650–1784* (paperback), Aberdeen, 1995.

Lenman, Bruce, *The Jacobite Risings In Britain, 1689–1746* (paperback), Aberdeen, 1995.

Lord, Steve, *Walking With Charlie: In the Footsteps of the Forty-Five*, Witney, 2003.

Maclean, Fitzroy, *Bonnie Prince Charlie*, New York, 1989.

McLynn, Frank, *Charles Edward Stuart: A Tragedy In Many Acts*, Loxford, 1991.

McLynn, Frank, *France and the Jacobites*, Edinburgh, 1981.

McLynn, Frank, *The Jacobites*, London, 1985.

Monod, Paul, *Jacobitism and the English People, 1688–1788*, Cambridge, 1989.

Murray, George, *Marches of the Highland Army*, in Chambers, Robert (ed.), *Jacobite Memoirs of the Rebellion of 1745*, London, 1834.

Pittock, Murray, *The Myth of the Jacobite Clans*, Edinburgh, 1995.

Reid, Stuart, *1745: A Military History of the Last Jacobite Rising*, New York, 1966.

Reid, Stuart, *Like Hungry Wolves: Culloden Moor 16 April 1746*, London, 1994.

Robins, Benjamin (ed.), *The Report of the Proceedings and Opinion of the Board of General Officers, On Their Examination Into the Conduct, Behaviour and Proceedings of Lieutenant-General Sir John Cope, Knight of the Bath, Colonel Peregrine Lascelles, and Brigadier-General Thomas Fowke*, London, 1749.

Steuart, A. Francis, *The Woodhouselee MS.*, London, 1907.

Szechi, Daniel, *The Jacobites: Britain and Europe 1688–1788*, Manchester, 1994.

Tayler, Alistair and Tayler, Henrietta (eds), *1745 and After*, London, 1938.

Tomasson, Katherine, *The Jacobite General*, Edinburgh and London, 1958.

Tomasson, Katherine, and Buist, Francis, *Battles of the '45*, New York, 1962.

Woosnam-Savage, Robert (ed.), *1745: Charles Edward Stuart and the Jacobites*, Edinburgh, 1995.

LIST OF ILLUSTRATIONS

INDEX

TEMPUS REVEALING HISTORY

William Wallace
The True Story of Braveheart
CHRIS BROWN
'The truth about Braveheart' **The Scottish Daily Mail**
£17.99
0 7524 3432 2

The Roman Conquest of Scotland
The Battle of Mons Graupius AD 84
JAMES E. FRASER
'Challenges a long held view' **The Scottish Sunday Express**
£17.99
0 7524 3325 3

An Abundance of Witches
The Great Scottish Witch-Hunt
P.G. MAXWELL-STUART
'An amazing account of Scots women in league with the Devil' **The Sunday Post**
£17.99
0 7524 3329 6

Scottish Voices from the Great War
DEREK YOUNG
'A treasure trove of personal letters and diaries from the archives'
    Trevor Royle
£17.99
0 7524 3326 1

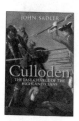

Culloden
The Last Charge of the Highland Clans
JOHN SADLER
£25
0 7524 3955 3

The Pictish Conquest
The Battle of Dunnichen 685 & the Birth of Scotland
JAMES E. FRASER
£12.99

The Scottish Civil War
The Bruces & the Balliols & the War for the Control of Scotland
MICHAEL PENMAN
'A highly informative and engaging account' **Historic Scotland**
£16.99
0 7524 2319 3

Scottish Voices from the Second World War
DEREK YOUNG
'Poignant memories of a lost generation... heart-rending' **The Sunday Post**
£17.99
0 7524 3710 0

If you are interested in purchasing other books published by Tempus, or in case you have difficulty finding any Tempus books in your local bookshop, you can also place orders directly through our website

www.tempus-publishing.com

TEMPUS REVEALING HISTORY

Scotland
From Prehistory to the Present
FIONA WATSON
The Scotsman **Bestseller**
£9.99
0 7524 2591 9

Flodden
NIALL BARR
'Tells the story brilliantly'
The Sunday Post
£9.99
0 7524 2593 5

1314 Bannockburn
ARYEH NUSBACHER
'Written with good-humoured verve as
befits a rattling "yarn of sex, violence and
terror"'
History Scotland
£9.99
0 7524 2982 5

Scotland's Black Death
The Foul Death of the English
KAREN JILLINGS
'So incongruously enjoyable a read, and so
attractively presented by the publishers'
The Scotsman
£14.99
0 7524 2314 2

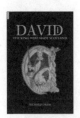   

David I The King Who Made Scotland
RICHARD ORAM
'Enthralling... sets just the right tone as the
launch-volume of an important new series
of royal biographies' *Magnus Magnusson*
£17.99
0 7524 2825 X

The Second Scottish Wars of Independence 1332–1363
CHRIS BROWN
'Explodes the myth of the invincible Bruces...
lucid and highly readable' *History Scotland*
£12.99
0 7524 3812 3

The Kings & Queens of Scotland
RICHARD ORAM
'A serious, readable work that sweeps across
a vast historical landscape' *The Daily Mail*
£12.99
0 7524 3814 X

Robert the Bruce: A Life Chronicled
CHRIS BROWN
'A masterpiece of research'
The Scots Magazine
£30
0 7524 2575 7

If you are interested in purchasing other books published by Tempus, or in case you have difficulty finding any Tempus
books in your local bookshop, you can also place orders directly through our website

www.tempus-publishing.com